Dead Pretty

by

Joy Wood

Dedication

*To my dear friends who I was lucky enough to share
two special years at the wonderful
Harlow Wood Orthopaedic Hospital.
Alison, Linda, Lynne, Maureen, Michelle, Andrew & Kevin.*

Thanks for the memories.

PROLOGUE

1977

Killing was a desire that saturated every minute of his waking day. Adrenaline surged through his veins as he fantasised about vibrant, young female flesh trapped within his deadly hands as he tightened his grip around her milky white neck and strangled the final breath out of her. It was an evil, depraved craving, he knew that, but nevertheless, it overwhelmed him. There wasn't even a hint of trepidation; right now a last kill was as vital to him as water. But the burning question he couldn't answer was – would he be able to stop at one girl? Especially now he had a death sentence hanging over him.

There was a certain irony that he was in a perfect place to find a victim. A smirk twitched at his lips as he ran his hand along the windowsill of the old sash window, desperately in need of a coat of paint judging by the flaky chippings dropping onto the burgundy carpet. The heavy embossed dark brown curtains shielded him as he peered outside. It was a crisp autumn day, mild for the time of year and his heart rate quickened watching the new intake of excited students as they arrived to embark on a two-year nurse training course at the cottage hospital nestled in the woods. The renowned Harlow Wood Orthopaedic Hospital, built in 1929 and situated on the A60 between Mansfield and Nottingham, with a reputation as a centre of excellence for anything to do with bones.

The car park was bustling with an array of cars with their boot lids open, crammed with endless items to make the new recruits comfortable in the new life they were about to embark upon. The contents were emptied out by dutiful parents as they followed their young, clutching letters explaining which nurses' home they needed to be in out of the two positioned on the hill. The seventeen-year-olds were always in the red brick North House, those eighteen and above were in the rendered South House, often labelled the white house, but over a period of time, appeared more a shade of dirty beige. Today, there was a greeter in each doorway with a list of names and the room number allocated to individual students. They came in the guise of second year student nurses, both with a beaming smile and a willingness to share their experience of Harlow Wood and the wonderful place it was.

A new entrant letter would be in each room instructing the students to meet at 6pm in the communal lounge of North House where they'd be told the rules they must adhere to while residing there. Nothing too onerous – it was essential that the nurses weren't overwhelmed, forcing them to quit. Not when they were the workforce of the future. They'd have to listen to the instructions about quietness, respecting fellow students, keeping the communal kitchen and bathrooms tidy, and using the in/out notice board so that in the event of a fire, they could ascertain who was inside the building.

Most would stick to the rules religiously, while others would bend them accordingly. He'd seen it all before . . . many times. And he hated them all. He hated their youth, their eagerness, and their couldn't care less attitude. Professional training would undoubtedly ensure their lives would change. He knew categorically that for one of them it would. And the reason he knew was because he was going to extinguish it.

The task ahead now was to pick which one . . .

1.

Kym

Kym surveyed the gloomy room 15 she'd been allocated on the upstairs floor of North House, a far cry from the cosy bedroom in the detached house by the seaside she lived in with her mum and dad. And, as if the room wasn't depressing enough with its murky walls, single bed, and old wardrobe with a door which didn't appear to shut properly, her eyes were drawn to the wall above the bed and the pieces of tape hanging down which to her indicated the room had barely been prepared for a new occupant. The previous nurse must have ripped off her posters, no doubt in an eager bid to be out of there.

"It's not too bad," a degree of sympathy was etched on her mother's forty-five-year-old face as she scrutinised the well-used sink unit in the corner of the room. "I think it'll be better when you put your own quilt on the bed and some pictures around to brighten it all up."

Despite Kym's reticence about upping and leaving home the last few weeks, the last thing she wanted was for her mum and dad to drive eighty miles home and be worried and upset about leaving her. They would be anyway, their only daughter moving away, but she didn't want to pile it on by appearing apprehensive about the room, even though in her young and naive mind, she'd expected something a little more palatial.

"Yeah," she forced some positivity into her voice, "it'll be fine." She smiled encouragingly at her dad as he lifted her case and bag onto the bed. "Like Mum says, it just needs making a bit more homely." Her eyes flicked towards the old wooden desk in the corner where numerous student nurses must have sat over the years. It was tatty and scratched, the wood embedded with stains of various colours from endless spillages.

Her mother took a step towards the window, "At least the view's nice, you can see the whole hospital from here." She reached towards the thick burgundy curtain and moved it slightly away from the window, "Shame these are heavy, they're blocking so much light out of the room."

Her dad undid the latches on her suitcase and opened it wide onto the bed.

"Leave it, Dad, I'll do it when you've gone."

A tap on the half open door interrupted them. All eyes turned towards the petite girl with a short pixie haircut and a warm friendly smile, "Hi. I'm Carol, one of the second-year students. I can give you a quick tour if you're ready, or I can come back if you need a bit more time."

"Right now would be lovely," her mother replied eagerly, no doubt keen to get out of the oppressive room. Kym knew she'd want to check the bathrooms had been suitably cleaned and bleached. Dirt bred germs and none were allowed in her mother's world. She was a nurse herself and didn't they know it. Their home life had been governed by her work as a senior nurse in a private hospital as far back as she could remember.

A wave of impatience descended on Kym as she made her way to the door. She wanted her mum and dad to leave her to it, but her mother wouldn't be satisfied until she'd inspected every inch of her daughter's living accommodation for the next two years. Kym dutifully followed her out of the door while her dad stood back to let them both go in front. As they made their way along the corridor, she couldn't resist peeking into the rooms with the doors half open. Most appeared crowded with family members. There was a girl of a similar age sat on the bed in the room opposite to her. Their eyes met briefly as she passed. Did she, like her feel disheartened and had expected so much more?

The first place Carol took them to was the kitchen which wasn't far down the corridor on the upstairs floor. It was large, functional and basic. There was a cooker, a toaster, a sink and a pine table that appeared to accommodate eight judging by the chairs.

"This is where most people congregate. You can cook in here if you want to, but there's not much point as we get all our food paid for in the canteen. But who doesn't get hungry at night for a snack? And you can bet when you do, everywhere's closed." Carol opened a cupboard door, "There are some mugs and plates, but not many. Most of us keep our own in our rooms."

"Yeah, I wasn't sure so I've brought some stuff with me," Kym said.

"That's good then. I'll show you the bathrooms next."

The door was on a spring and closed behind them as they made their way to the communal bathrooms which were through another door to the end of the corridor.

"There are three bathrooms on this floor and three shower rooms. There's the same downstairs if these are all occupied and you're in a rush for your shift. But they're for the locum male doctors or those on call so don't whatever you do, venture down there without your dressing gown. The cleaners come each day but you are expected to clean up after yourself. There's stuff in the bathroom cabinets to swill round the bath after use. I always do," Carol screwed up her face, "but I'm warning you, not everyone does unfortunately."

Nobody couldn't fail to hear her mother's 'Oh dear' and see the disgruntled expression on her face. Carol's eyes twinkled as if she was a mind reader. "Most parents like to get off after they've had a look round," her eyes met Kym's knowingly, "it gives you a chance to get unpacked and be ready for the meeting at six."

"Oh, right," her mum nodded and turned to her dad, "we'd better do that then, Ron, shall we?" She wasn't asking, she was telling as her dutiful dad only ever did what she said. Kym nodded at Carol, grateful for her intervention to hurry them along.

She waited while her parents used the toilets and walked with them both as they made their way back down the stairs, out of the nurses' home entrance and around to the back of the main hospital to the car park.

"Now you've got change to ring us tomorrow haven't you?" her mum asked.

"Yeah, Dad gave me plenty."

"Make sure you use it on us then and not on that sailor boy of yours."

"Don't call him that, you know I don't like it."

"And you know we don't like him, but it doesn't stop you seeing him, does it?" The usual pained expression reared its head when her boyfriend Tony, a rookie in the Navy, was mentioned. They stopped in the car park at her dad's pride and joy, his gleaming dark green Citroen GS which he diligently washed and buffed every Saturday morning. Her mother folded her arms across her chest and straightened her posture, which meant one thing – there was more to come from her. Any mention of Tony spurred her on with a derogatory tirade.

"The way I see it, that's one good thing about you coming here, you'll not be at his beck and call every time he fancies showing up."

"I'm not as his *beck and call*, I want to see him when he's home on leave."

"Yes, well things are going to be a whole lot more difficult now. You'll have off duty to comply with. You might not be off the same time as he is."

"I know that. But we're determined to work it out."

"Work it out?" Her mum widened her eyes. "I don't see how with you here and him in Portsmouth. And anyway, with your looks, you'll probably find the young doctors here will be flocking round you."

Kym sighed, she'd heard the doctor spiel so many times. So had her dad who was shuffling uncomfortably from one foot to the other clearly wanting to be off.

"I've told you loads of times, I'm not interested in any doctors."

"Yes, well things change, you might one day. That's all I'm saying."

Her mother would be delighted if she spilt up with Tony, but she wasn't going to do that. She cared about him too much to let her nurse training get in the way. She'd make it work. They had a future to look forward to once she was qualified. And although they'd both acknowledged the difficulties, they'd promised to be faithful to each other.

Kym checked her watch, "I'd better get a move on for the six o'clock meeting."

"Oh yes, you'd better. You won't forget to ring us, will you? Not before six mind, otherwise the phone will eat your money up."

"Yeah, I know."

"We're stopping at the Little Chef on the way home," her dad said. "I've cut a voucher out of the paper. It's offering twenty percent off, so we're going to have our tea there."

"Ah, that'll be nice then. I wonder what the food will be like here?" Kym glanced again at the imposing white hospital building.

"I'm sure it'll be lovely. Make sure you eat plenty," her mother barely took a breath, "working on a ward is completely different to working in an office, I can tell you. You'll need all your energy for all that lifting."

Kym smiled affectionately at her mum. She never let her forget she was a nurse. "I will, don't you worry."

She reached for her dad to hug him and he held onto her tightly. Her mum wasn't good with overt displays of affection, but he loved it.

"Safe journey home," she smiled lovingly at them both, "and enjoy your tea."

"We will," her mother gave her a quick hug and opened the door to sit in the passenger seat. "I'm dying to hear tomorrow how it goes," she said positioning her handbag at her feet.

"There won't be much to tell I wouldn't have thought." Kym raised her voice over the engine starting up, "It's just a first day in school, that's all."

"I know it is, but still, I want to hear all about it."

"Okay, I'll ring." Kym closed the car door. Despite wanting them to go, a wave of sadness clenched her tummy as she watched her dad reverse the car out of its space and then ease it forward. She waved cheerily as the Citroen disappeared through the car park exit and towards the main road. There was no doubt she was going to miss them but now she had an exciting future to look forward to. A surge of excitement rushed through her as she made her way back up the stairs to room 15. It was the realisation she was about to begin a completely new life. She'd worked since leaving school in an office and had quickly realised admin work wasn't for her. As soon as she knew she could begin her orthopaedic nurse training at seventeen, she quickly applied to do so.

The next half hour was spent unpacking. There was a large wardrobe and chest of drawers so plenty of room for the clothes she'd brought with her. Her empty suitcase and holdall fitted underneath the bed. The sink by the window was encased in a unit so she unpacked her toiletries and stored the surplus in the cupboard underneath with the disinfectant her mother had insisted on, even though she'd reassured her from the information booklet that there were cleaners coming in each day.

She purposely kept the door to her room open and smiled at anyone that passed, not entirely sure if they were the new intake like her, or nurses that had already began their training. She knew there had been an intake in January of that year, but she hadn't reached seventeen then so had to wait until the autumn intake.

The scrappy hanging bits and pieces from the previous occupant's posters were irritating her so she slipped off her shoes, climbed on the bed and reached to pull them off. As she did so, she decided when she was home at the weekend she'd buy some posters to cover the marks that were left. She had a couple of nice photos of Tony she'd had enlarged that she wanted to put up close to where she slept. Despite her mother's prediction their relationship wouldn't last, she was confident it would. They were going to write to each other, speak regularly on the phone, and he'd told her not to worry, they would make it work as they cared about each other. Warmth flooded through her thinking about him and how much he meant to her. She tossed the old Sellotape and Blue Tack into the bin next to the sink and moved towards the window to peer out. Her spirits had lifted thinking about Tony and she couldn't wait to ring him the following evening. They'd laugh together about her crap room – he'd joked it would be dire and she hadn't believed him.

2.

Louise

Her mum got up from her sitting position on the single bed in room 12. "We'd probably be better getting off then and leaving you to it."

Her young sister sitting at the small desk adjacent to the window, jumped up too, eager to be off – at fifteen she found everything and everybody irritating. But Louise wasn't too worried about her, it was her mum she was concerned about and the huge wrench it was going to be for her having to leave. She swallowed down the lump forming in her throat, forcing herself to see her off with a smile. It had only been three months since they'd buried her beloved dad and today was a massive hurdle for them all.

"Now, you're sure you're going to be alright?" her mother's eyes looked forlorn as they swept around the basic room.

"Course I will," she dismissed brightly, "come on, I'll walk with you to the car." Louise had to suppress an overwhelming urge to gather her things and leave with her mum and sister. It wasn't as if there'd be any shame in that. Shutting the door on the dreary nurses' home and recognising it had been a mistake would quickly be forgiven. They'd soon be home in their cosy semi in Sheffield, drinking hot chocolate and watching the escapades of JR Ewing in Dallas. And she could always do her general nurse training the following year when she was eighteen if she wanted to.

"I wish I could leave home and live here," her sister Karen said as they made their way down the stairs.

"Well, you can in a couple of years, but right now Mum needs you at home, don't you, Mum?" Louise held the entrance door open for them both.

Her mother linked her arm in hers as they exited into the sunshine and made their way towards the car park. "Yes, I must say I'm relieved I've still got Karen at home, she'll keep me busy. We'll miss you though love, but maybe not your music blaring out all hours."

Louise grinned. "Yeah, there are some benefits, I guess. I'm really going to miss home but I'll be back at weekends, especially while I'm in school. It might be a bit different when I start on the wards and have to work shifts."

Her mum's eyes glistened with unshed tears, "You mustn't think you have to come home on your days off all the time. I know you've got studying to do, but your life now is about having fun and enjoying yourself. That's what young people do. Your dad wanted that for you."

"I know, it's still hard though," Louise said, swallowing down the lump that was back in her throat.

"It will be. It'll be hard for us all. But we'll cope. The most important thing is you work hard and get that qualification. I can't remember a time in your life that you haven't wanted to be a nurse. Can you remember all those times you dressed in your nurses outfit and bandaged us all up? In the end Aunty Cathy said she'd only come round on the proviso she wasn't a patient."

They were laughing as they made their way towards the car remembering how obsessed she had been with bandages and applying them. Poor Karen, as a younger sister she'd more often than not been the recipient of her childish medical endeavours. As they stopped in front of the family blue Opel Kadett car, Louise noticed another girl saying goodbye to her parents. It looked to be the girl she'd seen earlier from the room opposite.

"Give me a quick ring in the week won't you so I know you're okay?" her mum said rooting round her handbag for the car keys. "If we've forgotten anything, then you can get it on Friday when you come home. And bring your washing."

"Oh, I will. I'm not paying to do it here. That second year who showed us round said it's really expensive to use the machines. I'll wash my bras and knickers out each night in my room."

"Yes, do that, love. Right, we'll get off then," she reached forward and Louise went into her mum's arms. Just a few more seconds of being strong and then she could go back to the privacy of her room and cry. It was evident from her mum's tears as she pulled away that she was struggling too, so Louise quickly turned to hug her sister – not in a loving way like she had her mother. Karen was at that awkward age where displays of affection were uncomfortable.

"Look after Mum, won't you? Promise?"

"Course I will," Karen said using her bubble gum to blow a bubble of indifference.

"And behave at school. You've got to knuckle down this last year. It won't be long now until your O-levels."

"Yeah, yeah, I know."

Louise painted on the brightest smile she could as they got into the car. She raised her hand and waved positively as her mum switched on the engine, put the car into gear and slowly moved away. Once the car had turned the corner and was out of sight, the tears she'd been holding back flowed down her cheeks. She reached in her jeans pocket for a handkerchief and blew her nose. If anyone questioned her, she was going to say she had hay fever. The last thing she wanted was anyone thinking she was upset about her family leaving, even though she was. The tears were for them but also for her dad that hadn't lived long enough to see her start her training. A huge void had appeared in her young life since he'd gone.

She took the stairs two steps at a time, eager to get back upstairs to room 12. Even though the place was busy with people milling about checking the facilities, she managed to avoid engaging with anyone along the way. She closed her room door on all the corridor mutterings and footsteps of parents checking every nook and cranny where their daughters would be spending the next two years.

A huge sigh escaped her lips. She'd been hoping on the way back that the room wasn't as dismal as she'd first thought – but it was. The single bed was against the wall, it had to be, there was no other place for it. The desk occupied the window which had a pleasant outlook to a small courtyard with some benches and tables. The

15

wardrobe looked like it had been bought off the set of Upstairs, Downstairs, and she'd tried to open a drawer earlier and it had been a struggle to close it again. But there was no good wallowing in grief; she had to make a start. She blew her nose and reached for the rucksack she'd carefully packed at home and offloaded the lemon cleaner, Dettol disinfectant and Domestos into the cupboard under the sink. Despite being told on the tour that cleaners came in each day, she hated dirt and germs of any description so needed to be sure she removed them all. Only then would she be able to relax.

She glanced at the notices on the cork board and the Housekeeping one caught her eye. Seemingly, once a week on a Monday she had to strip the bed and leave the sheets outside her room and she'd be left a clean set folded on the bed. So it appeared the cleaners weren't going to be making the bed. Good. She didn't particularly want them in her room anyway. But she daren't say that. They'd think she was crackers with her little cleanliness idiosyncrasies.

By the time the sink had been disinfected, the wardrobe wiped out with warm soapy water and the bed headboard damp dusted, it was almost 6 pm. There had been a letter on the desk in her room explaining that she needed to attend the welcome meeting at 6 pm in the communal sitting room. She hadn't yet unpacked her clothes but decided she'd do that after the meet and greet. She checked her appearance in the mirror inside the wardrobe door, her jeans and sweatshirt looked fine, and the makeup she'd put on at home earlier was still okay, but her mascara was smudged. She reached for her makeup bag and quickly applied some more before running a brush through her long thick black hair she'd inherited from her dad.

Checking first that she had her room key, she slung her bag over her shoulder and left the room. The latched door closed behind her as she turned right and made her way along the corridor, through the door to the communal sitting room that she'd been shown earlier. It was at the end of the corridor – the door she'd come through separated it from the rooms which was a good thing as she imagined it'd get noisy at night. The second-year student had said they could have TV's in their room if they wanted and some did, but most just used the lounge for TV and had radio and record players in their rooms.

As she approached the sitting room, her tummy churned. After her dad died, although reluctant to do so, she'd seen a bereavement counsellor. Her mother had persuaded her, "What harm can it do? Why don't you just try, it might help." So she had.

And as she paused at the sitting room door, she remembered the counsellor's words if she found herself becoming anxious . . . "Stop. Breathe. And slowly count to ten."

3.

Louise

The door to the sitting room was ajar and busy inside with chatter. A stout lady, mid-fifties and plump, particularly round her middle girth, turned as Louise tentatively stepped inside.

"Come in. I'm Mrs McGee, the matron, and your name is?"

"Louise Allard."

Mrs McGee had a long angular face framed by straight shoulder length hair. As she scanned the clipboard in her hand, her grey hair, parted down the middle like a pair of curtains, flopped forward. It seemed too long for a woman her age. She was a tall lady, wearing some sort of soft neck collar similar to one her aunt had once worn when she'd been in a car accident. But unlike the one her aunt had worn, this lady's was covered in a navy fabric.

"I've got you, take a seat," she gestured with her hand at those already seated, "anywhere you like."

The lounge was large and similar to her room, tired and dated. Woodchip paper adorned the walls, painted a dull beige colour, and thick mustard drapes with a matching pelmet dressed the sash window. The coloured two-seater sofas with their old-fashioned wooden arms appeared not to be in their usual position judging by the carpet indentations, but put together for the purpose of the meeting. They'd been positioned facing a small table and chair in front of the fireplace and the television has been pushed in the corner against the wall.

Louise moved towards a vacant seat on a sofa next to the pretty girl she'd seen earlier walking past her room and again in the car park saying goodbye to her parents. Dressed similarly to her in jeans and a tee-shirt was a relief due to her earlier uncertainty about whether to change for the meeting. The girl broke off her chat to two girls on the adjacent sofa and smiled welcomingly.

"Hi," she said in a plum voice, "I think I saw you earlier." Her vibrant turquoise eyes had been enhanced with blue mascara, and her thick lustrous hair secured at the top of her head in a long ponytail. It was a striking blonde colour, almost white, which was a complete contrast to her dark hair.

"Yes, that's right. I'm Louise. Is this seat taken?"

"No, go ahead."

Louise took the seat, shiny and worn from frequent use.

"I'm Kym," the girl's full lips smiled. Her skin was flawless, adding to her prettiness. Everything seemed perfect about her. One of the other girls on the adjacent sofa, a little bit taller judging by her long legs, leaned forward, "I'm Zoe," she said, curling her brown wavy hair around her ears. The smaller olive-skinned girl occupying the same two-seater as Zoe nodded, "Vanya, Vanya Mann."

"Pleased to meet you all, Louise nodded, "I wonder how many of us there are starting today?" The two males opposite and chatting together had surprised Louise. She hadn't considered there might be male nurses in their group.

"Ten of us, I think," Zoe's head turned as if mentally counting those in the room, "so the girl that showed me around said."

She'd somehow imagined there'd be more. "Whereabouts have you all come from today?" she asked, directing her question to Kym first of all.

"Not sure if you'll know it. Cleethorpes."

Louise did know the small seaside town. "Yes, I do. We used to go there for our holidays. My dad was a miner. We stopped at the Fitties."

"That's right, Humberston Fitties, a mini version of Butlins, loads of chalet accommodation with a pool and clubhouse. It's still there. What about you, where are you from?"

"Sheffield." Louise leant forward, "What about you, Zoe?"

"Boston."

"Gosh, that's quite a way."

Before Vanya had time to join in, the tapping of a biro on a glass halted their chatting. Mrs McGee had taken a seat at the table in front of the fireplace.

"I think everyone's here now, so we'll make a start." Not a hint of a smile as she cleared her throat, "I'd like to welcome you to Harlow Wood at the beginning of your training, which I hope will be two fulfilling years for all of you and shape your future as nurses. I'm going to go through some important information so I want you to listen carefully and then you'll be free to go for your supper and all get to know each other. And I'll apologise in advance if it appears like you've joined the military," there were a couple of muffled sniggers, "that isn't my intention. The management at Harlow Wood want you to enjoy your time here. But there are rules that you all must follow. Any breaches in these rules and there will be consequences. If you can keep any questions until I've finished speaking and then there'll be an opportunity to ask anything you're not sure about."

Louise's eyes were drawn to Mrs McGee's purple painted fingernails clutching a piece of paper she glanced down at. The nails seemed flashy for a woman her age.

"We'll start by going round everyone and each of you give your names and where you've come from today. It'll take me a while to get to know you all individually, but it won't take you long to get to know each other as you'll be spending a lot of time together in school for the next six weeks. I'm Barbara McGee, Mrs McGee to you all, the matron of the nurses' homes. I'm responsible for you all in terms of pastoral care and any issues you might have unrelated to your hospital work. I'm nothing to do with your training programme, any issues you have with that you need to take up with the School of Nursing, but anything else is down to me. So, for example, I'll be making sure you're all registered with a local doctor and a dentist, and if anyone is ill and unable to work for whatever reason, I need to be informed so I can keep a check on you in your rooms. You'll see me regularly around both nurses' homes and if you need me at anytime, I reside in South House. I'm sure those of you in North House will have seen it on your way in."

Her pause and stare indicated she was waiting for a response. Once they'd nodded, she continued.

"Mr McGee and I have rooms on the ground floor and my name is on the door. Mr McGee works here at the hospital too. He's a caretaker stroke maintenance man so you'll see him around as there always seems to be something to fix, but he does work in the hospital too. Okay," she turned to the males sitting to her left, "it's quite unusual to have one male on the course, let alone two. She looked at the one closest to her who had a completely bald head, a bit like the Olympic swimmer Duncan Goodhew.

"Would you like to start us off?"

"I'm Guy Logan, from Derby," he smiled showing a perfect set of even white teeth. His eyes twinkled as he spoke, and Louise noticed they were dark brown kind eyes, with long lashes any female would die for. Maybe his hair was dark when he had hair? Why had he shaved it?

The shorter chap at the side of him was the complete opposite with a head of blond unruly curls.

"Simon Buckingham from Leeds."

Mrs McGee followed on with the girls. It was a nice way to break the ice amongst them all as none of them appeared to have met before. Louise felt an immediate affinity with Kym sat alongside her, who was not only attractive looking, but she had a lovely voice too, like she may have had elocution lessons or something similar. Louise listened intently along with the others to Mrs McGee. Despite her denial, her persona implied she did run the place like a military operation. After discussing the expectations of them living in the nurses' home and the etiquette that went alongside that, she began winding the talk up.

"So, tomorrow you're due in the School of Nursing at nine thirty. Please don't be late. It's adjacent to the other side of the hospital. You have to go out of the hospital building to get to it. You'll find it signposted in the main entrance as you walk through the hospital to the canteen. During your first day in school, you'll be given a guided tour of the hospital by the tutors so there's absolutely no need for you to be rooting around it tonight. Breakfast is served daily in the canteen, which is just past the reception, from seven-thirty until eight-thirty and there is a seating area at the side of the dining room for drinks."

Mrs McGee glanced at her watch. "I'm about to finish now so you can head to the dining room for your evening meal and familiarise yourselves with it. It's in the main part of the hospital near reception. As you'll know from the communication you received, payment for your accommodation and meals are taken out of your monthly wage. You'll see the opening times for the dining room displayed on the door, and further in the hospital near ward 9, there's a visitors canteen where you can purchase snacks if you so wish and chocolate bars etc. Again, the opening times are displayed on the door. Are there any questions?"

Zoe put her hand up. "When I was shown around earlier, I was told we couldn't have any boyfriends in our room. Is that just while we're in this house because of our age?"

"No, it's either of them. And the same applies to you both," she turned to Guy and Simon, "no member of the opposite sex in your rooms. Any breaches of this and I'll be forced to have you suspended from the course, which will mean you'll be asked to leave and then consideration will be given as to whether you may rejoin the programme at a later date."

"But how will that work," Zoe scowled, "if say for example Simon or Guy called at my room maybe to borrow a book or ask a question? Do they have to stand in the doorway?"

A couple of the girls were bold enough to snigger.

Mrs McGee took a deep breath in – an obvious breath of irritation. "Remind me of your name again, would you?"

"Zoe."

"I think, Zoe," she glared, "that you, the same as everyone in this room, understand perfectly well what I'm referring to when I speak about no boyfriends and girlfriends in your room. If you don't, then I suggest you stay behind at the end and I'll explain it to you. Now," she turned back to the rest of them, "any other questions?"

Guy raised his hand.

"Yes?"

"Is it far to the nearest pub?"

His question lightened the mood in the room judging by the fidgeting. And even Mrs McGee's lips twitched slightly.

"It's the Rushley, down the road towards Mansfield," she indicated the direction with her head, "I'd say it's about three miles, so it's quite a walk. There are buses, of course. They stop directly opposite the hospital entrance and the timetable is posted in the shelter. They aren't too bad in terms of frequency, which is good as you'll have all noticed on your way here today, the hospital is very isolated. But it's a lovely place for training and any of you that like walking or running, there is plenty of space in the woods."

"It's fine, I have a car," Guy said.

Mrs McGee's eyebrow raised, "How fortunate. In that case, you might be interested to know that in the opposite direction, left as you exit the hospital towards Nottingham, there's the Hut. It's a Berni Inn and serves good food if you did want to eat out at all. Again, it's quite a distance to walk so you would need transport."

"Both sound great," Guy said and quickly added, "for our days off." Louise spotted him give Simon, sitting at the side of him, a nudge. Although she didn't know either of them, she thought it unlikely that they'd only be frequenting the pub on their days off.

"If there are no more questions right now, I'll let you make your way to the dining room where you can spend some time getting to know each other and having supper. And may I suggest you aren't late to bed tonight. It'll be a busy day for you all tomorrow."

As they stood up to leave, Mrs McGee turned to Guy and Simon, "Could you stay behind and help put the furniture back please before you go."

4.

Kym

After the session with Mrs McGee, the girls made their way to the dining room chatting excitedly. They passed the reception area and the dining room was almost opposite as Mrs McGee had advised. The dining room was clean and functional with printed orange and brown wallpaper. There were rows of long dark wood tables with eight seats around each. At the entrance to the dining room, there was a large counter with an array of food on display and a smaller counter with a selection of sweets, fruit and plated cheese and biscuits.

Kym queued with the others and once she'd made her selection, followed Louise to a table that Zoe and Vanya were seated at. There appeared to be two tables labelled for the new entrants but the first one was pretty much occupied with the girls that had been in the meeting, and it appeared like a couple of second year nurses had joined them, no doubt to fill them in about the place.

"So are we all in North House?" Louise asked once they'd all sat down.

"I think most of us are," Vanya said, taking an elastic bobble from around her wrist and securing her long dark hair into a ponytail. "I have to tie it back otherwise it can dangle in my food."

Louise spread out a napkin on her knee. "I don't think I've ever known anyone with such long hair."

"Would you believe I've had it cut for coming here? I knew it'd be a problem tying it up for work and getting the hat over the top so I've had loads cut off. I used to be able to sit on it."

"Gosh, really? It looks to be in great condition for hair that long."

"Thank you. I only wash it once a week, or twice at the most so maybe that's why. The first thing I packed was my hairdryer. I didn't think there'd be one in the rooms."

"No, they're really quite basic aren't they?" Kym said, pulling a face. "I'm guessing they're all pretty similar?" Zoe and Vanya nodded.

"I wonder if they're any better in South House?"

"They're bigger apparently." Zoe rested her knife and fork down, "So I was told on the tour. Mine's tiny. Good job I don't have claustrophobia that's all I can say."

As Vanya began to explain that her room was likely to be noisy as it was next to the kitchen, Kym's eyes were drawn to the door as Guy and Simon walked in. Guy was in front and scanned the food through the Perspex glass. No one could fail to notice he was really attractive, one of those she was certain the nurses would flock round. Even his jeans and sweatshirt with a logo on the left breast seemed classy, and the fact he had a car made her wonder if he was from a rich family. She wondered about his age. Guessing ages wasn't her thing although she could tell Simon was older, quite a bit older.

"What can I get you?" she heard the girl in a white uniform with her hair pinned in a net asking. She couldn't hear what Guy said as his back was to her, but whatever it was, the young server girl coloured, confirming her first thoughts that Guy was a complete charmer.

"How's your cottage pie?" Louise asked.

"Really nice, is yours?"

"Yeah. I hope all the food's not this good otherwise I'll soon be like a barrel."

"Me too."

Guy approached their table with the 'new entrants' sign displayed boldly in the centre. "Can we sit anywhere?" he asked, eyeing up the vacant chair adjacent to Kym.

"Course you can," she reached to take her bag off the seat.

"Cheers." He put his tray down, "I'm sorry," he said taking the seat and dragging his chair in, "I'm rubbish with names, it's Kym isn't it?"

"Not that rubbish, you're spot on."

Simon approached the table. "Room for a little one?" he asked pulling out the empty chair opposite, next to Zoe. Once they were both seated, Guy asked, "Does anyone mind going round again with names. I don't know about you all, but I've forgotten everyone already."

"Good idea. I'm Kym," she turned towards the others expectantly. Once they'd all re-introduced themselves, Guy reached for a knife and fork from the holder in the centre of the table, "I've read somewhere that to remember names, you should try and think of someone you know or have met with that name. Not sure if that helps though," he looked at Simon, "we'd have been better with name badges or something, even if it's just a sticky label."

"We get them tomorrow in school apparently," Simon said buttering a bread roll, "when I was given the guided tour earlier, they told me."

"Good. It would have been better this evening though, I would have thought. Anyway, how's the food?" he asked sprinkling his with plenty of salt.

"Great," Simon answered, "it always is here."

"How do you know that?" Kym asked.

"I was in here as a patient for a while."

"Really?"

"Yeah. I was in a motorbike accident a couple of years ago and ended up here on traction."

"And you're back now to do your training here, they must have looked after you well?"

"That's exactly what I said earlier when we met," Guy said forking some food into his mouth.

"They did, that's why I'm here really. I was on a ward with a male charge nurse, Nick Feeney, and it was him that inspired me to apply for my training."

"That's a lovely thing. Good for you."

"Well, it's all down to him really."

"Is he still here?"

"Yeah, he is. He's the charge nurse on Ward 7. It's one of the newer wards with bays opposed to the old Nightingale ones. I think they were added about eight years ago."

"I wonder if you'll be allocated his ward to work with him once we've finished in school?" Guy asked.

"I hope so. I think we get to go on most wards. Anyway, enough of me," Simon poured himself some water from the jug on the table, "what did you all make of Matron McGee? Do you reckon she's as fierce as she makes out?"

"Christ knows," Guy scowled, "she's a bit odd, isn't she? I wouldn't want to get on the wrong side of her. She reminds me of that singer, what's his name . . . erm, he's Greek . . . oh, I know, Demis Roussos."

Kym laughed, "Hey, she does look like him a bit. It sounds like she's going to be doing her rounds along the corridors each night to check we haven't smuggled any men into our rooms."

"Christ, imagine bumping into her when you're nipping to the loo. She'd frighten the life out of you. Hey, Zoe, she's got your card marked asking your name."

"Yeah, sounds like it. But how stupid saying we can't have the opposite sex in our rooms. It's a ridiculous rule if you ask me."

Guy raised an eyebrow questioningly. "Have you got a boyfriend? Is that why you asked?"

"Sort of."

"Well, don't invite him to stay over that's all I say. I wouldn't put it past Mrs McGee having a master key and coming into your room to catch you in the act."

The image made them all laugh.

"What about you," Zoe asked, "do either of you have girlfriends?"

"Nooooo not me," Simon said emphatically.

Guy nodded, "Yeah, I have."

Kym knew he would have. Someone as good looking as him wouldn't be on their own for long. Which nurses' home are you two in?" she asked.

"North, on the ground floor with the locum doctors," Simon said, putting his knife and fork together. "That was good. I might have to get a pudding though, I'm still hungry, my portion was only small." He scowled playfully at Guy, "How come you got a massive piece of pie and so many chips?"

"The girl server took pity on me when I said I hadn't eaten all day and I was a growing lad."

Simon laughed and got up out of his seat, "I must try that next time."

They'd stretched out the meal with desserts and chat, most probably because nobody wanted to head back to their dismal rooms. During supper, they branched off from the group conversation and picked up with those closest to them. Kym spoke more to Louise and Guy, while Simon had turned to talk more to Vanya and Zoe.

"I take it you two are only seventeen, with being in North House?" Guy asked.

"Yeah, that's right," Louise fiddled with a napkin, "I'm almost eighteen though so I guess I'll be moving to South House then."

"I'm not eighteen for a while," Kym said. "How old are you, Guy?"

"Twenty-two. And before you say it, I know I look much older." He scratched his bald head, "It's the lack of hair that does it."

"I wasn't going to say that at all."

"Sorry. It's just that most people want to know why and there's no great mystery. It just dropped out when I was thirteen and never grew back."

"Well, I think it suits you."

"Thank you, that's nice. People usually say something sympathetic like, what a shame, or maybe it'll grow back one day."

"Really? That seems a bit insensitive."

"Yeah, I know. But I'm used to it now. Anyway, enough about that. Have either of you got boyfriends?"

"I haven't," Louise said, "and I'm not looking for one either." She winced, "I didn't mean that to come out quite that way."

"No worries. What about you, Kym?"

"Yes, my boyfriend's in the Navy."

"That'll be a bit of a challenge, seeing much of him while you're here?"

"Yeah, it will be, but we'll manage. He's currently at Portsmouth and comes home to Cleethorpes when he can."

"That's good then."

A voice from the serving hatch interrupted their conversation. "We're closing up in fifteen minutes."

Guy checked his silver watch which at a glance looked much more expensive than an average Timex. "It's still early," he turned to include the others round the table, "is anyone up for checking this Rushley pub out if it's going to be our local? I can get five of us in my car," his eyes drifted towards Vanya who was the smallest of them, "and maybe at a push, squeeze six in."

"I'm in," Simon said eagerly, "never been one to turn down a beer."

Kym shook her head, "I want to finish unpacking and getting settled in, so not for me . . . not tonight anyway."

"Me neither." Louise raised her eyebrows, "Maybe another night though?"

"I'm up for it," Zoe said eagerly, "what about you, Vanya?"

"No, thanks. I've still got unpacking to do and I want an early night."

"Oh right," Zoe sighed, "I'll leave it then. I don't want to come on my own."

"Why not?" Guy frowned, "we won't bite. Well I won't, I can't speak for Simon."

Simon grinned, "I won't either," and then added cheekily, "not unless I'm asked to."

Zoe laughed, "Maybe another night then if nobody else is coming."

Kym caught Zoe's eyes focussing on Guy as she made the suggestion, but he seemed oblivious as he turned to Simon. "Looks like it's just thee and me then, mate."

"I'd love to come another night," Vanya said eagerly, "but just not tonight."

"Yeah, me too," Louise tossed her napkin onto her dessert plate, "I think tomorrow would be good though, so shall we say it's a date? Unless you two won't want to go to the pub two nights on the trot?"

Guy screwed his face up at Simon. "Is she for real? It looks like we're going to have to explain how important it is for us to get our cards marked regularly at the pub."

"Long as it isn't to the detriment of studying," Kym warned playfully, her eyes twinkling, "it said in all the bumf we got, there'll be homework while we're in school. That's why we have a desk in our rooms."

"Is it really?" Guy said with a straight face, "and here's me thinking that was a place to stand my telly on. Now, you're telling me that I have to study while I'm here?"

Kym wasn't fooled by his dismissal of studying. She'd come across people like him at school. Those that always portrayed themselves as the least academic invariably were often the brightest. And something told her that Guy was no dummy.

"Right," Kym grabbed her bag from the side of her chair, "I'm going to head to the nurses' home, anyone joining me?"

"Yep," Louise pushed back her chair at the same time as Vanya.

"Me too," Zoe said, "we'll see you in the morning then at breakfast. Don't drink too much if you do go to the pub. You want to make a good impression on your first day in school."

"Okay, Mum," Guy saluted her playfully, "advice noted."

Kym pushed back her chair and stood up. "See you both tomorrow." It was going to be good having the two of them on the course. In her experience working in a female dominated office, girls could get a bit bitchy, whereas males balanced that out. And she could just tell Guy and Simon were going to be fun.

"You bet," Guy smiled charmingly.

5.

He'd been sat in the coffee lounge area adjacent to the dining room where from his viewpoint he could see the girls as they ate their supper. Out of the two tables allocated to the new students, the one with the two males sitting on it interested him. It had surprised him that out of the eight girls in the new intake, there wasn't an ugly one amongst them. At a glance, he excluded a couple as definite *No's*, mainly the tubbier ones. He wanted one he could hold with ease. Overcome with ease. Easily dispose of, which meant carrying her. So he kept a watchful eye on the four slim ones as they laughed and interacted with each other around the table.

Although he was turning the pages of the Daily Mirror newspaper, he wasn't really interested in it. No highfalutin academic paper for him, he just liked to keep abreast of basic news. He liked to unwind at night, reading every article on every page. But unwinding at night was proving more difficult now since the beginning of the week and was only going to get worse – the consultant at Nottingham City hospital had seen to that. Since returning, he hadn't been able to sleep. It had been the worst news imaginable.

Dr Brompton, a stuck-up old git, sporting a grey suit and waistcoat and wearing a bow tie at his neck, was sat behind the desk as he took the seat the nurse had offered. In front of the consultant was a folder of patient notes with his name written in bold on the front. Not the name he'd been christened with; it was the fictitious one he'd taken on and changed by deed poll.

The consultant raised his head in a greeting, and without any further pleasantries, went for the jugular.

"We have all your recent tests and investigations back and I'm afraid it isn't good news." The conversation paused for a moment as Dr Brompton peered over his gold-rimmed glasses, as if he was gauging if he was ready for more.

"The shadow on your lung indicates cancer." He steepled his fingers, "Fortunately . . . if there can ever be any fortunate's in this sort of situation, we are able to offer treatment. Treatment that we would hope would be successful."

It hadn't come as a surprise. It had been initially when he'd visited his GP for some antibiotics for a cough he couldn't shake off. And even when he'd gone for the routine chest Xray, he still didn't think too much about it. It hadn't crossed his mind it could be anything sinister. He'd been religiously taking the tablets as the pharmacist had instructed 'until the course was complete' thinking to himself they weren't doing any good and he may need something stronger, but he hadn't thought any more than that. Until the telephone call came. The doctor was referring him to the hospital for further tests as it was evident from the Xray, there was a small shadow on his lung. Of course the doctor made all the right noises, 'It might not be anything to worry about' – 'it could be an infection', but he knew it was more than that – he developed a foreboding sense. Maybe it was karma?

Dr Brompton had continued, "I understand the news is a shock and a lot for you to take in and process. We will need to do further exploratory work to assess whether the tumour has spread."

He kept his expression deadpan. "How long?"

"All in all, it will take a few months. And I need to be honest, it will be gruelling."

"No, I wasn't asking that. How long have I got?"

"Oh, I see. Well, I'm afraid that's not easy to answer. Each patient responds differently to treatment. I do need to discuss further with the surgical team about removing either part of the lung, or the whole lung. And as graphic and frightening that sounds, it is a procedure we do all the time in cases like yours. Once the operation is over and after a short recovery period, you'll have radiotherapy."

"What if I don't have any treatment?"

"It's hard to judge. Your tests indicate you're relatively healthy, so I would urge you to consider the treatment offered. It could prolong your life for quite some time."

"Yes, I hear that. But can you give me a ballpark if I don't have treatment?"

He took a deep breath in. No doubt not used to patients considering their own mortality. Most would want any treatment offered. But he didn't.

"Maybe three or four months . . . perhaps longer. However, it could be less than that. It's always hard to put a time frame on these things. But the quality of however many months it is, the last months will be poor. We can offer palliative treatment that will keep you comfortable and pain free for a significant period we would hope. Initially you'd not notice any difference. You'll still have your cough, but things may not progress for quite some time. It's only a small lesion, that's why I'm encouraging you to have treatment. And I need to be clear, if you don't have any intervention, which is entirely your prerogative, your health will deteriorate as the cancer progresses."

"But there are no guarantees if I have any surgery?"

"No, I'm afraid there aren't. But I've been working as a physician for many years and my role is to advise using my experience on the best course of action, although I can't of course insist. The treatment options are entirely up to individuals themselves. I have learned to respect their choices."

"Thank you. I appreciate your directness."

"If you go with the nurse now, she'll sort out another appointment for you to come and see me. It's been quite a shock today and a lot to process. Think carefully about the options. The nurse will give you a patient information booklet about the surgery that you can study in depth. And then when you come back and see me again, we'll go from there on what you decide."

He stood up, shook the consultant's hand and followed the nurse into the adjacent room. No way was he undergoing surgery. The thought of anyone poring over his body, and to have strangers dissecting his insides, was to him, the stuff of nightmares. It was abhorrent. He'd been there once, and he was never going to let that happen again. There did seem a certain irony that the thing he'd thought about and dreaded most of his adult life was the day his freedom would be curtailed – but that was with handcuffs and a prison sentence, not cancer. He was adamant he wasn't going down the surgical route and nothing would make him change his mind. Nature would take its course. Maybe four months the doc had said, and he'd deteriorate during the latter part of those months.

"Do take a seat," the nurse smiled with a hint of sympathy in her eyes. "I'm just going to check Dr Brompton's next two clinics and see if we can fit you in for that further chat as he suggested. Just bear with me."

He watched her flicking through the appointments diary. She was attractive, but too old for his liking. He preference was young girls. Fresh and vibrant, not married ones or any that'd been round the block. Not particularly a virgin, but ones with a degree of shyness or inexperience.

"I've got a date for you," she looked up at him and he appeared attentive as she questioned if it was convenient to him. He just nodded his compliance, even though he wouldn't be attending.

A shriek of laughter brought his thoughts back into the present. It was coming from the table with the males on. He hoped they weren't going to be a problem; he'd clocked the bald one making for the prettiest one on the table, no doubt wanting to get in her knickers. She was stunning and the darker girl sat next to her was interesting. She'd been laughing and joining in but her eyes didn't seem quite so bright as the other girls. The tiny one was cute as hell. He pictured her in her underwear, and then naked. Imagined the soft feel of her skin. And the girl to her right was an option too, a looker with long wavy hair and pouty lips, but she seemed taller than the others so might be a problem. And she seemed more confident somehow, sort of holding court with the blond bloke and the tiny girl. Confident girls fought back. Confident girls opened their mouths and screamed.

"Do you mind if we join you?" A domestic and her buddy nodded to the vacant chairs next to him.

"Of course," he said moving towards the edge of his seat. "Don't think it's anything you said though, I was leaving anyway." They smiled at him as he picked up his newspaper.

He made his way out of the coffee lounge, excitement dancing in his gut. If he was going out of this world – he most definitely wasn't going alone. He'd go with a bang. And his impending death sentence meant there was no time to lose. So, if his cancer diagnosis was Karma's way of paying him back for previous murders – then Karma could go fuck itself. Because all it had done was whetted his appetite for the thrill of another kill.

And looking at those young beauties . . . one might not be enough.

6.

Louise

Louise and her new friends, their steps echoing on the tiled floors, walked together towards the hospital exit. Joining them were the other new starters from the adjacent table. The corridors were wide with numerous windows which, because it was dark, the benefits wouldn't be noticeable, but in the day the place would be light and airy, Louise thought.

Two of the girls, Marie and Helen, were chatting together just ahead of Louise. They were both in South House, and the other two girls, trailed behind. As they came out of the main hospital building, the cool night air hit them as they paused for the others to catch up.

"Gosh, it's cold," Louise said folding her arms across her chest. She always felt cold, her mother used to say it was because she wasn't eating enough. And there was a time when she did just graze and pick, but at least she was now eating more, which was a positive.

"It's not really," Vanya tightened her cardigan, "it's because we've just come out of the lovely warm hospital. They keep it at a high temperature for the patients."

"You're probably right," Helen said, rubbing her bare arms. "Anyway, I guess we'll see you all at breakfast in the morning. I don't suppose we're going to get much

41

sleep tonight somehow. It all feels a bit strange, doesn't it?"

"Yes," Vanya agreed, "it certainly does."

"We'll get used to it though," Kym said, "I just think this first night will be weird for all of us. But yeah, we'll see you in the dining room for breakfast in the morning. Shall we say about eight?"

"Sounds good. See you then. Night."

"Night," Louise said, pasting on a smile.

Louise and the others made their way up to North House which wasn't a great distance away, just a little higher up the hill. A tightness in her chest and an ominous feeling of dread ran through her at the thought of returning to her room. As nice as the girls appeared to be, it'd seemed for ever since she waved her mum off. Did she really want to be at Harlow Wood for the next two years? Had she made a mistake? It was the question at the forefront of her mind as she walked with the others towards the imposing nurses' home. Should she have deferred her place until the following year?

Zoe pulled a face, "Pity we're not going with them if their rooms are better than ours. Mind you, silver lining and all that, at least we have males on the ground floor with the locum doctors, and I reckon it's going to be a blast having Simon and Guy on our course, don't you?"

"Yeah, they're both really nice aren't they?" Vanya smiled, "I wonder why Guy's shaved his hair off like that?"

"He hasn't," Kym shook her head, "he told us that he started with alopecia when he was thirteen and it never grew back properly."

Vanya screwed her face up, "Oh, God that's awful. I wonder what happened? You don't just lose your hair. A significant event must have caused it. Maybe he was ill or something?"

"I think it suits him," Louise said, and she meant it. Guy was really attractive, anyone could see that. From just meeting him, she could tell that he wasn't an in-your-face good-looking bloke, he simply oozed charm and had an infectious appeal. "Simon's the opposite isn't he with his head of thick curly hair? It's quite a contrast."

"I didn't catch what age Simon was, did you?" Zoe asked as they continued walking.

"I don't think he actually said. But he must be a bit older than us," Vanya replied, "He did say he'd spent years working at the City hospital in the theatre supplies unit."

Louise frowned, "What do they do there?"

"It's where they sterilise everything for use in theatres."

Sterilising stuff sounded like a perfect job because of her desire for cleanliness. She almost voiced that she'd love to do that job but kept it to herself. "Well I think Simon is going to be a great nurse, especially after what he's been through with his motorbike accident. He'll be able to see things from a patient's perspective."

"Yeah, he does seem really nice," Kym said as they reached the pathway to the nurses' home entrance.

"Hey, what is this," Zoe grinned, "an appreciation society for Simon? Are any of you seeing him as boyfriend material?"

"Not me," Kym dismissed, "I've already got a boyfriend."

"Me neither," Vanya said, "I like him, but not like that. I just think they're both going to be a good laugh."

"If we're laying our cards on the table," Louise interjected, "I'm not interested either. My dad died recently, so I want to try and concentrate on the course and support my mum. She's taken it really badly. The last thing I need is to get entangled with anyone and certainly not with someone on the same course."

What she couldn't say was her last encounter with a male, still disturbed her and was no doubt responsible for the compulsive behaviours she'd adopted and couldn't shake off. But she wouldn't share that. If she was totally honest with herself, it was one of the reasons she'd wanted to get away from home. But nothing was to be gained by dwelling on that. Her counsellor had told her that moving away and onto something completely different may actually curb some of the obsessions. And she so wanted to believe that. It was a constant struggle having to pretend each day that everything was normal, and that she was the same as any other seventeen-year-old, bright, excited and care-free, when in reality, it was a massive struggle each day to put one foot in front of the other.

"What about you," Louise strode alongside Zoe, trying to dismiss the awful images that had crept in, "you asked the question?"

"I think Guy's quite nice."

"Yeah, but he did say he had a girlfriend, you'd be better going for Simon, seeing as he's single?"

"Nah, not for me."

"Didn't you say you had a boyfriend?"

"I have but he won't know what's going on here," Zoe winked. "Anyway, have you got a boyfriend, Vanya? You didn't say."

"I did have someone . . ." her voice faded . . . "but my dad wasn't keen. He's strict about anything like that. I had a devil of a job getting him to agree to me coming here. Thank goodness for my mother and her influence."

"Well, you'll be able to do what you like while you're here," Zoe said, "what goes on in Harlow Wood, stays in Harlow Wood, so your dad won't have any idea what you're up to."

Vanya playfully shuddered, "Oh, God, it makes me nervous just thinking about his disapproval."

Louise couldn't help smiling at her. "Yeah, but now you've cut the parent ties, you can get back with your ex if you want to."

"I'd like to but it's not as easy as that. He's moved on now with a new girlfriend. But I'm not bothered. I'm really looking forward to getting stuck into the training. Anyway, Louise, I'm sorry to hear about your dad. He can't have been that old?"

"No, he wasn't."

Louise didn't want to say anything more about her dad. It was still too raw and she'd said enough. She was barely coping herself. How many times she'd heard well-meaning people say it'd get easier? It was a stupid statement and a load of rubbish – in reality it seemed to get harder each day. She'd thought all evening about speaking to her mum and asking her to come and fetch her. There'd be no shame in admitting she'd made a mistake. Nurse training was what she wanted to do, maybe just not right now. But the little voice in her head reminded her to put one foot in front of the other, 'you only need to take one step at a time to get to the top of the stairs', her dad would always say.

Her tummy churned and the tightening in her chest accelerated her breathing as they reached the nurses' home entrance. Vanya held the door open and they all traipsed through. "You sound out of breath, Louise?"

She pasted on a smile. "Yeah, must be my asthma. Some days are worse than others."

"Oh, I am sorry," Vanya looked genuinely concerned, "I didn't mean anything by it."

"Don't be daft, I know you didn't." Louise quickly changed the subject, "Hey, we mustn't forget to do the in-out board," she reminded them, "we don't want to get on the wrong side of Mrs McGee. She seemed very intent on us all using it at that welcome meeting. She must have said it four times."

"Yeah, she did," Kym nodded, "But like she said, in the event of a fire, they have to know who's inside so they can rescue us. So it is a good thing."

"Blimey," Louise shuddered, "that doesn't bear thinking about." She had enough worries that would keep her awake without adding another to the list. Sleeping was really hard for her. Some nights she barely got to sleep before dawn, which resulted in grogginess most of the following day.

"It's just a precaution," Kym reassured, "I can't see anything happening like that. And there are fire escapes at each end of the corridor. So we'd easily get out in an emergency."

"Gosh, I hope you're right." If Kym only knew. If any of them knew how she'd been trapped once before. But she'd got away, she had to keep reminding herself.

They approached the wall board at the bottom of the stairs with all their names neatly written on. Vanya flicked the tiny window to *IN* alongside each of their names. Guy and Simon's were flicked to *OUT*. Although they'd just met them both that evening, Louise had a feeling both of them were likely to be socialising a lot during their training so their names would have *OUT* beside them more often than theirs.

They climbed the stairs to the first floor and waited at the top for Susan and Lisa who were following behind.

"Shall we go down to breakfast together?" Kym asked as they congregated at the top of the stairs, "I can tap on your doors, say about eight?"

"Sounds good to me," Zoe said, "or is it easier to meet here at the top of the stairs?"

"Yeah, that sounds better as I'll probably not remember all the numbers."

"We'll do that then," Vanya said, "and let's hope we manage to get some sleep at least."

"Let's hope so," Louise said, "See you all in the morning."

Louise closed the door to room 12. She leant against it, barely able to move. A tingling sensation enveloped her limbs. *Change your thought process, quickly onto something else,* her counsellor's voice was telling her – anything to suppress the anxiety that was flooding in. She thought about the evening and how much she had actually enjoyed it. For a little while, she'd been able to escape her woes, which was good. *A positive.* Everyone seemed really nice. And she loved Kym. Who wouldn't? She seemed to be a lovely person all round. So strikingly pretty, but it wasn't just her appearance, she had internal warmth about her. No wonder Guy wanted to sit next to her and chat to her most of all. They made a really attractive couple.

After breathing deeply through her nose, a technique she'd been taught, she felt more in control and moved towards the bed. She opened her suitcase and began to hang her clothes up in the wardrobe she'd cleaned and disinfected earlier. The air freshener she'd brought from home and hung in the wardrobe had made a difference. The wardrobe smelled lemon fresh.

She put her underwear neatly in the drawers, each bra paired up with the matching knickers and her toiletries and makeup underneath the sink. Her mother had packed a small linen bag for her dirty underwear which she stuffed underneath the bed. It was unlikely she'd be using it. The thought of dirty underwear under the bed wasn't something she could contemplate. She'd have to wash them out daily.

Once she'd unpacked everything, she clutched a cherished photo of her dad with his arm around her, taken on their last holiday in Scarborough. They'd laughed and screamed together with the crowds at Peasholm Park as the battleships fought on the water and her mum has snapped them both just at the right time. She placed the frame on the bedside table, caressing it as if she was touching him. In its position she would see him last thing at night and first thing in the morning.

She moved towards the washbowl and stared at her reflection in the mirror as she removed her makeup, washed her hands and face and brushed her teeth. It had been a lovely supper, meeting everyone. She felt an affinity with Kym, but also thought Vanya was really sweet. Zoe she wasn't too sure about. She was nice enough, but a little overconfident. Maybe it was nerves?

She'd brought a small travel wash powder with her so it was easy enough to wash her bra and knickers, squeeze them out, and place them on the radiator which was blasting out heat. They'd be dry by the morning. After putting on her new Snoopy pyjamas her mum had bought her, she proceeded to go through what would become a ritual each night. She put the plug in the sink and filled it with water, adding a squirt of Domestos, confident it would take care of any germs. She splashed some in the chipped overflow, just to be sure. Before she got into the single bed, she brought the bed sheet to her nose and inhaled it. It smelled clean and freshly laundered, like vanilla, which was a relief. Sleep eluded her as she laid down. There seemed to be a lot of music and door banging coming from down the corridor. But it wasn't just the noise. The tap had started dripping and she knew she'd turned it off properly. She got out of bed, turned the tap on, let it run and turned it off again.

Hours of tossing and turning followed before the noise eventually quietened down. Finally people must have headed to bed as the constant footsteps up and down the corridor, the slamming of doors, and the music and TV's blaring out, ceased. She took a deep breath in and she started to finally doze, exhausted by the full day. But the drip drip of the tap was back. She thought about her dad and how handy he was with any DIY – he'd have a dripping tap sorted in no time.

Despite trying to stifle the tears she'd been holding in all day, she couldn't any longer. They flowed down her cheeks and, as her crying gained momentum, she was forced to muffle her uncontrollable sobs in the pillow. If only her dad was there to hug her.

7.

Kym

The following morning, the trip along the corridor to the shower was an effort and a poignant reminder to Kym of her lovely home in Cleethorpes where her mother would wake her up with an early cup of tea. In the Sullivan household, they'd all be rushing round to get to work, her mum to the small private hospital, her dad to his teaching job, and her to the accountants where she'd been an office junior. It seemed much longer than Sunday afternoon when she'd said goodbye to her mum and dad.

She stared at her clothes neatly lined up in the wardrobe. Nobody was dressed that smartly the previous evening so she selected a bright turquoise jumper and black cords. As she dressed, she thought about Louise, saying that her dad had recently died. How sad that must be for her. God forbid, Kym couldn't bear to lose her dad, he was the calm to counteract her mum, the storm.

She applied mascara as she did religiously each day, as her eyelashes were fair, and thought about Tony and speaking to him that evening. Was he thinking about her right now? She hoped so. Their relationship was so much easier when she was at home in Cleethorpes. He could ring in the evening and catch her at home. It was going to prove more difficult once she started working shifts on the ward. But she'd promised herself she'd work it out and she would do. Tony was the most important thing in her life.

After brushing her hair and tying it up in a ponytail, as she did most days, she cleaned her teeth, grabbed her bag she'd packed the previous evening with a notebook and pencil case, and went to meet the others for breakfast.

They'd sat themselves at the same table in the dining room they'd been sitting on at supper. The only difference was, the rest of the group who'd been sitting on the adjacent table the previous evening had joined them pulling up extra chairs. The lads were nowhere to be seen. Kym enjoyed getting to know the other girls in the group. They all seemed really nice. She reeled off their names in her head, Louise, Vanya, Zoe, Marie, Helen, Susan and Lisa before checking the clock on the wall.

"Do you think we'd better be making a move?" she suggested, addressing the whole table, "It's quarter past and we don't want to be late." She hated being late for anything. It was something that had been installed in her since being a child. Sadly Tony didn't share her timekeeping need. He was always late and completely oblivious to the tension it caused between them.

"No, we don't or we might get the cane from Mrs McGee," Zoe laughed cynically.

"You could be right," Vanya smiled, "although she did say she was totally separate from school and our training programme."

"Yeah, that's true. But I reckon she's the sort that will interfere in everything. Probably getting a weekly report from school about how each of us is doing."

Louise shook her head, "I wouldn't have thought so somehow, I reckon it'll be a full-time job looking after the nurses' homes and everyone."

"Let's hope so," Zoe said, "I reckon where possible, we need to give her a wide berth. I definitely will. Hey, who was it Guy said she looked like?"

"Demis Roussos," Vanya said, laughing.

"That is so funny," Zoe laughed too, "although maybe a bit unkind to Demis Roussos."

The girls left the dining room together and followed the signs to the School of Nursing. Kym fell into step with Louise while Vanya and Zoe walked in front. Side by side, their height difference was obvious. Zoe must be about five foot nine, while Vanya was barely five foot. Both were wearing dresses and looked smart. Even though Vanya was petite, she wasn't one of those females that looked like a tiny girl, she was feminine with little breasts, a small waist and neat hips which her dress accentuated beautifully. Zoe suited her dress too which displayed her long legs in woollen tights as it was cut above the knee.

"I'll not be able to eat like this every morning," Louise said patting her tummy, "I'm stuffed. I'm having cereals tomorrow."

"Me too," Kym said, "my cords feel so tight, I don't normally have breakfast. Shame the lads missed it, I wonder why they didn't come?"

"They've probably slept in until the last minute, especially if they were at the pub until late. They're daft for not coming, especially when the food's paid for. Anyway, how did you sleep last night?" Louise asked.

"Awful, what about you?"

"Not very well. It was noisy, wasn't it? I hope it's not like that every night."

"It will be, I bet. We'll just have to get used to it."

They found the exit from the hospital towards the School of Nursing. Kym held the door for the others and followed them out. As they continued walking down the concrete path, the beautiful lawned area at the side of them was being tended by a tall man using shears to trim off the lawn edges but once he saw them, he stopped and tapped his red cap, "Lovely morning."

The girls nodded back, though Kym noticed his gaze seemed to linger on Vanya.

A few steps further, they reached the building they were looking for. The School of Nursing was more modern than anything they'd seen so far. It almost looked like two huge portacabins linked together. It appeared to be on one level, spread out and surrounded by beautiful, manicured lawns with several wooden benches. Each had an ornate plaque on them which Kym would have loved to look at, but there wasn't time. Maybe she could look at lunchtime?

All eyes were on the walls as they entered the School of Nursing. There were blue signs indicating numbered classrooms, toilets and even a practical ward. Someone had handwritten a notice and put it on the wall, 'New students classroom 1'.

As they continued down the corridor, a woman peered out of a doorway. "New intake?" she asked.

"That's us," Zoe replied.

"Then you're in the right place. This way."

They passed a small cordoned off area where a man was squatting down and painting a door frame. The lady in the doorway spoke to him. "When you're finished this morning, Mr McGee, would you put a notice up reminding us the paint will be wet. I'd hate for any of the students to accidentally brush past it and get their clothes covered in paint."

The man reached for a sheet of paper stating 'wet paint'. "All ready for when I leave."

"I should have known," she nodded, "thank you."

"Welcome girls," she smiled through a mouth enhanced with pink lipstick. "Come in and find a desk." Kym noticed the woman was wearing heavy makeup. Almost too heavy, as if it was some sort of camouflage to cover skin issues.

The tables were set up in twos in the bright classroom with a huge window making the room airy and light. The trees in the woods were displaying gorgeous berry reds and strong brown colours. As it was almost autumn, many had begun shedding their leaves.

Kym pulled out the modern chair next to the window, the complete opposite to the dated worn seats in the nurses' home they'd sat on for the meeting the previous evening. Louise sat beside her. In a short space of time, it seemed like they were meant to be friends. Zoe and Vanya took the table next to them.

"We're becoming the four musketeers don't you think?" Zoe laughed.

"Yes it seems like it. Hey," Kym whispered, "that painter must be Mrs McGee's husband."

"Yeah, he must be," Zoe nodded, "he seemed almost normal compared to her."

Kym watched as Louise took a tissue out of her bag and began wiping the desk.

"What are you doing?"

"It feels a bit sticky."

"Oh, right." It didn't feel at all sticky to her. Louise reminded Kym of her mum. It was just the sort of thing she'd do. Her mum was obsessed with cleanliness and disinfecting stuff. Her dad said it was the nurse in her. They used to play tricks on her and leave crumbs about to see if she spotted them, which of course she did, every single time. Her mum never missed a speck of dust or a smear on a window.

The teacher remained in the doorway, looking down the corridor, clearly waiting for Simon and Guy. "Did anyone see the missing two at breakfast?" she asked.

"No, they weren't there," Kym offered.

"I see. Well, it's almost nine thirty, maybe we ought to make a start. I'll leave the classroom door open. I can't imagine where they've got to. It's not a good impression on their first day."

As she was about to take her seat at the desk in front of them, Simon and Guy were ushered in by a tall man, about fifty with hair that looked too dark to be natural, it was almost jet black. He was dressed smartly in a grey suit and, judging by the lenses on his thick rimmed glasses, terribly short-sighted.

"I found these stragglers outside," he said in a voice that indicated his displeasure. "Seemingly, they thought it was okay to sit and have a bacon bun outside completely oblivious to the fact everyone's waiting for them."

"We're really sorry," Guy looked genuinely remorseful, "It was entirely my fault. I think my watch battery's on the way out." He pulled back his shirt sleeve, "It's not yet even saying nine thirty."

The man still had a look of annoyance but before he could say any more, the female teacher smiled. "You're here now, that's the main thing. Take a seat," she gestured Simon and Guy towards the tables.

"Do you want to speak now while you're here?" she asked the man.

"No. I've got something to do in the library. I'll come back at our agreed time."

"That's fine. See you shortly."

Simon and Guy took the vacant table at the front of the classroom. Guy looked really attractive in a white shirt and blue waistcoat which complemented his flared jeans. Simon was much more casual in a thick fisherman's brown polo neck jumper and jeans. As they emptied their rucksacks of pens and notebooks, Kym inhaled the rich, sharp aroma of aftershave. She wasn't normally a lover of male scent, especially the horrible Brut they all seemed to wear, or the older ones like her dad with his Old Spice. Both were more off-putting than anything as far as she was concerned, but this smell was the kind that commanded attention. Sort of earthy and all masculine, giving a rush of excitement that was alien to her. And she was sure it emanated from Guy, not Simon somehow.

The teacher waited until the lads seemed ready. She gave them a kind look, as if to say not to worry. She certainly didn't seem as perturbed as the man did.

"Good morning again everyone, and welcome. I'm Linda Beaumont, Mrs Beaumont to you all. I'm the senior tutor here in the School of Nursing. I'm leading the programme and will be joined by various tutors both from the hospital and outsiders for your tuition during the next two years. This morning is all about your training programme and then after coffee you'll get a tour around the hospital. And this afternoon, you have appointments in the sewing room to be measured for your uniforms. You'll be pleased to know as it's your first day and there's such a lot to take on board, you can go as soon as you've finished in the sewing room and you'll have the rest of the afternoon off. But please, don't get used to it. There's a lot to be done during your time in school."

Mrs Beaumont reached for a small box on her desk. "I'll pass this round; it's your name badges. Please identify your own and wear it in school until all the teachers are familiar with your names, and of course when you're on duty. And while you're doing that, I'm passing round a paper for each of you. The names are at the top left-hand corner. Select your own and then we can go through them."

"Hey," Guy turned to her and Louise to pass them the box, "that's fortuitous, finishing early. It gives us more drinking time at the pub."

Kym rolled her eyes, "You're pub mad."

"Team building, that's what it's all about," he winked, "spread the word."

She couldn't help but be amused. Guy had a charm and a sort of energy about him. As she'd only met him the night before, she wasn't able to articulate exactly how she felt but it was almost like having a mini adrenaline rush around him.

"Has everyone got a programme with their name on?" Mrs Beaumont asked. They all nodded.

"Before we go through that, I want you today to make sure you familiarise yourselves with the School of Nursing. It's not that large, there are three classrooms, the library, the practical room, which is like a mini ward, and of course there are toilets and the tutor's office. Have a look round today. I have a timetable for your week in school which I'll give out shortly.

"But first of all, I'd like to concentrate on the programme you have in front of you. These are your entire programmes for the two years you are with us. The different ward allocations for each of you are written in red. They are in blocks of eight weeks, and following each placement, you'll return to the school of nursing for tuition. Those are blocked out in green. The weeks blocked out in blue are your holidays and they are non-negotiable. You will have all received notification when you took up the offer of this course that any previous holiday bookings will not be sanctioned. So the allocated holidays will be the ones you will get during your training. I know currently it won't mean a great deal to you as you won't know what each ward is, but it will become clearer in the next few days. The main thing is, now you have a timetable, you'll be able to plan your holidays with your family. Any questions?"

Zoe raised her hand. "Are we all off at the same time?"

"No. The holidays have been allocated individually. There might be two of you off at the same time, but no more than that. And if you haven't been allocated a holiday during Christmas, and I don't think many of you have, then you'll be working. But the ward may give you your days off during that period. However, before you get too excited, permanent staff on the wards will all be vying for Christmas or New Year off so it is highly likely as a student nurse, you'll be working."

Kym heard Simon's mumble that both years he was working Christmas.

"Me too by the looks of things," she heard Guy reply.

Mrs Beaumont continued, "Your responsibility during your placement is to adhere to the duty rota allocated to you. The wards do have a request book so you are permitted to make requests. But let me say now, don't abuse it. Senior members of staff who have the job each week of staffing the ward, expect students to work hard. And that includes their share of weekends and late duties."

"Why is Wednesday next week crossed out?" Lisa asked.

"That's your first day on the ward. But don't be worrying about that at this stage. It's very much orientation. You won't be expected to do much more than familiarise yourself with the wards you have been allocated, talk to patients, and maybe filling water jugs, that sort of thing. We'll be discussing it further in the week.

"Now, I want to go through the shift patterns. Please make a note of these. An early is seven-thirty until three, a late shift is eleven-thirty until eight forty-five and night shifts which you'll only do in your second year, marked on your timetable in yellow, are eight-thirty pm until seven-thirty am. So for the first year you will do early and late shifts, and for your second year you have three blocks of night duty. When you see the off duty on the ward, you'll see your name with either a letter E or a letter L next to it for each day. Obviously DO means your days off and are nearly always two days together. Sometimes you might be lucky and get the weekend off and Monday and Tuesday of the following week off which gives you a nice long weekend. But of course by having a Monday and Tuesday off, it means a long stretch until your next days off the following week."

A tap on the classroom door halted her speaking.

"Good morning again," the man from earlier who brought Simon and Guy in was back. "Am I too early?"

"Not at all Mr Duffield, come in."

She turned back to the class as he closed the door and walked towards her desk.

"This is Mr Duffield, one of the nursing officers. He's going to show five of you around the hospital and I'll take the other five. It's easier to split you up rather than crowding ten of you on each ward at the same time." She smiled at Mr Duffield, "Do you want to tell them a bit about your role?" She stood up, "You can have my seat."

"No, I'm happy to stand." He turned to face them.

"I'm Derek Duffield one of the nursing officers you'll be coming into contact with during your training. There are three nursing officers, myself, and my opposite number Mrs Valance. And we have a night nursing officer who is Miss Hogg, who you'll come to know more of during your second year when you'll be doing blocks of night duty.

"Our roles as senior nursing officers is to ensure that high standards are maintained at all times in terms of care giving. And, if you don't already know, this is an elite orthopaedic hospital with a reputation for excellence. We must therefore strive always to ensure that we are giving quality care. You'll see us regularly around the hospital checking on wards, the operating theatres, outpatients, in fact everywhere in the hospital. We're all qualified nurses and a large part of our work is ensuring that we have excellent students that all eventually qualify. So, please make sure when you're on the wards that you know about your patients, what their diagnosis is and what care they are receiving as we will be doing spot checks during the two years you're here. And before you get too anxious about that, first of all, the intention isn't to worry you. But as you become more competent, we expect more. Okay so far?"

They all nodded their compliance.

"And just one other thing. I know you won't have come onto this yet, but Mrs Beaumont will be explaining this to you. For each practical assessment you carry out on the ward as part of your training, you are observed and signed off for that competence by a senior member of staff. All of your competencies have to be signed off also by a nursing officer. So, you may have applied some pelvic traction to a patient, learned the skill of aseptic technique, or scrubbed up to assist in the operating theatre – whichever one you get signed off for we, a senior nursing officer, needs to sign you off too. So make sure you know your stuff. Nights out are fabulous at your age, but you need to balance that with study also. It's the only way to get through this course. It's fifty percent practical, fifty percent academic. But as I say, don't get worked up about that for now. Mrs Beaumont will explain more as the course goes on."

Mrs Beaumont glanced at the wall clock, "I think it's probably best if you go for coffee now, and in half an hour, come back and Mr Duffield and I will begin showing you round. So, we'll say ten forty-five back here."

The word 'coffee' sparked Kym's interest. There seemed a lot to take in. She was looking forward to getting into the practical room and learning nursing tasks. They interested her far more than anything in the classroom. There had been occasions prior to starting the course that she'd worried about her academic ability. But her mother had reassured her that bedside care was far more important than anything written in a book.

8.

Kym

After the coffee break, Kym made her way out of the school of nursing following Mr Duffield whose group she'd been assigned to along with Guy, Vanya, Marie and Lisa. The other five were in front with Mrs Beaumont.

Guy walked beside her. She liked his height. Tony was much smaller, more her height really, so if she wore high shoes, she was slightly taller than him. Next to Guy, she felt quite feminine and petite.

"What on earth happened this morning?" she purposely kept her voice low, "I'm not sure you fooled anyone with the watch excuse."

"Do you think not?" he grinned cheekily, "I thought maybe Mrs Beaumont believed me?"

"I doubt it. It was a bit feeble. And I certainly don't think Mr Duffield was convinced."

"No, I don't either. That's why he's split Simon and me up for this tour."

"Yeah, you're right. He's got your card marked, that's for sure."

"Who cares about him? When you went for coffee to the dining room, me and Simon stayed behind and chatted with Mrs B, she was fine about everything."

The group pausing prevented them saying any more. The man mowing the lawn had stopped and seemed to be looking expectantly at them. With his hand, he brushed his navy-blue sweatshirt with a Harlow Wood logo on the right breast, as if it was dirty.

"Good morning, Lloyd," Mr Duffield said to the middle-aged man with the receding hairline. It was the same man they'd seen earlier, but he'd taken his cap off.

"Morning, sir."

"These are the new intake of student nurses. I'm just giving them a tour of the hospital."

"Welcome to Harlow Wood," the gardener nodded, before starting to cough. "Excuse me," he took a handkerchief out of his pocket, "it's all the pollen. I'll be glad to see the last of it."

"It's quite alright," Mr Duffield reassured before turning to the group. "This area is for patients and their relatives to spend some time together away from the hospital. Lloyd does a brilliant job. The lawns are always pristine, and the benches and tables are kept clean. Please feel free to use it at any time yourselves. It is a tranquil place and ideal for some quiet reflection."

As they were led on, Kym smiled an acknowledgement at the gardener and he smiled right back. She liked the fact that everyone seemed to know each other around the place. Almost like one big family.

They carried on following until the others stopped at the entrance to the hospital.

"We're going to visit Ward 1 first of all," Mr Duffield said, "it's a high dependency unit where patients spend the first twenty-four or forty-eight hours post operatively following major surgery before returning to their own wards. He held the door open for them all to pass through and then followed. "This way."

"You should have come with us last night," Guy kept his voice low, "we had a right laugh. The Rushley was full of Harlow Wood staff."

"I'm glad I didn't if it meant being late today. What time did you get in?"

"Not that late, but we came upstairs with some of the second years and were drinking coffee in the kitchen until God knows what time. I left my car at the pub as I had too much to drink, that's why I was late this morning. Francis, one of the locums, ran me back first thing to get it."

"Here we are," Mr Duffield paused at the door displaying the sign 'Ward 1, High Dependency Unit'. "We can go in as currently there aren't any patients. Two will be coming later today following their surgery this afternoon."

The group followed him down the ward and were greeted by a middle-aged woman in a navy-blue uniform, with a gleaming silver buckle holding a belt around her waist. The frilly white hat complemented her smart, professional uniform.

"Good morning," she smiled welcomingly, "I'm Sister Smyth."

They all listened attentively as Sister Smyth explained about the ward and what their placement would entail. It seemed quite high-level stuff and a sense of relief ran though Kym as she explained to them they wouldn't be allocated there until either the end of their first year, or during the second one.

"We'll head for Ward 3, the children's ward," Mr Duffield said after thanking the ward sister, "I can show you on the way where the sewing room is for you all this afternoon."

He held the door to let them through. Kym went through the door last. "Turn right," he instructed to those in front who followed his directive.

"Whereabouts do you live?" he asked Kym. Guy scuttled forward to walk beside Vanya.

"Cleethorpes."

"Ah, Cleethorpes, I know it well."

"Do you?"

"Absolutely. I used to go there with my parents when I was little. My brother, sister and I loved our yearly trip on the train."

"It's changed a lot over the years, but it is still nice. I like it."

"I'm sure it's just as quaint as I remember," he smiled and called as he moved forward to those at the front, "right again please everyone."

Guy fell back into step beside her. "Did you notice I gave him a wide berth?"

"I did, yes. You'd do better trying to make it up to him a bit. He seems alright."

"Don't be fooled. They were saying last night he's a bit of a lech."

"What? I can't believe that. He's a nursing officer in a position of responsibility."

"I'm only telling you what the second years said. They reckon they don't like going to him to sign off their competencies as he makes stupid jokes and has an odd look, as if he's eyeing them up. And he hates male nurses, apparently."

"Why would he hate male nurses? He's one himself."

"I dunno, but that's what they said. He gives them a really hard time."

She nudged his arm playfully, "Then you'd better knuckle down."

As they continued to follow the others, Mr Duffield pointed out the patients' canteen which he said was only open during visiting times in the afternoon and evening.

"What did you do before you came here?" she asked Guy, "Did you have a job, or were you studying at uni or something?"

"Erm . . . sort of at uni."

"What do you mean, sort . . . "

They'd stopped at the entrance to Ward 3. "Okay, we'll go in and take a look round. And I'm telling you, you're in for a treat if you like kids. Remember the children aren't feeling sick, and they appear perfectly healthy. They're here because they have problems with their bones. So there are very few in their actual beds."

As they walked through double doors and onto the ward, a young child of about five ran excitedly towards Mr Duffield, and a second one of a similar age hobbled towards him on crutches. He reached in his pocket and produced a sweetie bag. "Go on pick one, no more though, you'll not eat your lunch. I've brought some new people to see you today and to have a look round your ward."

A sister came out of the office dressed equally as smartly as Sister Smyth they'd just met on Ward 1. She introduced herself as Sister Edwards and took them around the ward. Kym loved the ward, something about the children made her feel happy. It most probably would be a specialism she'd consider working in later on even if she could hear her mother already saying, *No, adult nursing is much more rewarding.*

The ward was full of noise, colour, pictures, toys. There were some children on their beds and in cots on various forms of skeletal traction. It was evident that the nurses attending them were skilled by the way they were interacting with the babies and children with giggles, gentleness and encouragement.

Kym glanced at a corner of the ward which appeared to be an area for learning judging by the wall with a frieze of numbers and letters.

Sister Edwards saw the direction of her gaze. "We have teachers that come in and work with some of the children. Many are here for such a long time; they need more stimulation than just toys."

Once they'd looked around the ward, segregated in two parts, one for the under tens, the other for the ten-to-sixteen-year-olds, they were shown the treatment and equipment rooms. Mr Duffield spent a few minutes chatting to the sister and they headed off.

"We're going first of all to the two of the older wards, eight and nine. They're more traditional nightingale wards and then we'll go to the modern wards with bays for patients and you can compare the difference. Eight is an all-female ward, next door is nine, an all-male ward. They mirror each other completely. Does anyone have eight or nine as their first placement?"

"I'm on eight," Lisa said.

Guy raised his hand, "I'm nine."

"I'm nine too," Kym said realising for the first time that her and Guy would be working together for eight weeks on their first ward. The thought made her smile.

"Okay then, follow me." Mr Duffield placed his hand gently on Lisa's back. "You'll be interested in this ward then."

"See what I mean," Guy whispered, nodding at Mr Duffield as they fell into step into the ward entrance.

"He's just being friendly."

"Yeah, too friendly I reckon. You need to watch out for him. Nobody normal has hair that colour."

"Just wait here a minute," Mr Duffield said, "while I check we can go in. It's still relatively early so some may still be attending to their personal hygiene."

Once he was out of earshot, Guy asked, "You're coming to the Rushley tonight, aren't you?"

Kym pulled a face. "I'm not sure."

"What aren't you sure about?"

"I want to ring my parents tonight and then Tony. They're expecting to hear how I've got on today."

"Right. Well that's not even going to take up more than half an hour I would have thought, so you can come. We'll wait for you."

"Don't you take hints?" she joked, "Have you considered I might not want to come?"

"Nope. I'm rubbish at social cues," he grinned. "So we'll wait for you while you make your calls. I can't say fairer than that, can I?"

"Okay," she rolled her eyes at his persistence, "I'll come."

9.

As he made his way through the car park he spotted two lads and four girls from the new intake heading towards a blue Ford Capri. Tall slap-head obviously wasn't too worried about breaking the law if he was going to fit four in the back.

"Are you sure?" the tiny girl asked, "What if we get caught?"

"We won't," slap-head dismissed, "just get in. It's only down the road."

He watched surreptitiously as the girls squeezed in the back and the boys got in the front, no doubt they'd be heading for the Rushley. Four pretty young girls. Were any of them virgins? He doubted it. He liked innocence in a girl, there was something about purity he found refreshing, but accepted that these days girls were sexually active from a young age with the pill being readily available.

The Ford Capri was in front of him now and slap-head slowed right down and indicated with his hand for him to pass. He raised his own hand in thanks, passed in front of the car and stepped onto the pavement. As he did so, he caught sight of the dark girl with the sad eyes in the back. Her name was Louise. They all wore name badges during the day, so it was easy to remember their names. The little lass was hunched up on the taller one's knee. She was Vanya. Maybe there was Romanian or

Bulgarian in her family as her skin tone was darker than the others? A tightness formed across his chest as that reminded him of dear Angela with her olive skin – but he couldn't go there. It was too painful. Best to focus on the excitement brimming within him, back now with a vengeance after having been dormant for a while. He'd always adored beautiful things, particularly females. And most of the time he was actually harmless; he only watched and admired their lithe movements, soft hair, slender limbs, and pert young breasts. Female shapes attracted him. Right now, the urge was overwhelming to touch one of them and feel their warm vibrant skin beneath his own fingers. Either of the pretties would do, Louise or Vanya. And maybe, if luck was on his side, he'd kill them both before he finally left God's waiting room himself.

As he continued through the grounds of the hospital, a black van caught his eye, parked close to the mortuary with its back doors open ready to collect a deceased patient. There weren't many deaths at Harlow Wood, it wasn't a hospital with loads of sick patients. They were there to have their bones fixed, but that didn't make them ill as such. He thought about family mourners – there were bound to be some. Not like when the grim reaper called for him, there'd only be his brother to mourn his passing. And if anything had the power to crush him, it was his brother. He'd had to be his mother and father as well as his brother over the years. He hadn't been strong, mentally or physically, their father had seen to that. But for a while they'd had their mother, a protector against that odious piece of shit, until she'd died and left them both in his evil clutches.

The acute emotional trauma had forced him, a thirteen-year-old boy, into early adulthood while his brother became an introverted child. He could still remember the endless crushing pain as he pined for his beautiful mother who'd kiss the bruises inflicted by his father's belt and cuddle him tightly after yet another beating. "Daddy has a high-pressured job which requires him making decisions all the time that affect us all. That's why sometimes he gets angry. He doesn't mean to. He loves you and your brother dearly."

He'd had to learn to cope with all the beatings, the bruising and swelling, the pain that lasted for days afterwards – and he became used to meals being withdrawn and being ostracised to his bedroom, because he had a mother that loved him. But when she died, all that was left was a depraved monster and no referee.

A shudder ran down his spine as he recollected preparing for his mother's funeral. It was to be the following day and until then, their mother was in a casket in the front lounge of their terraced house. The curtains were closed and one solitary candle was lit which only added to the macabre for two young boys.

"Go and kiss your mother goodbye," his father had commanded. But he didn't want to kiss her goodbye – he didn't even want to see her in the coffin. That would mean it was final and he could no longer close his eyes and pretend, that she was coming to tuck him in bed and kiss him goodnight.

"Go on, I said," his father shoved a fist into his back, "and take your brother with you."

His brother's face was a ghastly pale colour, as if he was going to throw up. "Here," he reached out his hand to him and they walked tentatively towards the open casket. Their mother lay with her eyes closed, and her hair had been combed in an odd way. Whoever had done it, hadn't got her parting on the right side. She'd been put in a white dress and a rose had been placed in her hands which had been positioned across her chest. But it didn't look like their mother. She looked like a waxwork model, with transparent skin. He daren't do any other than stand on his tiptoes, lean over and kiss her cheek. She was cold. Just a carcass. She'd gone to heaven, that's where all lovely people went, he'd read. Unlike his father who'd rot in hell. His brother looked terrified but duly kissed her also. Neither of them would dare defy their father.

"Now go to your room. The funeral's in the morning."

They scurried off, yet another night with nothing to eat and no mother this time to smuggle crisps and biscuits into their room. Tears flowed from his brother as soon as he lay on his bed and the sobs gained momentum as he tried to stifle them in the pillow.

He got out of his bed and climbed in with him, wrapping him tightly in his arms.

"I want Mummy back," his brother sniffed, "I don't want to stay here with him."

"I don't either, but we have to for now. We can leave later when we've finished school."

"But that's ages away. Can't we run away now?"

"No. We'd be found and brought back. And he'd beat us for doing that."

"What if he won't let us go when we're old enough? He said that when we leave school, we'll be working and paying our way and then he won't have to work anymore."

"Yeah, but that's a long way off. He'll most probably be dead by then."

"How do you know?"

"I just do."

"But how? He might live 'till he's ninety," he wiped his nose on his pyjama sleeve, "some people do."

"Well, he won't, I promise you that."

"You can't promise it. Nobody can."

"I can. If I give my word on something, I make it happen. We will get away from him and I'll always look after you. He'll definitely be long gone by then."

And he'd followed through. Their father had died a gruesome death just before his forty-fifth birthday.

As he'd told his brother . . . he never broke a promise.

10.

Kym

The lounge in the Rushley pub was warm and inviting with navy velour seating, wooden tables with cast iron legs and a rich patterned burgundy carpet. Small wall lights and numerous framed pictures on the walls, gave it a cosy feel. The focal point was the huge wooden bar which dominated the room. There weren't many punters spread about, but of the ones smoking and drinking at tables, some Kym recognised from Harlow Wood.

Guy led them to a vacant table near the glowing fire and they all took a seat apart from him. "Right," he clapped his hands together, "what we all having, my shout?"

"No, mate," Simon objected, "we can't have that. Why don't we have a kitty?"

"That sounds like a good idea," Zoe said, "saves getting in rounds. Someone always ends up buying more. How much?" she asked opening her bag.

"Honestly, I'm happy to get you all a drink."

"No, Guy, Simon's right," Kym agreed, "let's start as we mean to go on."

"Yeah, let's," Louise said, "if we don't spend it all, we can save it until next time. How much are we all putting in?"

Simon put two pound notes on the table. "How about two quid for starters."

"Sounds fine," Vanya said tossing hers in as well.

"I'll give you a hand with the drinks," Simon stood up and took the kitty money, "what are you girls having?"

Vanya gazed in the direction of the lads as they waited at the bar. "They seem really nice those two, don't they? It's kind of Guy to bring us here tonight."

"Yeah, we better make the most of them hanging around with us," Zoe said, "they soon dumped us at lunchtime for those second years, didn't they?"

It had miffed Kym, but she couldn't fathom out why. It was daft really – Guy had every right to sit with who he liked. But she wasn't about to let on. "In fairness, they are stuck with us in school all day, so it's nice to have a break with others."

"I know that," Zoe said, "but you're not telling me those second years weren't after them. I saw that Mary Best who showed me round on Sunday, hanging on to Guy's every word. If she got any closer to him at the table, she'd have been sat on his knee."

"You sound a bit peeved Zoe," Louise said raising an eyebrow, "maybe you better make it clear early on to Guy that you're interested, so at least you're in pole position."

"Hey, don't forget he's got a girlfriend," Kym reminded them, "he won't be interested in anyone."

"God, Kym, you're a bit naïve, aren't you?" Zoe smirked, "Whenever has having a girlfriend ever stopped anyone?"

The lads returning with a tray of drinks prevented Kym from replying but she was a good judge of character and she couldn't somehow see Guy cheating. She hoped not anyway. One of the reasons she liked him was because they both had partners. It seemed acceptable they were friends only. But Zoe not refuting she was interested in Guy irritated her. The thought of the two of them together didn't sit well with her. What she didn't get was why she was so bothered when she had Tony.

Simon took a sip of his pint. "I've booked next door in the bar for a game of snooker. The bloke's going to give me a nod when they've finished their game. We'll have two teams of three, so you girls are going to have to fight over which one of you is with me and Guy."

Kym put her hands up playfully, "I'll surrender now then as I can't even play snooker, so I'm happy sitting here."

"Me too," Louise said, "I'll stay with you. I'm useless at the game."

"Right," Simon grinned at Guy, "looks like it's you and me against Vanya and Zoe."

"Sounds good to me," Guy smiled at the girls and Kym didn't miss Zoe's cheeks turning pink.

"There you go," Guy placed two glasses of lager on the table in front of them. "I'll go join the others. It won't take us long to thrash the girls. We'll be back in no time," he said with a wink. Kym noticed he had a habit of winking. She found it quite attractive.

Louise took a sip of her drink, "That was nice of him. He didn't need to bring us a top up, we could have got our own."

"I think he's a sorter type," Kym said, "likes to make sure everyone's okay." Kym liked that in a person – easy going, self-assured. Add that cheeky wink and Guy was really nice.

"Yeah, you're right. I wonder what he did before he came here. Maybe he was in hospitality or something."

Kym shrugged, "I don't know. I did ask him but he was vague. I thought maybe uni. We'll ask him when he comes back, shall we?"

"Yep, let's do that." Louise took a sip of her drink, "Did you finally get through to your boyfriend? You seemed to be going up and down the stairs for ages earlier on."

"Sorry, I was in and out my room a bit. I must have got on your nerves."

"Don't be daft. I could have shut my door if I'd wanted to."

"Why don't you?"

"I'm not sure really," Louise frowned, "I just don't like being closed in, which is stupid because at home, I love being in my room. When I go home at the weekend I'm going to bring my running shoes back with me. I used to go a lot with my friend, so I thought it might be nice to get some exercise. Mrs McGee said that first night there were some lovely walks in the woods."

"That's a good idea if you like running." Kym took a sip of her lager, "I'm more of a reading and listening to music sort of person otherwise I'd come with you."

"Nothing wrong with that. I'm just not keen on my room. I might feel differently when we've been here a while, though."

"Yeah, it's still early days. Anyway, I kept ringing to speak to Tony but I never did. I'm not sure where he was. The man I spoke to jotted my message down and said he'd give it to him. I told him I'd try again tomorrow. I want him to have the nurses' home number so he can ring me."

"Did you leave the number with the man?"

"No, I didn't like to really. I was worried it could get into the wrong hands and some of the lads might have started ringing when they'd had a drink. Tony reckons they're a full-on bunch. I'll give him the number when I speak to him." She took a sip of her lager, "I did get through to my mother though, but not for long. I told her someone was waiting to use the phone, which isn't very nice." Kym winced, "I love her to bits but she does go on. She's not a lover of Tony, so as soon as she starts, I tend to switch off."

"Why doesn't she like him?"

"Erm . . . well he smokes for one thing, and she calls him a modern-day Casanova." Kym rolled her eyes, "All red flags to my mother."

"God, mothers, what are they like? Have you been together long?"

"About ten months."

"And he's just started in the Navy?"

"Yeah, he's only just gone in. He should have started in February, but he fractured his foot so it was put back.

He went to Portsmouth for his initial training last month."

"So when he's done that, does he get a ship and travel?"

"Yeah, that's the next bit in a few weeks. I'm dreading it because I'll not see him for ages then."

"Aw, yeah, that'll be hard."

"It will but we'll manage, plenty of people do. Anyway, did you get to speak to your mum?"

"Yeah, I did."

"I know you said before you'd lost your dad recently. I'm sorry about that."

"Thank you. I am finding it hard right now." Louise's voice lowered. She ran her hand across her fringe that framed her pretty face. It was a shame to see dullness in her eyes. "I'm not entirely sure it's right to be doing this course. Part of me wants to be at home with her."

"I can only imagine how hard it must be," Kym sympathised. "Did she have to push you to come?"

"Yeah, spot on. She's right though, it's what my dad wanted. I'm just not sure whether it's too soon."

"You're not thinking of jacking it in, are you?"

"I'm not sure to be honest," Louise said, but not convincingly. Had she already made up her mind to quit?

"My sister Karen's fifteen and a bit of a handful. Mum doesn't tell me half of it. If I was at home, I'd know more."

"Yeah, but isn't everyone a pain at fifteen – I bet you were."

"I suppose so. Maybe it's not just my sister. I'm not sure of anything right now."

"Please don't leave," Kym pleaded. "Once we get on the wards, things will be different. It's all so new and takes some getting used to. And you've had a massive shock in your life. Promise me you'll give it a bit longer."

Louise took a deep breath in. "Yeah, I am definitely going to try. I went and sat in the patients' garden while you were messing about on the phone, just for ten minutes. It was nice."

"It looks really peaceful, though it's probably best to go when it's not visiting hours. Mr Duffield told us it can get quite busy."

"I'd imagine it would. It was quiet at 5 o'clock though, I was on my own. Well, the gardener was there. He seemed friendly, but after he'd said hello and mentioned the weather, he left me alone."

"We met him on our tour round. Lloyd I think he was called."

"Is it? I didn't catch his name. He said to make the most of the sunshine as it would change in October."

"It is a beautiful garden. I must find some time to read those bench plaques. I like anything like that. That must make me such a saddo," Kym laughed.

Louise gave her a lovely smile. "No, of course it doesn't."

"I'm pleased you're going to give it a bit more time," Kym squeezed her new friend's hand, "I'd be lost without you already if you packed it in." She'd hate her to leave. It was hard to believe they'd only known each other two days, it felt like so much longer. "The depressing rooms don't help either, do they?" Kym said taking her hand away.

"No, they're bloody dire."

"I'm going to get some posters at the weekend when I'm home, anything to brighten it up."

"Good idea, I will too. I've got a tap that drips in mine would you believe, it's driving me mad."

"You need to get that fixed."

"I'm not sure what to do, or who to see."

"Mrs McGee in the first instance I would have thought. Remember she said she's the point of contact."

"Yes, she did."

"And her husband is the handyman, so he'll have that fixed in no time."

"You're right. I'll see her . . ."

Simon interrupted Louise as he and the others returned to the table. "Easy! Easy!" he chanted as they took their seats.

After sending the girls up about how bad they were at snooker, and the girls arguing back Guy and Simon had cheated, Kym decided to referee. "Enough about snooker, let's talk about something else. How about what we all did prior to starting here? You go first Vanya."

"I stayed on at school," Vanya said, "I was doing my A-levels but wanted to start my nursing early. I think I said before, I had heck of a job convincing my dad. But I'm here now."

"And we're pleased you are," Kym smiled. And she was. Vanya was so sweet.

"What about you, Zoe?"

"Boots, in the city centre, and I hated every minute. The pay was rubbish too."

Simon wiped the beer froth off his mouth. "Did you get loads of freebies?"

"Not a single one," Zoe said, "They even checked your bags when you clocked off to make sure you hadn't stolen anything."

"That's awful," Kym said, "Surely they shouldn't be allowed to do that."

"Well, they did. Random searches every now and then as well, and they didn't mind emptying out your bag in front of everyone. It was so embarrassing. What about you, Kym?"

"Office work for me," Kym said, finding Zoe hard to believe. It seemed almost like she said things for effect. "I liked it but knew I couldn't do it all the time. One year was more than enough. What about you, Louise?"

"Waitressing," Louise said, "I knew I wanted to come to Harlow Wood, so it was just biding my time, trying to earn some money. I didn't particularly like it though."

"You know my story," Simon said, "a motorbike accident and all that and how I worked in the supplies unit at the city hospital."

All eyes turned to Guy. He gave a huge sigh.

"Go on," Simon grinned, "tell them."

"Tell us what?" Zoe asked eagerly. "You're not an undercover reporter doing an article on student life at Harlow Wood, are you?"

"No," Guy laughed, "nothing as exciting as that."

"What then?"

"I was at medical school."

"You're joking."

"Nope. That's where I was."

"Why the hell did you leave to come here," Zoe pulled a disparaging face, "to train as a nurse?"

"Because I didn't want to be a doctor."

"Whyever not? You could earn loads more as a doctor than you'll ever make as a nurse."

"Yeah, I know that, but becoming a doctor is more my old man's dream, he's a GP so is obviously biased. And life isn't always about money."

"I agree," Kym said. Just as she'd suspected, Guy was clearly exceptionally bright. And she liked him even more, knowing that money wasn't his driving force. "You need to do what's right for you."

"Thank you, Kym," he reached and squeezed her shoulder and she liked the feel of his warm hand. "I knew you'd be a good ally." He turned to Zoe, "I'm not a hundred percent sure I am going to be a nurse. If I finish this course, I can train as a physiotherapist and get a much-shortened course. This course cuts it in half, almost."

"Why didn't you go straight into a physio course then?"

"Because I'm not sure that's what I want to do either. Anyway, enough about me." Guy glanced at his watch, "A quick one for the road, anyone?"

11.

Louise

Louise was up early. It gave her a chance to get to the shower before anyone else. She liked to give the cubicle she used a quick spray round and a wipe down so it was clean before she stepped in it. The previous evening at the pub had been fun, she'd really enjoyed it, particularly speaking to Kym. It was obvious to anyone that she was a lovely person. And so kind that she encouraged her to not jack the course in. She was going to listen to her advice and give it time. As she stood under the warm water and rubbed the lemon soap into her body, she felt slightly less anxious, which had to be progress? Her counsellor's voice was forever on her mind – *small steps at a time*.

After breakfast, they made their way to the classroom. Zoe was in front of them alongside Guy as they walked through the garden to the school of nursing. She let out a loud laugh, leant into him and whispered something in his ear.

"I think she's really into him," Louise whispered to Kym.

"Definitely."

"I wonder if he likes her?"

"I don't know. He's not said much about his girlfriend, only that he has one."

"No, he hasn't really. Hey, it's a surprise he left medical school, isn't it. I wonder what that's really all about."

"Who knows? It must have been a big step to pack that in."

"His dad won't have been pleased, especially as he's a GP."

"Yeah, I bet."

As they walked into the classroom, a man was perched on the edge of the desk with his legs stretched out in front of him and crossed at the ankles. According to their timetable, he was Mr Feeney, the morning tutor for anatomy and physiology. Simon had said he was the charge nurse that had taken care of him after his motorbike accident and encouraged him to train as a nurse.

"Morning," he said with a smile as they made their way towards the desks they'd taken on the first day. "Many more to come?"

Louise took a quick glance at those already seated. "Just two more, they were still in the dining room as we left."

"Okay, that's fine," his eyes drifted towards the wall clock, "we'll give them a bit longer, it's not quite nine thirty." He reached for a book from the desk and turned to a bookmarked page.

"Hey," Kym said quietly as they took their seats, "make sure you see Mrs McGee about your tap, if it's still dripping that is."

"Yes, it's still dripping. But I've put a flannel under it and that stops the noise at least." Louise couldn't add though that the flannel was interfering with the Domestos she wanted to fill the sink with each night.

"That's good then. But you still need to get it sorted."

"I know. I'll give her a knock after school today."

Louise emptied her bag and placed her pencil case and note book in front of her as the teacher moved towards the classroom door and glanced down the corridor. His dark blond hair was sort of feathered, a bit like a David Cassidy cut. He was wearing a smart jacket and tie, and his shoes were gleaming. What was it her father used to say, *you can tell a lot by a man's shoes?* She wondered about his age, he didn't look that old, in fact, he looked almost hot for a teacher. Maybe he was late twenties. Simon would know.

"Ah, I do believe it's them coming now," Mr Feeney said.

Simon sauntered in alongside Helen. Mr Feeney reached his hand out to Simon, pleasure lighting up his face.

Simon gave his hand a hearty shake. "It's been a while."

"Yes, hasn't it just. We'll catch up properly at break. Grab your seats and we'll make a start."

Mr Feeney came round to the front of the desk and perched himself again on the edge of it.

"Morning everyone, I'll start by giving you a bit of background on me. I'm Nick Feeney, the charge nurse on ward seven, and I work here in the School of Nursing delivering some sessions to both first and second-year students. Eventually I'd like to be a full-time tutor, but for now I enjoy the balance of both. So, while you're in school, you're going to be bored to death with me for at least a couple, if not three sessions a week. And don't be worrying about the patients on the ward, I have great support from a sister who works opposite shifts to me, and the staff nurses. In fact, I think they like it best when I'm teaching and not on the ward." He grinned cheekily. That wouldn't be true. Simon had said he was a brilliant charge nurse and staff loved him.

"Have any of you been allocated to my ward as your first placement?"

Louise raised her hand.

"Brilliant," he said, "you'll be doing your first shift next week so I'll look out for you. Ward seven is a special ward, you'll love it, I promise. That said, they're all great wards, it's a great hospital, I love it here. Now, before we start some serious work, let's have a bit of fun. I thought we could all say something about ourselves that the others may not know. It could be a hobby, an achievement, an ambition. Just something light though, we don't want to know any gory, hard luck stories. That okay with everyone?" He waited for them to nod.

"Great, I'll start us off. As far back as I can remember," he indicated with his hand a small child, "I wanted to join the RAF at eighteen and fly those beautiful planes. Alas, it was not to be. I failed the medical on the grounds that I'm colour blind. I could have still got in, but not doing the job I wanted to. It's an understatement to say I was gutted, but hey ho, that's life, and here I am. Okay, let's start on the back row shall we."

It was fun listening to the four girls behind talk of their achievements and ambitions. Nobody had any inhibitions; Marie had studied ballet dancing as a child and would have liked to pursue it further but grew too tall and Lisa used to run long distance for the county. Helen seemed to be an accomplished horse rider winning many trophies and Susan explained she was torn between the police and nursing as a career but saw a fortune teller at a fair who said she was destined to be a nurse.

Louise watched Nick Feeney as he concentrated on each of them speaking. He had lovely warm hazel-coloured eyes, kind eyes her mother would have called them. They seemed to have a bit of a twinkle when he smiled, and the skin around the edges crinkled. He smiled encouragingly as each person spoke and was enthusiastic about everyone's comments.

Next it was Kym's turn and then it was going to be hers. For some bizarre reason, her heart rate seemed to increase.

She heard Kym's intake of breath. "When I was twelve, we visited family in Jordan and I was taken on King Hussein of Jordon's speedboat."

"Really?" Mr Feeney's eyes widened, "tell us more."

"Yeah, I was having water skiing lessons and would wait on a raft for the instructor with the other kids to take turns. On this particular morning, along came King Hussein and took some of us on a speedboat boat ride around the bay. I hadn't realised at the time that the boats following us were his protection team, or exactly who he was. I was more interested in his fabulous looking boat. Our instructor came so it was all above board."

"I'm delighted to hear it."

"I think it's fair to say royalty out there is very different to our royalty."

"I'm sure you're right, but still, it's a great story."

Louise just knew Kym would have something interesting to tell. She was like that, engaging as well as pretty.

"What about you . . ." he scrutinised her name badge, "Louise?"

"Erm . . ." she liked the way he said her name. "Sticking with royalty, I was chosen to present the Queen with a bouquet when she visited the leisure centre I used to go to for gymnastics as a child, and despite practicing for days and days on how to do a curtsey, I completely forgot that bit. My mother was not pleased."

Mr Feeney smiled, "I bet the Queen wasn't one bit bothered."

"No, she didn't appear to be. She just took the flowers and asked kindly if I liked spending time there."

"That's really sweet," he said and Louise found her cheeks were flushing. She glanced down at her note book, hoping he'd move on.

"And Vanya, how about you?"

Vanya surprised them all by saying she could speak a second language. Her grandmother was Bulgarian so she spoke it fluently. And Zoe was equally surprising. She had an identical twin she hadn't mentioned to them at all.

"What about you, Simon?" Mr Feeney asked.

He crinkled his nose. "I'm a bit of a geek. I quite like train spotting."

"Nothing wrong with that, I like steam engines myself. And you . . . Guy?"

"Erm," Guy's face looked pained, almost as if he was apologising. "I was head boy at school."

"Were you? That's quite an achievement."

"Yeah, I suppose so, although I did get loads of grief, but my dad loved it as he'd been head boy at the same school too, so the way he saw it, I was following in his footsteps."

"Quite right too. He must have been proud."

"I guess so," Guy shrugged in a non-committal way which lacked any enthusiasm. It sounded like there was more to it. Possibly Mr Feeney felt it, as he swiftly moved on.

"Okay, we'd better get down to some academic work or I won't be getting paid and I need the money," he joked. "Thank you all for doing that, I really enjoyed hearing everyone's story."

He stood up and moved round the desk and took his seat. He picked up some papers, but hesitated. "I've got a handout for you all which I think I'll give you at the end of the session. Feel free to make your own notes as we go along. I personally find I retain more information writing my own notes.

His lips twitched into a smile. Louise felt her heart lurch slightly. For some bizarre reason, he reminded her of her dad. He didn't physically look like him, but he had an easy-going manner, a sort of infectiousness which her father had in spades. He'd been a popular man with many friends and associates from the company he worked for. They'd been overwhelmed at the funeral at how many had attended. It was comforting how many lives he touched during his life.

Nick Feeney's approach was engaging. The subject matter of the heart and circulatory system was dry to say the least, but his personality made it entertaining.

"You all thought I was going to be discussing fractured femurs or something of that nature, and I will as time goes on, but we have to understand the rudiments of how the body functions, so we can understand what happens when something threatens that system such as trauma to the bones. As nurses, we have to care holistically for the patient. That's what nursing care is all about. Looking at the patient as a whole, not just at the problem they've presented us with."

Louise did her best trying to focus on the topic and take notes. Mr Feeney managed to combine the academic work with amusing anecdotes on patient care which made the lesson engaging. She listened to the tone of his voice. She liked it. She liked him, which was reassuring as she'd avoided boys after her last hideous encounter which she tried daily to eradicate from her mind. For the first time in ages, a wave of excitement flooded through her. The ward placement was more appealing knowing she would be spending time in his company. But she quickly came back down to earth as her eyes drifted towards the third finger of his left hand.

Of course anyone as attractive as Nick Feeney would be married.

12.

Kym

Kym headed along the corridor to the bathroom and passed Vanya near the stairs.

"I'm just nipping down to use the phone," Vanya said, "I tried earlier but there was a queue."

"There always is. You could go into the hospital near the patients' canteen."

"Yeah, I know. I might if I go down and there's still a queue."

"Okay, see you later. Good luck."

While the bath was running, Kym poured bubble bath into it and watched it froth up. The fruity lemon aroma made the wrought iron bath a little more inviting. She turned off the taps and climbed in, resting her head on the small inflatable pillow she'd brought with her. A soak in the bath was her guilty pleasure. She wanted to kill a bit of time before she rang Tony. He wouldn't finish work until 9pm, that's when he'd call her usually at home. It sounded like his residence for initial training had a similar layout to hers with a communal payphone on the corridor.

She was enjoying it at Harlow Wood. She'd always liked company, so it was great getting to know everyone. Although it was early days, her, Louise and Vanya seemed to gel well together. Zoe hung around with them, but she still wasn't keen on her. She just didn't seem genuine. She liked the lads tagging along too, although if they got a better offer, invariably they would take it. Simon made no secret of the fact he was attracted to the nurses, whereas Guy seemed friendly enough but had a girlfriend so didn't appear to be on the lookout quite as much. She liked that about him. He was really good looking, but he never flaunted it. And he seemed to like her as a friend which was reciprocal.

As she headed back to her room after her bath wearing her dressing gown and clutching her toiletry bag, Vanya called from her room doorway. "Kym, have you got a minute?"

"Erm . . ." she looked down at her dressing gown, "sure. Shall I put some clothes on?"

"No, don't do that. I just wanted a quick word."

Vanya's room was neat and tidy as well as being homely with two plants on the windowsill and some framed photographs on her bedside table.

Kym closed the door behind her.

"The weirdest thing has happened," Vanya said, her eyes moved towards her bed. "You see my underwear."

Kym looked at where she pointed. On the bed was a plain, powder-pink-coloured bra and knickers set, and a more ornate cream lace bra with a tiny black bow.

"Yeah," she said.

Vanya screwed her face up, "The cream knickers that match my bra have gone missing."

"What?" Kym frowned, "I don't understand."

"The cream knickers that match my bra have disappeared. I have a bag in the cupboard under my sink for my dirty underwear so I can wash them out every couple of days, but the cream knickers have gone. She scratched her head, "Just disappeared. The bra's still there, but no pants."

"Gone? They can't have gone. How could a pair of knickers disappear?"

"I don't know. I think I'm going mad. But they have."

"Maybe they've fallen down the back of the unit, or have you slipped them off in bed perhaps?"

"No, I don't think so. I've stripped the bed to check, but they aren't there."

"Let's pull your bed out and have a look down the side."

"Okay," Vanya shrugged, "it won't do any harm to check."

They heaved the bed away from the wall and Vanya climbed onto it and looked down the gap. "No, nothing."

"What about the cupboard under the sink where you keep the bag, let's take everything out and see if they're at the back."

They knelt on the floor as Vanya lifted her toiletries out and checked at the back of the cupboard. "Not here, either."

"How odd," Kym frowned, you couldn't just lose a pair of knickers. "If it was anything else I'd say someone was playing a trick, but not stealing knickers. Nobody would take those, even for fun."

"I know. And I'd worn them, so that's even worse."

"Oh God," Kym said, "that's bloody awful. Who would steal dirty knickers?"

Vanya visibly shuddered. "I dread to think."

"But no one has a key to your room. What are you going to do? Are you going to mention it to Mrs McGee?"

"God no, I don't think so. What can she do?" Vanya widened her eyes playfully, "Launch a full investigation into a pair of missing knickers. Last thing I want is everyone knowing my dirty knickers are somewhere out there."

"No, you're right," Kym agreed, smiling, "but it is odd. I don't know what to say."

"Well at least we know they're no good to anyone as they'll not fit them. I'm much smaller than everyone else."

"Now there's a point," Kym grinned, relieved Vanya didn't seem too worried. She still couldn't believe anyone had been in her room and taken a pair of knickers. A thought struck her, "I bet I know what's happened. You'll have dropped them when you've had a shower or a bath. If you go down to the bathroom, someone may have hung them on a tap or something. I bet they're there."

"Do you think?"

"It's worth a try."

"Yeah, I'll go take a look now." They both got to their feet.

"Oh, here," Vanya took an Orthopaedic text book off her desk and handed it to Kym, "this is the book you wanted to have a look at."

"Thanks." Kym took it from her. "I got some WH Smith vouchers as a leaving present from the girls in the office so I want to get something that'll be useful."

"This one was on the reading list we got and it does seem really good."

"Great, I'll have a flick through and give you it back tomorrow."

"No rush," Vanya said, closing the door behind them. "Don't say anything about my missing knickers will you?" she whispered, "I'd hate to be the butt of the lads' jokes."

"Course I won't. But I'm sure you've dropped them in the bathroom."

"Yeah, that's the likeliest explanation. Thanks for helping me look."

"You're welcome. See you in the morning."

"Will do."

Kym headed down the corridor towards her room with a feeling of unease. Surely no one would have taken Vanya's worn knickers, would they? She felt a bit uncomfortable, determined to check her own laundry bag straight away.

13.

He pressed the gusset of Vanya's cream knickers to his nose and inhaled the femininity of them. The soft cotton felt sensual as he stroked the side of his face and pictured them covering her pert little bottom. It'd be tight and firm, just how a female should be, not big and flabby like some of them. He couldn't stand overweight, sagging women. As far as he was concerned, they should have firm breasts, a small waist and neat hips. So many let themselves go and carried weight around their middle. That's not how a female should look. They should all look like dear Angela who was perfect in every way.

His whole focus for the past week had been on the new intake of students. He surreptitiously watched them moving around the hospital. He liked sad-eyed Louise, but tiny Vanya held his interest most of all. She was a sociable little thing, and rarely alone, which might be a problem. He'd need her on her own eventually for his plan to succeed. He'd been patient long enough. Now was the time to act, which he was going to do the following week. They'd all be going home this weekend anyway. *Patience was a virtue* his father used to say, but he didn't have that luxury. Time for him was running out. He needed to act quickly now he'd identified it was Vanya he was after. He inhaled the feminine scent one more time before placing the knickers deep in his pocket. He liked the idea of keeping them on him – walking round the hospital with them close gave him a thrill. He'd hide them when he got home at the back of his own underwear drawer where they couldn't be found. His stomach rumbled. It had to be lunchtime.

As he made his way towards the hospital entrance he spotted a mother clutching a child's arm, heading towards the outpatients department. The image brought back a painful memory of himself at a similar age, living in Marpole Street where he'd spent his childhood. Images were imprinted on his mind that he couldn't erase. The terrace house with the pretty nets at the window, steeped scrupulously in bleach to keep them as pristine as the neighbours'. But hidden behind their meticulous nets was a household of horrific abuse. He winced . . . remembering.

"I haven't," he protested, sobbing as the second blow to his head came from his father.

"Give it back now, boy or you'll feel my belt next."

His insides quivered as his father started to remove his black leather belt holding his oversized trousers up over his pot belly.

"One of you has taken my money." Sobs racked his brother's body. His father glared at him, "Have you taken it?"

His brother shook his head vigorously. "No."

"Then if neither of you will own up, you'll both be punished. Right, you boy," he barked at him, "trousers down."

He knew what was coming. That belt with the huge buckle would leave marks that would do more than hurt.

They both pulled down their trousers as he instructed – not doing so wasn't an option.

"It was me," he cried feebly, anything to stop what was coming. "I took it."

"Too late." The first blow came sooner than he'd anticipated. And then another, and then another. Each one harder that the first. He tried not to scream, but he couldn't help it. One after the other, it was persistent. His feeble legs eventually buckled under him and he slouched down, but the leathering kept on going. When it eventually stopped he was barely in the room. He felt like he was floating off somewhere, until he opened his eyes and watched his brother get the same.

Their beatings had been relentless.

All had gone quiet. His brother had curled himself into a ball on the settee and had gone into a deep sleep.

His father moved towards the fireplace, reached for a lighter and lit a cigarette. "Get out of my sight," he dragged hard, glaring at his younger brother, "and take him with you."

As he stood on weak, spindly legs that could barely hold him upright, he kept his gaze averted. No sense in looking at his father, he'd get another beating for insolence.

"I have a housekeeper moving in at the end of the week. So you two better learn to behave yourselves or there'll be trouble like you've never seen before."

With each step, the pain from the beating was evident. It would take days to heal, weeks even. They'd been there before. And there'd be more beatings in the future – that certainly wouldn't be the last. Hate crawled through his veins like hot syrup. Even now as an adult, he was sure it was his father's violence that had rubbed off on him. As if it was in the genes. Yet, his brother was mild, rather like their beloved mother. Warmth flooded through him as he remembered her warm bosom and sweet smell when she cuddled him at night in bed and told him how much she loved him and his brother. She was a beautiful woman. He loved everything about her.

Angela was a beautiful woman too. But he'd lost her as well. The sweet aroma of Vanya's knickers evoked memories of how he'd slip Angela's panties on and wear them in private around the house. He loved nothing better than to go through her underwear drawer, taking out the delicate fabrics, caressing them and inhaling the female sweetness. But he had to stop himself from going there. The pain was too acute. His focus had to be on pretty little Vanya right now. The sand was running out of the glass for him. He had to act.

"What can I get you?" the serving lady asked from behind the food counter.

14.

Louise

Once school had finished for the day, she'd walked with the girls back to her room. After dumping her bag and giving her hands a good wash, she headed towards South House to find where Mrs McGee lived. She'd considered late afternoon was a better time to knock than first thing in the morning, but she was still apprehensive about doing so. The main thing though was getting the tap fixed, so she was ready for the wrath of Mrs McGee if she was in trouble for disturbing her.

As soon as she entered South House, she could see it was much nicer than North House. It had a cosier feel with patterned wallpaper opposed to their beige woodchip, and even though the flowery carpet was well used, it was a more vibrant blue than their dark brown one. And it felt spongier, as if it had underlay, whereas in North House the corridor carpet was a thin nylon one.

Several paces along the ground floor corridor, she stopped at the door that had a sign that said *Mrs McGee (Matron)*. She ran her sweaty hand down her jeans and gently tapped, psyching herself up to apologise for disturbing her.

The door was opened by the man they'd seen on their first morning in the school of nursing. He'd been doing some painting. He was in a blue boiler suit sporting the

Harlow Wood logo. He looked to be about mid-forties with receding hair and his glasses were of an aviator style and heavily tinted so she couldn't quite see his eyes.

His smile was broad despite missing one of his front teeth.

"Hi. I'm really sorry for disturbing you. I was looking for Mrs McGee . . . I've a dripping tap in my room which is driving me mad, particularly at night when I'm trying to sleep."

"Oh dear, we can't have that can we? What's your room number?"

"Number twelve in North House. It's upstairs . . ."

"Yes, I know. I'm Eric McGee, the caretaker or," he grinned, "handyman. I answer to both."

"Ah, right, that's good to know. I did leave a note for the cleaner on the first day but I haven't heard back, so I thought I'd let Mrs McGee know."

"No worries. I'll make sure it's fixed for you."

"That would be brilliant."

"I'd come across now, but I need to fill out a requisition first. All paperwork I know, but it's evidence I am actually working and not stood gazing out of a window all day."

"Yes, I see . . . er . . . not that anyone would think you'd be doing that."

"I would hope not. But you never know."

She wasn't sure if he was messing about or deadly serious. She couldn't see his eyes properly through his glasses. But he was staring at her as if expecting her to say more.

"Well, thank you anyway."

"What are you working tomorrow, an early or a late shift?"

"Pardon?" Why was he asking that? She was so busy focussing on his glasses, she'd lost track of their conversation.

"So, I can fix the tap . . . while you're out."

"Ah, I see. Sorry. I'm actually in school all day."

"I'll get it done first thing for you then."

"That's kind. Thank you so much."

"You're welcome."

As she made her way along the corridor she was acutely aware he hadn't gone inside and closed the door. Sensing he was watching her, she quickened her pace towards the exit, relieved when she finally reached it.

Outside, she checked her watch. Her, Louise, Vanya and Zoe had got into a routine of going at six thirty each night together for supper, but that wasn't for a while so there was a bit of time for a walk before then. Anything was better than sitting in her room. She strolled towards the patients' garden intending to go to the part of the woods they could see from the classroom window when she spotted Vanya walking towards her.

"Hi, what are you up to? Extra curriculum in the library so you can get ahead of us all?"

"I don't think so," Vanya laughed and held up a small purse. "I couldn't find this so went back. It must have dropped out of my bag in class, Mrs Beaumont had it. Where are you off to?"

"Just for a quick walk, do you fancy coming?"

"I can't." Vanya pulled a face, "I've got to call home, my gran's round for tea and I said I'd speak to her tonight."

"No probs, I'm only going to be half an hour or so. I just want to check out the woods next to the school of nursing. I keep staring at them each day promising myself I'll go take a look."

"You'll be okay on your own?"

"Course I will. It's daylight."

"Yeah, I guess so. The gardener's around somewhere, anyhow, I've just seen him. He seems nice." She lowered her voice, "A bit boring on the plant front though, so don't stop to chat whatever you do."

"Crikey, thanks for the warning, I'll keep my head down if I spot him. See you at supper then."

"Will do. I'll give you a knock."

She carried on walking, pleased she'd spoken to Mr McGee about her tap. It sounded like it'd be fixed tomorrow, and after school had finished that afternoon, her mum was picking her up and they were all heading home for the weekend. She was dying to see her mum, sister and their Labrador Bess.

As she made her way into the woods, an array of greens and browns greeted her alongside an earthy smell of rotting wood, animal scents and wild flowers. Immediately, she felt a sense of peace which was probably unheard of for a girl her age. She couldn't think of a single friend that would enjoy the solitude of the woods with the insects and birds, yet she loved it. She'd always been an outdoor person. Family holidays usually consisted of walking in the Lake District. Mentally, particularly now, she wasn't strong, but physically she was. She'd had to be with the outdoor pursuits she'd been brought up with.

She continued along the uneven ground, with the pine cones, needles and twigs crunching underneath her feet and spotted a male figure squatting down with a camera in his hands. She stood still, even if she didn't recognise immediately who he was, the flutter in her chest suggested who it might be. Nick Feeney, the talented tutor and charge nurse who somehow had the ability to make her jittery by just standing near him. As much as she had an urge to tell him she was there, she watched quietly as he twisted the camera to different angles trying to get a shot of what appeared to be a foxglove wild flower. He looked even more attractive in jeans, boots and a thick jumper. He seemed almost lost in a world with only him and the flowers. Eventually, guilt got the better of her and she cleared her throat.

He turned and quickly brought himself to a standing position. "Hi. It's . . . Louise isn't it?"

"Yes it is." He'd remembered her as she didn't have her name badge on.

"How's it going? You're just having a walk I take it?"

"Yes. I see the woods from the classroom each day and they look inviting so I thought while I had a bit of time before supper I'd take a look." She nodded towards his camera. "You're taking photos?" She inwardly cursed – of course he was taking photos.

"Yeah," he glanced at the camera in his hand, looking as awkward as she felt. No doubt he wasn't expecting to be disturbed. "My brother bought me the camera for my birthday so I'm just learning really, but I like taking unusual shots."

"It's great isn't it? There's something about still photos."

"Ah, you're bit of a photographer yourself then?"

"Not really. My dad was though."

"Was?"

"He died recently."

"Oh, I am sorry to hear that. How recent . . . if you don't mind me asking?"

"Eleven weeks . . ." she tried to interject a bit of humour, "not that I'm counting."

"Expected or sudden?"

"Sudden. Seeing you with your camera . . . sort of . . ." she swallowed the ball forming in her throat which was doable, controlling the tears filling her eyes was harder. Desperate not to make a fool of herself, she tried to breathe them away.

"Hey, it's okay." He moved closer to her and squeezed her arm. "Grief hits us at the most unexpected times," he reached in his pocket, "here, it's clean."

"Thank you." She used the hanky to wipe away the stray tears. "I'm sorry. I've disturbed you."

"Don't worry about that. I'm often out here. I like the solitude after a busy day on the ward." He glanced at his watch, "But it's getting late now and I'm losing the light. Are you carrying on walking, or heading back?"

"I'd better head back too." Anything to walk with him.

"Shall we walk together then?"

"Of course."

She smiled and fell into step beside him. What was it about him that her body responded to? He was totally out of bounds, she barely knew him, yet her tummy was fluttering just walking alongside him. What would it be like to hold his hand – or wrap her arms around his waist and lean into him? He seemed almost magnetic. It was only the second time she'd met the man and she was behaving stupidly, fantasising about getting close to him. As if a teacher would fraternise with a student, anyway.

Of course he wouldn't. Especially not when he had a wife.

15.

Kym

Kym was leant against the wall fidgeting while she waited for the girl to hang up on the phone. It had been a long day in school, she was bloated from a heavy supper, and all she really wanted was to get into bed, flick through a few pages of her book, and sleep. She'd already gone back to her room once and returned, but the same girl was still on the phone. There was a large notice above the phone about being fair and not hogging it, but clearly this student hadn't got the message.

She gave up waiting and left the nurses' home and headed for the hospital. There was the patients' cafe with a phone outside. She'd see if that was free. Tony had told her he would be heading out for one of the lads birthdays so she wanted to catch him before he left. Fortunately when she got there, the phone was free. She dialled the number in Portsmouth and it sounded like a similar set up to theirs in the nurses' home. Whoever answered had to go to the room the person required and tell them there was a phone call.

Eventually after six ten-pence pieces, the familiar voice she'd missed picked up.

"Sorry to keep you waiting," he sounded gentle and apologetic. "Have you spent loads?"

"I have a bit, but never mind. I thought you said you'd hang around the phone for me to ring."

"I did, but gave up. I thought maybe you'd decided not to."

"Don't be daft. Why wouldn't I ring – I said I would, didn't I? I just had to wait for a phone to become free. Anyway, how are you? It's lovely to hear you."

"I'm okay, shitting myself about the one-to-one tomorrow."

"You'll be great. It's just a formality, isn't it?"

"Not really. They tell you how you've done at basic training, and if it's okay, you get a commission. If it's not so good, you stay on land in Portsmouth for a bit longer."

"That seems awful when you've joined the Navy to be on a ship."

"Yeah, but that's the way it is."

"It'll be fine I'm sure. You have bags of charm."

"Nice of you to say," he sniggered, "but they aren't big on charm here. It's more about skills and leadership."

"Yeah, I know, but you've got that in spades. They'd be mad not to have you."

The pips beeped and she quickly put in another ten pence.

"Are you still there?"

"Yep, but not for long. The lads are waiting to go out."

"Yeah, well they can wait a minute can't they?"

"I'm not sure about that, they're desperate for a pint."

"You go steady though with tomorrow being a big day. Don't let them wreck it for you."

"They won't." Someone spoke to him in the background. She sensed him taking a deep breath. "I'm going to have to go."

"Really, must you? I've got loads to tell you."

"We can speak properly tomorrow. I can let you know about the interview."

"I'm going home tomorrow after school remember."

"Yeah, I know. I'll be able to ring you there."

"I wish you were coming home."

"Me too. But it's not long until next weekend."

"I know." There was a pause. He didn't try to fill in the gap. "Okay, I'd better let you go then. Best of luck for tomorrow."

"Thanks. Speak tomorrow night."

The line went dead. Disappointment kicked in. No, how was she doing, how was school, how was she finding the academic work? Nothing. She left the phone area and made her way to the patients' cafe. She needed chocolate to console her and ended up with a large bar of Cadbury's. As she broke off a couple of squares and slipped the rest into her bag, she thought about their one-sided conversation acknowledging Tony must be anxious about the following day. And she was seeing him the following weekend. Maybe she needed to chill out.

Tony was still on her mind as she made her way through the hospital heading towards the nurses' home. Much as she cared about him, it did seem all about him, which was fine when he was embarking on his initial training, but now she was also, she expected a bit more from him. They had a long way to go in their distance relationship. Next weekend would be a great opportunity to talk about him needing to put the effort in, not just her.

As she continued down the corridor, Guy and Zoe caught up with her.

"Hi. Where have you two been?" she asked.

"To our wards to see what shift we're doing next Wednesday," Guy said. "I've got an early and you're on a late."

"Oh, right, I guess it gives me a lie in."

"Yeah, and we swap the following week. I'm the late, you're the early."

"That's fair then. What about you Zoe?"

"An early."

"That's better I reckon for the first day. But I don't suppose it matters really. Are you heading back to the nurses' home?"

"We were," Guy pointed to the cafe, "unless you want to grab a drink in the shop?"

"It's closing."

"Oh, right. We'll walk back with you then. We can get a coffee there."

As they walked together and exited the hospital heading towards the nurses' home, Mrs McGee was coming down the footpath towards them.

"Finally," she puffed, "I'm looking for residents of North House but can't find anyone. It's like the Mary Celeste on both floors."

Kym had no idea what she was referring to, but she wasn't about to ask.

Matron pursed her lips. "I've just put a notice on the entrance to keep the outer door closed. I don't know why people aren't doing that. Goodness knows what sort of person walks through a door and doesn't close it behind them."

She stared through her tiny grey eyes at them as if she wanted a reply.

"It's not us," Guy offered, "we always shut it."

"Well, somebody is leaving it open. There's a real mess in the doorway with debris blowing everywhere and there's no point in having heating on for it to be escaping out the doors."

All three of them stared. What more was she expecting them to say? She was such an odd-looking woman. Kym's eyes were drawn to her neck. Why was she wearing that collar with a scarf round it? If her intention was to cover it, it wasn't working. It looked stupid. And she had her hair pulled back from her face which didn't suit her. Not that the long lank hair did either.

"Right," Mrs McGee seemed to pull her shoulders back, "I must get on. Please do tell anyone you see about closing the door."

"We will do," Kym said as they made their way to the nurses' home entrance.

"What's she like," Zoe whispered out of earshot, "God help anyone she catches leaving the door open."

"Anyone fancy a drink at the Rushley?" Guy asked putting them *IN* on the board.

Kym shook her head, "Not for me."

"Hey, that's a good idea," Zoe said eagerly, "just us or shall I nip up and see if Louise and Vanya fancy it?"

"The more the merrier," Guy smiled, "I'll see if I can find Simon."

"Okay," Zoe said, heading for the stairs. "I'll be back in five with anyone I can rustle up."

Kym attempted to follow her but Guy stopped her by asking, "Why won't you come?"

She shrugged. "I'm not bothered tonight."

"Why not? It's better than sitting in."

"I just fancy an early night."

"We won't be late," he widened his eyes persuasively, "I'll have you home at a decent time, I promise Cinderella."

"No, honestly," she smiled at his humour, "not tonight. Busy weekend and all that at home tomorrow. You enjoy yourselves though."

"Are you seeing your boyfriend this weekend?"

"No, he's not home. He will be the next one though. What about you, will you see your girlfriend? You haven't said much about her."

"Haven't I? Yeah, I'll see her."

"What's she called?"

"Heather."

"That'll be nice then. Although you don't look elated to be going home?"

"That's 'cause I'm not. My old man will be on my case. He'll never get over me giving up medical school."

"He might be okay now you've started here, you never know. And your girlfriend will be pleased to see you."

"Yeah, I guess so. Won't you change your mind and come with us? Please."

"No, not tonight. I'm going up for a soak in the bath and then to bed." She put a foot on the stairs and playfully put on a stern voice. "And don't you forget to close that door behind you, it's letting out far too much heat."

He did that wink again. For some reason, warmth spread through her chest. She grinned affectionately back as she headed up the stairs to her room.

Why was he so bothered about her going to the pub when he had the others to go with? It couldn't be attraction. He knew she had Tony and he had a girlfriend also. Maybe he was just being kind? And even if he was free, nobody would get a look in. Not with Zoe eagerly waiting in the wings for her opportunity.

Nevertheless, soaking into the bubbles of her hot bath, she couldn't help replaying that wink over and over in her mind.

16.

Louise

There was a sense of anticipation flooding through Louise as she opened her door, dressed in her new uniform ready for the first shift on the ward. Her, Kym and Vanya were on late shifts, meaning they started on their wards at eleven thirty. Zoe, Guy and Simon had been allocated early shifts so had left first thing.

Kym, in the opposite room to her, had her door wide open. She was staring at herself in the full-length mirror on the wardrobe door. Louise couldn't help but appreciate how lovely Kym looked. The pale blue uniform with a tiny white check, nipped in at the waist with a matching material belt, suited her perfectly. It finished just above her knee and she was wearing the obligatory black shoes they'd been instructed to buy. Even the white hat with the single navy stripe around indicating their first year in training, suited Kym. Her hair was neatly ensconced in some sort of bun underneath the hat and not a stray hair was evident. She looked like the perfect nurse.

"You look fabulous Kym, the blue really suits you."

"Aw, thank you. You look nice too. The blue really suits your dark colouring."

"Thank you. That's kind of you. I do love the colour, I must say. I feel a bit naff in the hat though, do you?"

"Yeah, I do a bit, but we'll get used to it I suppose."

Vanya came walking down the corridor wrapped in the navy wool cape with a red lining. Two thick red straps held the cape in place, crossed over her chest and fastened at the back. "You both look nice," Vanya smiled, "are you about ready?"

"Yep, as ready as we'll ever be, "Louise nodded. "You look like the perfect nurse in your cape. I see you managed to get your hair under your hat."

"Yes, with about 50 hairgrips."

"Hey, we need a photo of us for posterity." Kym reached for her camera off the dresser,

"First day on the ward and all that."

Vanya held out her hand, "I'll take one of each of you, shall I?"

"You take Kym first of all, while I go get my cape and lock my door," Louise said nipping across the corridor to her room.

"Are you nervous?" Vanya asked as they made their way downstairs and put themselves *OUT* on the board.

"A bit," Louise said brightly, masking the butterflies swirling around her tummy. It wasn't the same anxiety they might be feeling. Hers was more about seeing Nick Feeney again.

"I'm looking forward to it," Kym said, "not that it sounds like we'll be doing much."

"Be nice to get a feel for the ward though," Louise said, "it won't be so strange then when we do start full-time."

Vanya nodded, "I just hope they don't expect too much. It's alright in that practical room in the school of nursing, it'll be totally different on the ward."

"Yeah, you're right, but remember what Mrs Beaumont said, they won't be expecting anything from us. So I'm sure we'll be fine."

They entered the hospital and made their way down the corridor. Louise felt special and proud in her new nurse's uniform. This was what it was all about as far as she was concerned. She liked being in school, but nursing on a ward was what she really wanted to do. They soon reached ward 9.

"This is my stop," Kym grinned, "good luck both of you. I'll see you tonight."

"Will do," Louise smiled, "have a good shift."

"Yeah, Vanya said, "say hello to Guy. Hope he's enjoyed the early."

Louise and Vanya carried on walking together to the newer part of the hospital. Ward 9 was the last of the old Nightingale wards. Eight and nine were adjacent to each other. Eight was female, nine male. The wards they were heading for were more modern and segregated into male and female bays.

"Kym looks stunning in her uniform, doesn't she?" Vanya said.

"Yeah, she does. She's not only pretty, but she's a really nice person."

"She is. I think Guy likes her you know."

"What makes you say that?"

"Just a sense really."

"I don't think she's interested in him. She has Tony."

"I know. I just have a feeling her and Guy might get together somehow."

"I doubt it. She'd have to get past Zoe first and she makes no secret about the fact she likes him."

"Oh, you're right there, she does."

As they turned the corner towards their respective wards, Mr Duffield the nursing officer was walking towards them. "Hello girls," he paused in front of them. "May I say how smart you are looking in your uniforms?"

"Thank you," Louise smiled feeling slightly awkward at the way he was staring. She'd remembered on their first day when he'd marched Guy and Simon into the classroom. His appearance was odd. He looked smart enough in a suit, white shirt and tie, but it seemed like he was trying to make himself appear younger with his dyed black hair, which didn't suit him. Neither did the thick-rimmed Michael Caine glasses.

"I'll call on the wards later to see how you're getting on if I have some time. I do have a meeting which may go on a bit, so if I miss you, I'll most definitely catch you next week when you do your early shift."

"Okay," Vanya said, surreptitiously glancing down at her new fob watch.

He noticed. "Oh, yes, you mustn't be late. Enjoy your shifts both of you."

"He's a bit weird, isn't he?" Vanya whispered as they carried on walking.

"Yeah, he is. But best to keep on the right side of him if he has to sign our competencies off."

"Too right," Vanya agreed stopping outside of ward 7. "Looks like this is you, then. Hope you have a good shift."

"You too," Louise smiled, "see you later."

"Will do, good luck," Vanya nodded as she carried on walking to her ward while Louise pushed the door open to hers. Finally she was going to be working as a nurse and she couldn't wait. She almost skipped along. The smell of her freshly laundered uniform excited her, and she'd spent an age that morning tying her dark hair in a ponytail, twirling it around into a bun and gripping it in place. It didn't matter that is wasn't perfect because the white nurse's hat covered it completely. And, as if she didn't feel proud enough, the gorgeous navy cape with the thick red lining completed the nurse's look. She was glad Kym had a camera and they'd taken photos. Her mum would love that. Kym had used up all the film and said she'd send it to Truprint at the weekend.

"Hi," a nurse greeted her as she tapped on the office door on the ward. "You must be Nurse Allard. Do you want to go and hang your cape up in the staff cloakroom to your left, and we'll be with you to orientate you to the ward."

"Thank you," she smiled and headed towards the cloakroom. She hung up her cape with the others, pleased the sewing room had labelled it. She didn't like the thought of anyone sharing her stuff. Not with her obsession about germs and cleanliness.

One last look in the mirror demonstrated her name badge was on wonky, so she quickly adjusted it and went and stood outside the office again. The door was ajar. A male voice she recognised caused a flutter in her tummy. It was what had kept her awake half the night.

Nick Feeney's voice was so soft, "We're missing Ralph, where is he?"

"With Mr Harvey in X-ray."

The nurse sitting down spotted her. "Come in."

Nick Feeney was sitting behind the desk looking terribly attractive in his navy tabard. It was short-sleeved and the hairs on his arms had her tummy doing somersaults.

"Good morning, Nurse Allard. This is Staff Nurse Oates who you'll be working with part of the day today. I'm going to show you round myself, but I have a meeting at two."

Louise smiled at the older lady. "Hi."

"Hello again and welcome, Nurse Allard."

"Thank you." She hadn't expected the formality. She'd thought they would call her Louise.

"Right," Nick Feeney stood up, "we'll leave Staff Nurse Oates to take reports from the early staff while we have the tour and get you orientated."

He held the office door for her to go in front of him. "You found the ladies' cloakroom?" He asked pausing outside of it, "next to that is the male one," he indicated with his head. "It's barely more than a broom cupboard but there are fewer males in the hospital, particularly student nurses. We do seem to get more physiotherapists on secondment than anything. Anyway, follow me to the most important room in the house."

They stopped at what appeared to be a utility area. "This is the sluice. Known as a dirty area because all the waste patients excrete go down there." He pointed to a huge machine. "Don't look so worried," he picked up a clean bedpan from the rack and a grey cardboard inset. "These are thrown in the incinerator when the patient has used them. You'll get used to it. It's often a case of learning to breathe through your mouth rather than your nose, opening the lid to the machine and throwing the inset in. The machine then does the rest. Of course then you must wash your hands. You'll have learned about the importance of hand washing in school?"

"Yes."

"Good. It is terribly important. Your first competency will be attending to a patient's hygiene. A little tip to give you the heads-up – whatever task you are carrying out, before you move onto another, wash your hands. So many nurses fail on the first attempt by not doing so." He smiled kindly out of gorgeous hazel eyes she could lose herself in. "You'll pick it up, don't worry."

She followed him down to a bay and he paused outside. There were six beds all neatly made but only three were occupied. The three patients turned towards them.

"Good morning all," Mr Feeney glanced at his fob watch, "yes it is still morning . . . just. I'm showing a new student round the ward today, this is Nurse Allard."

The three patients smiled and said hello. They seemed pleased to see a new face.

An elderly patient asked, "Am I going to OT this afternoon for my assessment?"

"As far as I know you are," Mr Feeney said, "I'll check that it's still on when I get back to the office." He turned to her, "Mr Sampson is going home on Friday and OT – occupational therapy – want to assess he is able to manage tasks such as making himself a cup of tea, managing the toilet etc. You'll get a chance to visit OT and the physiotherapy department while you're on placement."

"Sounds great, thanks," she said, trying to not bounce on her heels so much.

Louise was charmed by him. He was everything she could possibly want in a man. Good looking, kind, infectious and a great nurse as well as a tutor. Her gut tightened thinking about him having a wife. How did she get so lucky?

"Next comes the thing I want you to hear from me personally, even though anyone will tell you. I'm obsessed with tidiness, cleanliness, and infection control. So, I like the staff to keep all surfaces uncluttered and wiped regularly, and woe betide anyone that leaves anything out that shouldn't be. Particularly in the sluice we've just come from. Just because it's a sluice, doesn't mean it's a dumping ground for everything. All the staff know that and I'm pleased to say adhere to it without any nagging from me. Well . . . not too much nagging anyway."

Was that the precise moment she fell in love with him? She wasn't sure but he certainly ticked all the boxes with his cleanliness and tidiness regime. They were a perfect match.

She followed him around the rest of the ward and he introduced her to staff along the way. Some of the beds had curtains around them in the three male bays and a fourth female bay and he explained they might be having dressings done, or were being examined by a doctor.

"I like all patients to have had their personal hygiene needs attending to by eleven at the latest. Then it's time for the nursing staff to attend to any extras that are required. You'll soon see. I do love tidy and organised. I like the patients' lockers to be tidy, too. And, I have a certain way I like each bed to look. You'll get used to me, I can assure you. I sound like a complete tyrant, I know I do, but I can assure you I'm not."

"I'm sure you're not," she shook her head, not quite sure what to say. He was anything but a tyrant. Hero, more like.

"Right, how about I leave you with Nurse Clayton here and she can explain what she's up to. If there are any beds left to be made, you can get some practice in with all those endless envelope corners they've had you doing in school. And when the remaining beds are made, you can take each patient a fresh water jug, making sure the jug is spotlessly clean, of course. You'll get the hang of it. I have a dressing to do later today, so you can watch me do it if you like. I'm taking some stitches out of a young lad's leg. You'll see me use the aseptic technique that you've been learning about too."

He turned to the nurse who had two stripes on her hat, "Nurse Clayton, can Nurse Allard join you please, make up any beds left and after that do the waters. Perhaps you can show her the intake and output charts and explain how we calculate them."

"Yes, of course."

He turned back to her. "Happy with everything, Nurse Allard?"

"Very happy, Mr Feeney. Thank you."

Happy? She was on cloud nine.

17.

He gazed out of the corridor window onto the car park. It was time. He was poised. The essential implements he needed were in place and his car was parked close to the door of the disused corridor. All he needed now was the girl. He'd walked up and down the corridor several times, and even used the public phone while he waited. But there were only so many times he could call the talking clock.

The excitement brimming within him hadn't surfaced for a number of years. But it was back with a vengeance. He adored beautiful things, particularly females. And normally it was harmless, just watching. He loved their movements, their hair, their slender limbs, and their breasts. Their shape attracted him. But right now the urges were overwhelming to touch one of them, caress them and feel their warm skin beneath his own fingers. He loved the thrill of taking Vanya's knickers. The feminine smell was his driving force. He liked having something that belonged to her. He put his hand inside his pocket, caressing the delicate fabric. He'd hide them away after he'd finished with Vanya. He imagined her beauty without clothes. He just knew she'd be perfect.

The rain and hail was belting down on the corridor windows reminding him of the hours he spent as a child, looking out his bedroom window and watching the rain. It had fascinated him. He would draw pictures in his mind watching the drops cascading down the old windows. Despite not wanting to go back into the dark corners of his mind to his childhood, it continued to haunt him. It had been a thoroughly tortuous and miserable period. He could barely remember a time when he was happy. Maybe at school, despite being the victim of relentless bullying, he did love academic work. He was at his happiest in the classroom with the teacher. If things had been different, he could have made something of his life. But because of his wretched father, the disciplinarian, his life hadn't been pleasant. His advantage though was his mental strength, his brother was not quite so lucky. So he'd quickly become almost his brother's mother after their own mother took her last breath. Mrs Baxter the housekeeper arriving had helped. Before that, they'd had an intolerable year. Seemingly Mrs Baxter did some administration for the council his father worked for and had fallen on difficult times when her husband had died suddenly and she was left with an enormous amount of debt. She'd moved in with them and was given his bedroom, forcing him to share with his brother. He quickly realised that Mrs Baxter was barely occupying his bedroom at all. Well if she did, it was for only half of the night. The other half she spent in his father's bed.

Frustration was getting the better of him. He was tired of waiting for Vanya to leave the ward. He was banking on her being alone. If not, he'd have to abandon the plan. He checked his watch again. Despite not wanting to think about his life as a youngster with his brother, it was at the forefront of his mind as he waited.

He remembered the greasy spoon cafe he'd sat in with his brother after their beating. They'd relished the fried bacon, eggs, beans and chips washed down with tea that had been so stewed, a spoon would stand upright in it. They hadn't had much to eat at home for days. The old man was still harping on about the missing five pounds. He'd smiled inwardly. That would be the missing five pounds which paid for the meal they were eating.

"Where did you get the money to pay for this?" his brother had asked, tipping more tomato sauce on the side of his plate.

"I did some jobs for Mr Davis at the end of the road and he gave me a few quid. Don't say anything to Dad though."

"I won't. What we gonna do when we get home if Mrs Baxter has made us some food?"

"I dunno," he shrugged, "try and eat it I suppose. Or just say we don't feel like it. Friday's her day off, so I don't think she'll be there. She visits her mother or something so doesn't get back 'till late remember."

"That's right, I forgot," his brother said mopping the last of the sauce with some bread lathered in margarine. On the table next to them were two adults and a boy about the same age as them tucking into their food and interacting together and laughing. His brother screwed his face up and whispered, "I wish we got to do things like normal people."

"Yeah, but we're not normal in our house."

"Why though?"

"Dunno," he shrugged, "guess our dad's a nutcase."

"We never go to Gran's anymore do we? Dad says it's too far to travel but it's not that far to Derby. I looked at the map in the hall at school."

"Yeah, well he would say that. He doesn't want to go."

"Why doesn't Gran come and see us?"

"'Cause she doesn't like him."

"Is that really why?"

"Course it is."

"I miss seeing her."

"Yeah, well she's not coming. We're stuck with him . . . and Mrs Baxter."

"As soon as I'm old enough, I'm going to leave home and get trained to do something. Anything so I can get a good job and live somewhere else."

"Me too. But we're stuck with them a while yet. He says I've got to get a job somewhere at weekends to help pay the bills."

"But you've got a paper round and hand that over each week."

"He says it's not enough. I have to bring in more now I'm fourteen."

"What work can you get?"

"Dunno," he shrugged, "but I've got to go look on Saturday. I'll get it in the neck if I don't come back with a job."

His brother took a swig of his tea and wiped his mouth with his hand. "I hate him. I wish he would get run over or something and died. Then it'd just be me and you . . . and Mrs Baxter. She might stay and take care of us." He screwed his face up. "But we wouldn't have a house if he died I suppose."

"Yeah, we would. We'd live in our house. It belongs to Dad. He got it when Granddad died. It'd be ours if anything happened to him."

"That'd be good, wouldn't it?" He paused for a moment and then grinned. "I don't want anything to happen to him really, just when he's mean."

"You're soft. Right come on, and remember, not a word about this food. If Mrs Baxter is there, or Dad, we've been playing footie on the playing field and forgot the time."

"Okay."

His melancholy thoughts were interrupted when the delightful Vanya stepped out of the ward. She looked so perfectly beautiful, wrapped in her new cape, ready for the short journey to the nurses' home, which would require her to leave the warmth of the hospital at some stage, to walk up the hill.

"Good evening," he said approaching her. "Are you just finishing?"

"Yes," she said. "It was a great first day on the ward. Everyone has been so kind and welcoming."

"Good. Has it been busy?" he asked, sliding his hand into his pocket, touching her knickers.

"It was rather. But I've enjoyed it." She gave him the cutest smile.

He smiled back, breathing her in. Soon he'd be touching her flesh for real, inhaling her scent up close. He gestured with his head towards the corridor window.

"And now you'll be heading to the nurses' home in all this rain."

"Yes, I'll have to make a run for it."

"No need for that. I can show you a quicker way that'll take you directly to the nurses' home without getting wet."

"Oh, right," Vanya looked puzzled, "if you're sure."

"Quite sure. Follow me, it's this way."

And just like that, pretty little innocent Vanya followed his lead through the *do not enter* door, having no idea what she was letting herself in for.

18.

Kym

She hung her cape on the door inside her room and kicked off her shoes. It had been a long shift since eleven thirty that morning and her new lace-up shoes had caused her feet to throb. It was a relief to put on her soft slippers. She opened her bedside locker for a jar of coffee and her mug. The induction to the ward had been brilliant; she'd loved every minute of it. The charge nurse Mr Griffiths was really pleasant and she loved Diana Flynn the staff nurse she'd been allocated to work with for the duration of the shift. She'd escorted a patient to X-ray with a porter, helped serve meals to the patients, and even got to feed an old man in the side ward.

She tapped on Louise's door to see if she was back from her late but she didn't answer. She made her way down the corridor to the kitchen, her thoughts on a warm drink and a bath, then to bed. Louise had maybe thought the same and was soaking in some bubbles right now.

As she entered the kitchen, Louise, Simon, Guy and Zoe were sitting round the table with drinks in front of them. "Ah, this is where you all are. How was everyone's shift?" she asked flicking on the kettle.

"Great," Louise said, "I really enjoyed mine. The staff are lovely and Mr Feeney is so good."

"I told you," Simon said sipping from a can of Coca Cola, "he is a fantastic nurse."

"Isn't he just? The way he runs the ward is brilliant."

"Did you work with him the whole shift?"

"No, he kept getting called away. But he showed me around the ward and talked to me about how he likes the beds to look uniformed with neat counterpanes and also clean lockers. It sounds like he's a bit obsessive about stuff like that."

"Oh, he is. But it works. Very few infections or pressure sores on his ward. He runs a really tight ship."

"Yeah, I could tell that. Someone said he's married, is it to anyone that works here?"

"No, it's an anaesthetist from Mansfield General."

"Really?"

"Yeah. They live in that house as you come up the drive."

"The gatekeeper's cottage?"

"Yeah, if it was the gatekeepers. I think it's called Alan Malkin House. Something to do with a surgeon who used to work here when it was first opened in the thirties."

"Oh, right. I wondered who lived there. It looks ever so cute and homely." Louise turned her head. "What about you, Kym, how did your shift go?"

"Good," Kym leant against the kitchen unit while she waited for the kettle to boil. "I got to see loads. I enjoyed the late shift. Mr Griffiths the charge nurse is really nice, isn't he, Guy?"

"Yeah, he seems decent enough. I got a bit fed up with all the bed making though. And I'm looking forward to doing more than just observing. It was a long day with nothing much to do. I think we need some hands on."

"You speak for yourself," Zoe interjected, "I'm happy observing. We'll be full on before you know it. The staff nurse I was working alongside said the expectations are the students work really hard. And they get the crappiest shifts. So I'm going to enjoy the induction for as long as it lasts."

"Anyone want one?" Kym asked as she switched the boiling kettle off.

"I'll have another," Zoe leaned forward and passed her mug, "just milk, no sugar." She turned to Guy, "So, what did you make of the ward in terms of how different it is to medicine?"

"Fine. But like I say, I want to do more. Simon was saying he got to do a dressing."

"What sort of dressing?" Zoe looked at Simon.

"Cleaning some Steinman pins of a bloke on traction."

"Really . . . and they let you do that?"

"Not let me do it as such. I got to clean the trolley to prepare and open the sterile bits. But they said I'd be doing that maybe next week."

"That's really cool," Louise said. "I didn't get to do any stuff like that. Too busy damp dusting lockers and refreshing the water jugs."

Kym put a coffee in front of Zoe and sat down with hers. "Where's Vanya?"

"I don't know," Zoe shrugged, "she's not been in here."

Mary Best, one of the second-year students, opened the door causing Simon to jump up and go to the bin to throw away his empty can.

"Did you all have a good day?" Mary asked.

"We did, thank you," Kym nodded.

"Good. It'll be better next week, you'll get to do more. The first day can be a bit boring."

"No, I think we all enjoyed it," Louise joined in.

"Right," Simon moved towards the door, "I'll see you lot later." Mary nodded to them as they both left the kitchen together.

"What's going on there," Kym frowned, "are they together or something?" she stared at Guy.

"I think she's helping him with some revision for the test on Friday," he grinned causing them all to laugh.

"Oh, right. We get it. Quickly moving on, shall I go give Vanya a knock and see if she wants a drink? Be nice to see how she's got on today." She'd hate not to include Vanya when she'd have only just finished her late like the rest of them.

"I'll go," Louise said, "you have your coffee, I've had mine. I won't be long." She opened the door and it swung closed behind her.

"So what's happening in school tomorrow?" Guy asked, "not more anatomy and physiology I hope."

"It is if I remember rightly from the timetable," Kym said. "It'll be all about the test on Friday."

"Yeah," Guy shrugged, "but they are multiple choice questions so we should do alright."

"You might," Zoe said, "it'll be a struggle for the rest of us."

"You'll be fine," Guy said. "Hey Zoe, did you get Mr dyed hair Duffield visiting you on the ward. We did, didn't we, Kym?"

"Yeah, it was nice of him to come round."

"No," Zoe said, "I saw Mrs Valance the other nursing officer. She came to my ward first thing while we were making beds. She pretty much said what you'd expect about working hard and knowing the patients. She seems nice."

"I wish we got her," Guy pulled a face, "I'm going to look out for her, anything's better than Duffield."

"There's nothing wrong with him," Kym interjected, "you just got off to a bad start that first day. He's fine."

"Is he? He barely spoke to me, but he was all over you."

"He wasn't all over me. He only spoke for five minutes."

The door opened and Louise came back in. "I tapped on her door but she didn't answer. Maybe she's in the bath?"

"Or on the phone," Kym said. "She might want to tell her mum and dad about her first day."

"Yeah, probably. Talking about baths, I think I'll go and get one. Although I didn't do much hands-on today, I sort of feel I need a good scrub."

"Me too," Kym said standing up and rinsing her mug. "I'll come with you."

"Nobody fancies helping me with any revision then?" Guy said with a twinkle in his eye.

"You don't need any help," Kym grinned, "you'll walk the test."

"Well, maybe I can help you?" he tilted his head.

"No thank you. I'm fine. On that note, we'll leave you with Zoe. She might want some help. See you in the morning at breakfast. Night," her and Louise said in unison as they left the kitchen together. Louise was grinning as they made their way down the corridor to their rooms for their towels.

"You've set him up now, he'll not be able to get rid of Zoe."

"Yeah, I know. It's funny, isn't it?" But she didn't feel it was funny really. On hindsight she wished she hadn't suggested it. Zoe and Guy together . . . surely he wouldn't go there? Not when he had a girlfriend.

They reached their rooms, said cheerio and closed their doors behind them.

Kym took her uniform off and wrapped herself in her dressing gown. She collected her soap bag and headed off towards the bathrooms. As she passed Vanya's room, she could tell from the glass window at the top of the door, it was in darkness. Maybe she was tired after her shift and had gone straight to bed?

They'd see her first thing at breakfast and find out then how she got on.

19.

Kym

She opened her eyes and John Travolta was staring at her from one side of her room, and David Bowie from the other. The posters she'd bought when she was home the previous weekend had made the room look more homely and personal. She'd put a pink spotted duvet cover on with a bright pillowslip to match and brought a couple of bright cushions to make the bed more of a sitting area in the daytime.

As always, she was awake before the alarm went off. Tony, grinning back from the wall next to the bed, made her smile. She'd be speaking to him that evening and seeing him the following night at home. She couldn't wait. It seemed ages since they'd been together and she had loads to tell him. He'd be excited too as he'd got a commission and would be joining his ship, HMS Blake in two weeks. But as pleased as she was for him, it did mean she'd be seeing much less of him and that worried her. While he promised he'd write and telephone regularly, she wasn't totally confident he would. So, as much as she was looking forward to seeing him, she needed to explain how she was feeling. He had an abundance of charm and an innate ability to reassure, but it was following through that bothered her.

She reached for her dressing gown from the back of the door, collected her soap bag and towels and left her room, heading for the shower. Zoe, coming down the corridor towards her was a surprise. She was fully dressed with her hair still damp from the shower and it was still relatively early. Most startling of all was her pallor, she usually had a full face of makeup, but not today. And she had tiny beads of perspiration on her forehead.

"Morning," Kym said brightly as they paused at the stairs, "you're early, are you going for breakfast already?"

"Yeah, needs must. I stopped up with the lads and had a couple of drinks last night," she scrunched up her face, "well, maybe more than a couple. I need to get something greasy inside of me, quickly."

"Oh, right. I'll not hold you up then. See you in a bit."

"I hope so," Zoe sighed, heading down the stairs.

Tightness clenched at Kym's gut as she headed for the shower, which was completely ridiculous. Zoe could drink with who she wanted. And, she reminded herself, it had been her that encouraged the two of them the previous evening when Guy had joked about someone helping him with revision. It didn't sound like she was on her own with him though which was good. Guy had a girlfriend at the end of the day. There was just something about Zoe she couldn't warm to as she had to Louise and Vanya. They were both lovely and had already become friends, but with Zoe, it was relief she felt when she was with the other girls in the set.

Once dressed in her jeans, pale pink sweatshirt and boots, Kym opened her door and Louise's was open opposite. It had become a ritual each morning, as soon as her and Louise were ready, they'd open their doors. Usually Vanya walked down to meet them and they'd head off to breakfast together.

"Morning," Kym smiled at Louise who was picking up her rucksack from the chair, "I saw Zoe before my shower. She was hot-footing it to the canteen – sounded like a bit of a heavy drinking night with the boys."

"What, after we left them in the kitchen?"

"Must have been."

"Was she just with Guy then, because Simon was," Louise raised her fingers implying quote marks, "with Mary Best revising."

Kym shrugged, "Not sure. She didn't say much, but I could tell she was feeling rough."

"More fool her then," Louise said closing her door, "good job it's not the test today."

"Yeah, absolutely." Kym frowned, "Not sure where Vanya is this morning, we better go knock for her."

Kym and Louise selected their breakfasts in the dining room and joined Simon, Guy and Zoe at the table. Each of them appeared to be almost finished with what looked like a full fried breakfast.

Kym took her seat and reached for a napkin and cutlery from the centre of the table. "I take it you're all feeling a bit delicate," she said looking at Guy and Zoe.

"The breakfast's helping," Zoe said finishing off the last of her bacon and mopping it around some egg yolk.

"Never again," Guy rubbed his head, "bloody Schnapps, it's lethal."

"Schnapps?" Louise looked puzzled, "Where did you get that from?"

"Francis, the trainee doctor opposite us invited us to his room and we just sat listening to music and drinking."

"And you were with them, Zoe?" Kym frowned, "You better be careful. You'll have Mrs McGee on the warpath."

"I'm not bothered about her. We were all just sitting around if she had caught us. It's not like we were all in bed together." Kym noticed Zoe glancing at Guy but he was still tucking into the last of his bacon and seemed oblivious to any agenda Zoe might have. Had they already been together? She tossed the slice of toast she was eating down on the plate, it had somehow lost its appeal. The thought of any sort of liaison between Zoe and Guy, didn't sit well with her.

"How many did you all have?" she asked, looking directly at Guy.

He reached for his glass of orange and gulped it down. "Erm . . . two or three."

"Really?" she widened her eyes, "good job that's all you had then," she said sarcastically. Anyone could see by their faces, they'd all had a skinful.

"I might just get another coffee," Guy pushed his chair back, "anyone else?"

"I'll have another," Zoe said, "just black please."

Simon stood up. "I'll come with you. I fancy some more orange juice."

"What are you like," Louise rolled her eyes. "It's going to be a long day for you, Zoe."

"Yeah, don't I know it."

"What is it we've got on today?" Louise asked as she buttered a slice of toast. "I can't remember?"

Kym reached into her bag for the timetable and turned to Thursday. "Taking temperatures and blood pressures first thing, and then after coffee we've got Mrs Valance, the other nursing officer coming to talk on standards, expectations and professionalism. This afternoon, it's giving intramuscular injections and the safe disposal of sharps."

"God, how boring," Zoe put two fingers to her temple, "shoot me now. Hey, where's Vanya? Why isn't she here for breakfast?"

"We don't know. We tapped on her door but she never answered." Kym glanced at her watch, "She's cutting it fine if she wants anything to eat. We'll have to make a move shortly."

Louise wiped the corner of her mouth on her serviette. "She could be having a lie in and maybe skipping breakfast. I bet she's gone straight to the classroom."

"Yeah, I suppose so. Did you see her at all last night, Zoe after we'd gone?" Kym asked.

Zoe shook her head.

"I reckon she probably went straight to bed," Louise said. "I used the phone about half past nine and her door was closed then."

"Yeah, it was when I went for a bath. It seems odd though," Kym screwed her face up, "I hope she isn't poorly or anything."

"She'd have knocked and let one of us know, surely?"

"Maybe not, though. Remember what Matron said on our first evening. Anyone that was not well must first of all inform her and she would visit and make an assessment as to whether we needed to see a doctor."

"Oh, God, yeah, she did. Maybe Vanya's keeping her head down then. Who could face Mrs McGee examining them? It'd be your worst nightmare."

Vanya not seeing them the previous evening after their shifts and not joining them for breakfast, concerned Kym. Although they hadn't known each other long, the four of them went to and from school together as well as having their meals together; they'd formed a small clique. The other girls in the group were nice, but they'd developed their own friendship unit. And Guy and Simon floated around between the two groups.

They couldn't continue to do nothing about their friend, they needed to check up on her. "We'll see when we get to school if Vanya's gone straight there. If not, at break time I'll go across and give her another knock. If she doesn't reply, I'm going to see Mrs McGee."

"Good idea," Louise agreed, "I'll come with you."

The first hour of the morning was spent in the practical room taking each other's blood pressures under the watchful eye of Mrs Beaumont. She'd informed them that there was a change in the programme as Mrs Valance was off sick, so Nick Feeney was stepping in with a refresher on anatomy and physiology for the test on Friday morning.

It seemed a long hour until break time, but eventually, Kym and Louise headed for North House to check on

Vanya. They'd asked Mrs Beaumont if she'd received a message in school to say she was unwell, but she hadn't. The first thing they checked was the *IN/OUT* board on the ground floor which indicated that Vanya was *OUT*.

"Shall we knock anyway?" Kym asked, "she might have forgotten to click she's back in?"

"Yeah, best to try. Could be she's feeling better though and gone out for some fresh air," Louise said as they climbed the stairs.

Kym tapped on their friend's door. "Vanya?" There was no response. "Are you okay, Vanya?"

Silence.

"It doesn't sound as if she's in there," Kym said, with her ear against the door.

"Shall we go and see Mrs McGee then?" Louise asked. "Hey, you don't think she could have gone home, do you? You know, maybe a bit homesick?"

"Could have, I suppose, but surely she would have said?" Kym frowned. "We better say something. If Mrs McGee doesn't know, she might want to call her parents."

"Yeah, you're right. If we're quick, we can get back to the canteen and grab a drink before the next lesson."

They made their way down the stairs, out of the nurses' home and headed towards South House. "I'm pleased we've got anatomy and physiology now with Mr Feeney this afternoon," Kym said as they walked down the hill, "it might help with the test being on Friday."

"Hallelujah, that's all I can say. Only someone as hot as him could make such a boring subject worth listening too."

"Honestly, what are you like? He's married remember."

"I know. I'm only looking and admiring." Louise grinned cheekily, "Nothing wrong with that?"

"No," Kym replied as they made their way towards Mrs McGee's quarters in South House, "as long as that's all it is."

Kym tapped on Mrs McGee's door and it was quickly opened.

"Yes. What is it?" Mrs McGee stood in the doorway wearing what looked like an oversized overall. It was grey with a belt which would have to be big to fit around her ample waist. Kym could see down the hallway to a lounge. The gas fire was on and an open newspaper rested on the arm of the chair next to it. Mrs McGee would no doubt be irritated about being disturbed.

"Vanya Mann wasn't in school this morning," Kym said, "we wondered if she might be poorly? We knocked on her door but she didn't answer. We thought maybe you might know."

"I'm not aware of anything," Mrs McGee frowned and Kym couldn't help but stare at her painted-on eyebrows. They weren't done terribly well. They looked like they'd been hastily applied. She imagined Mrs McGee was one of those women who spent so long plucking her eyebrows, she had very little left, hence the need to crayon them on. "There are a lot of coughs and colds around right now though, so you're right, she might not be well."

"That's what we thought."

"Was she alright yesterday?"

"We didn't see her after our late shift. We think maybe she went straight to bed."

"I see. I'd better go check her room."

"Shall we come too?" Louise suggested.

"There's no need for that," Mrs McGee snapped, "where are you supposed to be right now?"

Kym looked at her watch. "We're on our break at the moment."

"Well, you'd better go get a drink. I'll deal with it. You did right coming and telling me."

"What if she isn't in her room? We wondered whether she might have just had enough and gone home?"

"I doubt that very much," Mrs McGee dismissed, "but if I'm concerned, I'll ring her parents. Leave it with me."

"Will you let us know?" Kym asked.

"Yes, of course I will when I know anything. Run along now. I'll come and find you later on when you've finished and let you know how Vanya is. I'll be keeping a check on her from now on."

"Thank you," they both said as she closed the door on them. Louise's puzzled face echoed Kym's thoughts. Mrs McGee seemed most irritated.

"Hey," Louise laughed, as they made their way back to the canteen, "imagine Vanya's face if she's in bed and Matron opens the door. You'd die wouldn't you? She scares me half to death."

"She's really odd, isn't she? What's that scarf around her neck supposed to be hiding? You can tell it's a brace of some sort."

"Yeah, I think it is. My grandma had one of those. She had a damaged vertebrae and had to wear it for support. She wore it right up until the time she died."

"Aw, that's sad. Maybe that's what Mrs McGee has then, some sort of damage to her neck?"

"It'll be something like that, I reckon."

In the canteen, they grabbed themselves canned drinks and made their way towards Zoe, Guy and Simon. They took their seats beside them in the linked leather easy chairs.

"Feeling any better?" Kym asked.

"Yeah, coming round a bit now," Zoe said, "I was a bit rough first thing."

"I'm fine," Guy said sitting upright, "It's just these bleeding men hammering away in my head."

"I've got some aspirin if you want some," Louise said opening her rucksack.

"Cheers," Guy said taking two from her.

"I've already taken some," Zoe said, "but thanks anyway. I might have some more in an hour or so."

"Just say if you want some. I've got plenty."

Guy washed his tablets down with a gulp of water. "Did you manage to find Vanya?"

"No," Kym said, "she's not in her room, or at least we don't think she is. We've just been to see Mrs McGee to tell her."

"You don't reckon she's jacked it in and gone home, do you?" Simon asked.

"No, definitely not," Louise dismissed. "She never mentioned anything yesterday morning when we were getting ready for our late shift. We took some photos and I walked with her to her ward. I said cheerio at the entrance to ward 7 but I never saw her last night and neither did anyone else by the sound of things."

"It's all getting a bit spooky," Simon wiggled his fingers, "I've heard there's a ghost that haunts Harlow Wood. Maybe she was abducted in the night as we all slept."

"Shut up, Simon," Louise slapped his arm, "that isn't helping." She turned to Kym. "Do you think we should knock on Matron's door again after school?"

"I wouldn't keep troubling Demis Roussos if I was you," Simon sniggered, "not now she's on the case."

"You are awful calling her that," Kym said, "she can't help being stocky."

"Fat you mean."

"You're just being rude. Wait until you're in your fifties, you might be like that."

"God, I hope not. I still wouldn't go bothering her though. She'll come and find you when she knows something."

"I hope so. Right, is everyone ready to head back?"

They all made their way out of the hospital towards the school of nursing. Simon was in front chatting with Louise, while Zoe walked with her and Guy. Kym noticed Zoe was becoming a bit like Guy's shadow. Wherever he was, she seemed to be.

The gardener was deadheading flowers at the edge of the path as they approached. "Good morning," he said, smiling brightly beneath his wide-brimmed hat that Kym thought was a bit over the top for the time of year.

"Morning, Lloyd. You okay, mate?" Guy smiled.

"Yep, all good."

"Great. Catch you later."

Kym waited until they were well ahead of the gardener so she couldn't be heard. "How come you're on first name terms with the gardener?"

"He was at the Rushley the other night. We had a great laugh with him didn't we, Zoe . . . and can he drink."

"Honestly, is there anyone you don't drink with?" Kym said playfully.

"Mmmm . . . no, not really. But there are some people I'd rather drink with more than others," he reached for the door and held it open for them to walk through, "if you get my drift," he winked.

Kym didn't know quite what to say. Did he mean her, or was he on about Zoe?

He must mean Zoe, surely?

20.

It was done. Over. And he was buzzing with adrenaline, lying on his bed in the darkness, curtains open wide to let the brilliance of the moonlight in. He was on a high and knew he'd be like it for days. Images were vivid of his abduction of Vanya and he replayed them over and over again. The stupid girl had complied when he'd offered to take her on a shortcut to the nurses' home by taking her through a door that said *no entry*. Although getting to where he wanted her, hadn't been easy. She was no dummy and had quickly become suspicious.

"Are you sure it's the right way?" she asked, the puzzlement clear in her dark eyes as they made their way along the dimly lit corridor swathed in cold, musty air, with the buzz of electricity the only sound apart from their footsteps.

"Of course I'm sure. We'll turn this corner and then I'll show you the shortcut."

"I think I'd rather go back through the hospital. It's eerie here."

"There's nothing to worry about, I wouldn't let anything happen to you."

"I know that, but still . . ."

"Here we are," they turned the corner into a patch of nothingness. This particular part of the hospital was shut off to the public. It had been a ward once-upon-a-time but had been redundant since the new wards were added.

Now, it had become a place to store old relics such as broken cabinets, rusted metal bed frames, and grisly medical equipment that looked like torture devices.

The girl's unease was evident by her sharp intake of breath. While she peered around at the cobwebs and dirty floor tiles, he reached for the rounders bat on the wall hook and gripped it tightly. His heart was pounding so hard as he raised the bat, savouring the moment before she turned around.

The gasp and the look of terror in her eyes when she did turn around was the trigger. One swift whack was all it took to knock her out cold. He caught her as she fell, a lightweight, so easy to handle. His excitement mounted as he dragged her further into the dark oppressive room. He hadn't felt such a high for years, not since his last kill.

He gently laid her down on the two rugs he'd prepared earlier and quickly undid her belt to remove her blue uniform and shoes. She was wearing a cream bra with a matching set of knickers he could see underneath her tights. He had to roll her slightly onto her side to undo the strap to expose her breasts, before easing her tights and knickers down her legs. He had to see her naked. It was the beauty of a female body he loved and Vanya was everything he hoped for, with her with pert little breasts, tiny waist, neat hips and pubic area. Nakedness to him wasn't about fucking. That could never be his driving force. All he wanted was to stroke and admire. He stared in awe at her beauty as her pink nipples tightened against the cold. She was perfect. Just as he'd known she would be. Petite but formed, and completely feminine. With flawless olive skin, just like

153

Angela, the woman he'd loved. The woman he'd seen naked so many times. Not that Angela ever knew that. She had no idea of the peephole he'd made from his bedroom to hers that allowed him to watch her every intimate movement. Everything had been fine until Angela met the waste of space that was Ricky Hurst. That's when his perfect life changed and he had to witness the groaning idiot pawing over his beautiful Angela, shoving his dirty prick inside her time and time again. And much as he tried, he still couldn't erase images of how she'd squirmed and moaned for him. His pure, pretty, perfect Angela. Surely she'd been faking enjoyment to please him? Sex was for animals after all.

He slipped off Vanya's hat, carefully taking the grips that held it in place, and loosened her thick hair from the tight bun on her head. He put the hair tie and grips in his pocket. He wasn't stupid enough to leave any evidence behind. The police would search the derelict part of the hospital, he was sure of that. He bunched her soft dark hair up and positioned it round one side of her head and loosely plaited it. Angela used to let him plait her hair. They'd watch TV and she'd sit on the floor at the side of him and get him to brush her hair and plait it. How he loved doing that.

He trailed his fingers down Vanya's slender neck, loving the softness of her skin, her perfect little breasts, and perfect nipples that were so hard. He stroked her flat stomach, her thighs, her pubic hair so neatly trimmed. Such a thrill to have her like this. Such a thrill to touch, to admire. He smoothed both hands over her breasts and down over her hips to her thighs, parting her legs

154

enough to get a glimpse of her beautiful femininity. He wondered if she was a virgin. To take the life of a virgin – a perfect virgin – would be so much more thrilling.

His hands wrapped around her ankles, they were tiny. And her toenails were cut neatly and painted a rich burgundy colour. She had pretty feet. She was so feminine and beautiful, just how a female should be. A whimper from Vanya made him pause. Once she opened her eyes, she'd have to die. She couldn't live, not now she recognised him. He'd go to jail, and even though his life wasn't going to last much longer, he didn't want to spend the last few months of it locked up. That wasn't about to happen. He covered his tracks well so there was little chance he'd be caught. He hadn't been before. But if he got a sniff the police were onto him, then he was going in the woods to hang himself.

The whimper turned into a groan. Her eyelids fluttered. He hadn't hit her hard enough to kill – the blow had been to stun her. The actual killing was what he wanted to physically do. Extinguishing a life, to him, meant satisfaction. Warped genes he must have inherited from his father, the evil bastard who thrived on hurting.

She groaned, as her eyelids flickered again. She managed to open them. He was kneeling across her – the first thing she saw. Recognition of her predicament was immediate. She tried to scream but he slammed his hand over her mouth. Nobody would hear her anyway, but he'd never been able to cope with screams. Her wide eyes displayed the sheer terror of the situation she was in. She'd feel her own nakedness. He swiftly moved his hands to her neck. She let out a squeal and her pretty little hands tried in vain to pull on his larger ones. But it was too late. He was about to squeeze the life out of her. This was what it was all about – watching her breathe her last breath. Seeing her die. She kicked and wriggled as his hands tightened. His thumbs overlapped around her neck as it was so slight. All the time he watched her eyes. Terrified eyes . . . pleading for her life eyes . . . tired eyes . . . exhausted eyes . . . defeated eyes.

Her airway was closed. No more oxygen was going in. Her once beautiful brown eyes were bulbous. Tiny thread veins had burst in her eye sockets. The kicking had stopped but still he squeezed. There was no room for error. He had to do the job properly.

He eventually loosened his grip. She was dead. Beautiful little Vanya's life, extinguished. His father had been wrong. He wasn't a useless piece of shit who couldn't tie his shoelaces properly – he could do anything he wanted to. And he could get away with it. Hadn't he proven that time and time again? He'd got rid of him, the bastard, hadn't he?

He took a moment to caress Vanya's perfect body one last time before wrapping her in the rug she was lying on. He packed her clothes into a holdall and placed the bat he'd hit her with inside. There wouldn't be any evidence. He was taking everything with him. All he had to do now was put her in the boot of his car which was parked at the disused exit and take her somewhere she wouldn't be found. There'd be no trace of her – nothing to lead the police to him.

He'd outwit them all.

Just like he always did.

21.

Louise

Barely touching their breakfasts, her and Kym hastily made their way to the classroom to see if there was any news on Vanya. Mrs Beaumont had told them to take their seats while she spoke with a man in the corridor. It was amazing how in the space of less than two weeks, she was growing in confidence and coming round to the idea that she would be able to do the course, whereas initially she thought every hour of the day she needed to leave. Part of it was down to Kym and their developing friendship she was sure, as well as interacting daily with the others in the group. But if she was totally honest, it was the presence of Nick Feeney that caused her the most excitement. Excitement which was good considering she'd stifled urges towards the male sex for months.

Nick Feeney was married, so completely out of bounds. But maybe that's why she liked him? Her spirits were certainly lifted just being around him. And as far as she was concerned, she wasn't hurting anyone lusting after him. It wasn't as if Nick Feeney would come on to her. It was just a harmless crush which brightened up her days.

The previous evening, they'd missed Vanya at supper and her and Kym spent ages talking about what could have happened to her. It appeared as if it was just her and Kym that were worried. Guy and Zoe had been dismissive and hadn't hung around long after they'd eaten supper. Too busy no doubt trying to rest having soldiered on with terrible hangovers all day, and Simon was nowhere to be seen, probably 'doing revision again' with Mary Best. They'd not heard a thing from Mrs McGee despite asking her to let them know, and neither of them felt they wanted to knock on her door again.

"We're spot on you know, something's very wrong," Kym whispered placing her notebook and pencil case on the desk, "I can just tell."

"Yeah. I don't know who that bloke was on the corridor when we came in but he looked official."

"Do you think maybe it's Vanya's dad come to tell us she's packed it in?"

"I honestly don't know. Hey, they're coming now. And look who's with them."

Mrs Beaumont came into the classroom accompanied by the man they'd seen earlier on the corridor. He walked with a limp. He appeared to be in his fifties, short with a dark moustache. Although he was wearing a suit, he looked dishevelled with his wonky tie and the neck of his shirt looked slightly frayed. He had a lanyard around his neck but it had flicked backwards so they couldn't read it. Following him into the classroom was Mrs McGee.

"Good morning again everyone," Mrs Beaumont said, "This is Inspector Hugh Porteous from the police who's come to talk to you this morning and Matron McGee you all know. Listen carefully to everything Inspector Porteous has to say, and if you can help, then please do."

Hugh Porteous attempted to take a seat at the front of the classroom, but before he did, he used his hand to assist his knee bending which indicated he may have some sort of prosthesis. Mrs Beaumont and Mrs McGee took their seats next to him.

He cleared his throat. "Good morning. As some of you may be aware, Vanya Mann is missing. Mrs McGee contacted her parents under the assumption that maybe she'd left Harlow Wood yesterday and gone home. But seemingly she hasn't. What we do know is, she was on ward 6 on Wednesday evening until 8.30 pm when she was let off the ward. What I'm trying to establish is, did any of you see her either leaving the ward that evening, or any time after that, say for example in the nurses' home that night?"

His question was met with silence.

"So when was the last time any of you saw Vanya? It's important that you think back to Wednesday."

Kym raised her hand. "We took some photos in my room and walked together to the hospital for our late shift. I was on ward 9 which we came to first of all, and said cheerio. She carried on with," she nodded to Louise sat at the side of her, "Louise. That's the last time I saw her."

Louise joined in. "I left her at the entrance to my ward at eleven thirty.

"And you didn't see her leave her ward that evening?"

"No. It sounds like she left before me. I was sent off at 8.45."

Mrs Beaumont interrupted, "That's the normal time a late shift finishes, 8.45."

He nodded as if he already knew. "Did any of you see Vanya after that?"

Nobody answered.

"So," he carried on, "we've established that Vanya left her ward at eight thirty. Presumably she'll have walked through the hospital to get to the nurses' home. Unless there's another way?"

"Well, there is," Mrs Beaumont said, "but it isn't one the students would use at night. I'm not sure it's actually any quicker really. It's more or less around the vicinity of the hospital grounds as opposed to walking through the hospital. It's actually longer. Fine maybe on a sunny day when you would want to be outside, but Wednesday night was stormy, so Vanya would have come through the hospital. It's only a short walk up the hill to the nurses' home once you've left the hospital so there's not much time to get wet."

"I see. So, can I ask again for you all to think back? Did any of you see Vanya Wednesday night after 8.30 pm?"

They all shook their heads no.

"Okay. What is currently happening is one of my officers is on Ward 6 talking to the staff to see if there is anything they can add about Vanya's shift on Wednesday. My intention this morning is speak to you all individually here in the school of nursing. Just informally, so nothing to worry about. It could be that I jog your memory about something significant that you hadn't thought about that might be relevant. Mrs McGee has agreed to sit in with each of you. The last thing I want is for any of you to feel worried or intimidated. I know you'll all be anxious, but we all need to do our best to find Vanya."

"I've set up some chairs in the library," Mrs Beaumont said, "so while the interviews are going on, the rest of you can stay in the classroom and do some work with me. It's going to be a difficult morning. We're all worried about Vanya, so we won't be doing anything too onerous. And our test scheduled for today will now take place next week."

When it was her turn, Louise made her way to the library on unsteady legs. Her heart rate seemed to have quickened which she recognised as anxiety and had to quickly deploy the techniques she'd been taught to calm herself. Unfortunately Vanya's disappearance had caused her a sleepless night. She feared something terrible had happened to her. Ugly memories had reared their head. Memories she fought to erase had reappeared at the forefront of her mind causing her to toss and turn into the early hours.

The school end of term party had all started off so well. It had been a celebration for the 6th formers from school who'd finished their A-levels and were departing for university. Not many of her year group had been invited, but her friend Alice was popular and she'd gone along with her. Louise could still remember the anticipation as she put on her new dress her mother had bought her which fitted perfectly. It was an off the shoulder type which she thought looked lovely as her neck and shoulders were nice features she had. It was a crimson colour which her mother said looked so vibrant against her dark hair. It was quite short, but she had pretty legs and was able to put some fake tan on them rather than wear tights. And she had some killer heels that she'd worn as a bridesmaid which complemented the look. Even though she'd been thrilled about looking nice, there was a greater excitement; Andy Moore was going to be there. He was one of those students that excelled at everything. And he was good looking which made her mad for him. He had a reputation for being a bit of a Jack-the-lad, sadly that was an understatement which she'd found out to her cost that particular night.

Although she'd had the warnings about not having alcohol to drink, she'd totally disregarded her mother's wise words and done the opposite. There was an abundance of alcohol for a house party, and not many mixers. She'd been stupid having too much wine. But the party was exciting and everyone was buzzing. When Andy invited her for a dance, she was elated. They'd smooched together for a while and he'd told her how gorgeous she looked, telling her that she was the prettiest girl in the room and why hadn't he noticed her before. She'd joked it must have been the drab school uniform.

He became more intimate in the quiet corner amongst others writhing to the music. She wasn't naive, she knew what the hands on her bum meant, and the kisses down her neck. She wanted it too, so when he suggested going upstairs, she'd readily agreed. But once in the privacy of the bedroom, laid on a bed full of coats, she began to have second thoughts. It somehow seemed torrid and dirty. Whether it was the wine wearing off, or the realisation that Andy was only interested in a quick shag and nothing else, she wasn't sure – all she did know was she wanted him to stop groping her.

"No don't," she pushed him away as his mouth slobbered down her neck, "I don't want this." She'd tried to sit up but he forcibly pushed her back down and became heavy handed, grabbing her breasts.

"Stop it. Get off me." She tried again to hoist him off but he was heavy and powerful. His big hands were hurting her breasts. One of his went up her dress and she heard her knickers rip.

She started to cry. "No. Stop. Please."

He nudged her legs open before sharp pain gripped her as he forced himself inside of her. He hurt as he began to move. He felt big. She wanted to get him off her, but couldn't. She was trapped in a darkened room with coats digging in her back and him thrusting frantically inside of her. How stupid had she been? She felt powerless. Grunt after grunt gained momentum. After what seemed like for ever, but maybe only minutes, he gave an enormous groan, "Fuck." The thrusting stopped. His breathing slowed. He moved away from her and muttered, "You okay?"

Of course she wasn't okay. She was dying inside. The urge to throw up was overwhelming. As quickly as she could, she pulled herself up, reached for her knickers from the bed and screwed them into a ball in her hand, at the same time pulling her dress down to cover herself.

"You okay?" he asked again sitting up and straightening his trousers.

She couldn't speak – she could barely breathe. On trembling legs, she ran out of the room to the bathroom on the landing which thankfully wasn't occupied and bolted the door behind her. After throwing up in the sink, she'd sat down on the toilet and, using reams of toilet paper, tried to wipe away the evidence of him. Sperm seemed to be everywhere. She sobbed her heart out at how easily she'd been violated. And as if that wasn't bad enough, a further anxiety kicked in. He hadn't used a condom. What if she got pregnant?

Several knocks on the bathroom door didn't budge her. She was almost glued to the toilet, crying. She knew she had to somehow get out of the house and home, but doing so scared her. The thought of seeing him made her want to vomit again. All she could think of was getting to the safety of her home. And once she eventually escaped quietly through the front door, as much as she'd wanted to tell someone about the incident, she never did. Her father would have been horrified and taken her straight to the police. So, she'd kept quiet and never told a soul. And fortunately there hadn't been any lasting repercussions, not from a pregnancy perspective anyway. The constant need for cleanliness and disinfecting most definitely had come from being covered in his sperm. You didn't need to be a psychiatrist to work that one out.

Louise took the seat in the library indicated by Mrs McGee. She was breathing deeply and squeezing her fingertips and thumbs together – techniques she'd been taught to do when feeling anxious.

"Hello again," Inspector Porteous looked down at his list, "Louise. I can appreciate you haven't known Vanya for long, but is there anything you can think of however small that might be significant."

She shook her head. "I can't think of anything."

"And she appeared her normal self as you made your way to the ward for your late shift?"

"Yes, she seemed fine."

"What did you talk about?"

"Erm . . . about how we wouldn't be able to do much on the ward as it was just a sort of induction day and how we were looking forward to working full-time and doing hands-on nursing. Just normal stuff really," she shrugged. "Oh, and Vanya did think that Guy and Kym would get together one day." Louise indicated with her head towards the classroom behind them, "They're fellow students. Vanya thought there was an attraction between the two of them. But that was about it really. And we did stop and speak to Mr Duffield the nursing officer on the corridor, but only for a couple of minutes as we didn't want to be late for our shift."

"I see. Has Vanya mentioned any troubles at home, boyfriends or anything? Not particularly that morning, but at any time?"

"No, nothing I can think of. She told us she had a boyfriend before she started her training, but that they'd split up. I don't think her dad approved. She said the ex had moved on and had a new girlfriend."

"And you're certain you didn't see Vanya at all Wednesday night in the nurses' home?"

165

"Positive. I tried her room to see if she wanted a coffee but didn't get a response. And I went to use the phone downstairs about nine-thirty and her room was in darkness. I assumed she'd gone to sleep early. But when she didn't turn up yesterday for breakfast and school, Kym and I let Mrs McGee know."

The Inspector nodded before turning to Mrs McGee, "How many keys are there to each student's rooms. I take it you have a master key?"

"That's correct."

"Are there any other keys?"

"There is another one kept in the main hospital reception in the key cupboard."

"And who has access to that?"

"Anyone who would need to go into any of the rooms, the cleaners, the caretaker, which is my husband, he can do odd jobs, but if we need to get say, an electrician in for example, he sees to that side of things. So he'd let a tradesman into any of the rooms."

"What about other members of staff in the hospital? Could they go into reception and access that key? Would they be challenged for instance?"

Mrs McGee's colour paled. "Well, I don't think they'd be challenged as such. But the key is inside a cupboard so anyone who wanted access would have to enter the reception area to get it."

"But the cupboard isn't locked?"

"I'm not entirely sure. You'd have to check with reception about that. It certainly has a lock. There are other hospital keys kept in the cupboard."

"Okay, that's really helpful. I can check with them. Thank you, Mrs McGee. And thank you, Louise for speaking to me."

"That's okay, I just wish I could help. But everything seemed completely normal that day. You don't think anything awful has happened do you?"

"Not at this stage we don't. We're working hard to locate Vanya so try not to worry. In the meantime, we have police officers around the hospital so please go about your daily business as normal. And if you do think of something, anything, however small, let us know."

Louise stood up. "I will. Vanya's lovely, I'm keeping everything crossed you find her soon."

"Yes, let's hope so. Can you ask," he looked down at his list, "Kym Sullivan to come in next please?"

22.

Kym

It was bitterly cold as she stood on Grimsby Town station waiting for Tony's train. Typically the train was late, which had eaten into their evening together. She'd been glad to return home early that afternoon and be with her mum and dad before having to catch the bus to meet Tony. Harlow Wood had somehow lost its shine since Vanya's disappearance. She'd been interviewed by Inspector Porteous but couldn't tell him anything. The last time she'd seen her friend was as they made their way to their respective wards alongside Louise. All day they'd speculated in class what could have happened to poor Vanya. Although she'd only known her less than two weeks, she was one hundred percent certain she wouldn't just leave Harlow Wood. Something awful must have happened to her. She tightened her coat around herself wiping away a stray tear with her gloved hand as she tried to push the horrible images of what might have happened from her mind.

The train finally rolled into the station and as it passed, she saw Tony waiting at the exit door. He raised a hand cheerily at her and she waved back. It had been two weeks since they'd last been together and she was so looking forward to seeing him, particularly now with feeling so vulnerable. His mother was away for the weekend again at her sister's caravan so they had the flat to themselves. She daren't tell her mother that though, she'd have a fit. She assumed that Tony's mother was around when she visited him at the flat.

Her heart raced as he came towards her, threw down his holdall and wrapped his arms around her, hugging her tightly. "God, I've missed you," he breathed in between kisses.

"Me too."

She savoured his safe warm arms and could have stayed there wrapped securely in them. Although she was near to tears, she suppressed them, knowing for certain they'd come later when she told him what had happened.

"Do you want to get a drink or go straight to the flat?" he asked, picking up his holdall with one hand and clutching hers with his other.

"Straight to the flat I think. We've loads to catch up on."

"Yeah, and we need to take advantage of the fact we have it to ourselves."

"Absolutely," she grinned as they made their way to the taxi rank. "We can go out tomorrow night."

"Sounds good to me."

After a short taxi ride, and once they were alone in the lift to the seventh floor, they cuddled up together. It was so good to finally be with him. Two weeks apart felt much longer. Although she'd embarked on a new start which she wanted to tell him all about, he was familiar and she liked that.

"Can't wait to get in the flat," he said breaking off from a hot kiss.

"Me too," she said, her skin prickling.

Tony dumped his bag in the bedroom and they took off their coats and hung them in the hall. Despite wanting to chat about Harlow Wood and Vanya first of all, Tony had a different agenda as they made their way into the lounge, his hand already squeezing her bum.

"Shall I get us a drink?" she asked.

"Never mind a drink, come here."

His tongue in her mouth inflamed her and their kisses deepened. Desire flooded through her as she kissed him back, hands in his hair. The talking would have to wait. She wanted to savour their togetherness. She needed him. She'd missed him.

They fell back onto the settee, his hands tugging at her jumper as they kissed, and she helped him ease it over her head. She had bathed, put on a nice purple bra and matching knickers and doused herself in the Charlie perfume her mother had bought her for her birthday, which she knew he loved the smell of.

The kissing continued as she reached for his belt, undid it and unzipped him. "Take your things off," she whispered, reaching to undo the top buttons of his shirt.

He pushed her hands away and slid his behind her back to release her bra. "God, you are perfect," he said as he eased her back and began kissing her breasts.

She tugged at his shirt as he sucked a nipple into his mouth. "Take it off," she said.

He ignored her, moving his hands to her jeans and pulling the zipper down, kissing down her stomach.

"Tony, take your clothes off," she urged again. He didn't. He continued to tug her jeans down her legs and off her feet. She was stripped down to just her knickers while he had his jeans down his legs and was still in his shirt.

"What's the matter?" she asked.

"Nothing," he said, with one hand caressing her tummy and the other slipping into her knickers.

"Yes, there is. Why aren't you taking your clothes off?"

The movement of his head backwards exposed his neckline, which immediately gave her the answer. A huge love bite was evident on the side of his neck.

"What the hell is that?" she snapped, quickly sitting up. She reached to the floor for her discarded jumper and swiftly put it on.

He tightened his collar around his neck, as if that would suddenly erase what she'd seen, and stood to pull up his jeans and fasten them. "It's not what you think."

"Isn't it?" It felt like he'd physically slapped her. She stood up and reached for her jeans. She needed to get dressed.

"I haven't been with anyone, I promise," he protested, facing her.

She didn't believe him, not one bit. He was young, attractive and sporting the evidence he'd been intimate with some female. He couldn't get out of that however much he protested.

He pulled a pained face. "I know what it looks like."

"I bet you do."

"Just hear me out."

Her insides were churning. She couldn't believe he'd cheat on her. She was on the brink of crying but held the tears back. It had been the crappiest few days and all she wanted to do was to be close to him. And he'd let her down by having sex with someone else.

"The lads did it for a laugh," he scratched his head, "they made the mark."

"What? Do you think I'm that stupid?"

"It's true. You've no idea what they're like. They held me down and did it. Honestly, I'm not lying. They did it 'cause they knew you'd react like this and bomb me out."

"Did they? Well, they were absolutely right. Not that I believe a word of it."

"I knew you wouldn't. But I've got Mucker's number so we can give him a ring. He'll vouch for me."

"Oh, I bet he will." She moved towards the lounge door. "I'm ringing a taxi to go home."

"Don't do that," he pleaded, following her into the hall. "Please. I'm really sorry. The last thing I want is for anything to spoil what we've got."

"You should have thought about that before you went with someone else."

She stopped at the ornate glass telephone table in the hall, lifted the receiver off the telephone and dialled the number which she knew by memory. "Hello. Could you send a taxi to 21 Tennyson House, please? I'll be at the entrance. Yes, right away."

"We can sort this out," he begged as she replaced the telephone on the hook. "I'm telling you, I haven't been with anyone. It's a joke. I'm as furious as you are. It's spoilt everything now."

"Too right it has." She reached for her coat off the hall stand and put it on.

"Don't go like this." His face was pained as she buttoned it up.

"I'm going. Why you'd think I'd stay after this, I don't know," she scowled, "what was your plan, eh? Have sex with me in your clothes. Is that what you were going to do all weekend?"

"No. Yes." He screwed his face up, "I don't know. I'm sorry. What more can I say?" His eyes looked sad but that wasn't going to sway her. "You'll come tomorrow though, when you've calmed down, won't you?" he asked trying to put his hands on her arms as if to stop her.

"I doubt it." She pushed him away, eager to get to the front door. She couldn't look at his pleading eyes. They might make her weaken and she didn't want to. She needed to get out of the oppressive flat. As she undid the chain and reached for the door handle, he put his hand on top of hers.

"I'll ring you tomorrow then, to see how you are."

"Do what you like." She opened the door which swung closed behind her and made her way towards the lift, praying it wouldn't take long to come as she pressed the button to call for it. Not that he'd tried to follow her, he hadn't. He'd stayed in the flat. Too ashamed no doubt.

Once inside the lift, she pressed for the ground floor, and let the tears flow. Her precious little world had been crushed. Just when she'd needed him most.

* * *

"You can't mope around all weekend," her mother said the following day. Her dad had gone fishing and she was mooching around the house. She'd only told her mum that she'd fallen out with Tony, nothing more. It would play right into her hands if she'd known exactly why she wouldn't take his phone calls that morning and afternoon, although she was sure it gave her mother great pleasure telling him she didn't want to speak to him.

"Why don't you ring Wendy and Jayne to see what they're doing?" her mum suggested as she stood ironing in the lounge, "They'd love to see you. Do they know you're home?"

"Yeah, and I will later," Kym said reaching for one of the magazines in the rack at the side of the settee.

"I bet they'll be out tonight at the Dolphin and Clouds. That's where you usually go to on a Saturday night, isn't it?"

"Yeah, I'm sure they will be. I'll see, I might go with them."

"You do that. You don't want to be moping around after him. He isn't worth it, love."

Her mother was right, she always seemed to be. But she didn't want to hear that. Her tummy was churning with anger and jealousy about what he'd done. How could he? He was supposed to care about her. She'd never do that to him.

"Anyway," her mother switched the iron off and came and sat down next to her on the settee, "Put your

174

magazine down a minute, there's something I need to tell you."

She looked at her mother's eyes. She was paler than usual, almost gaunt. What was wrong? She'd been too wrapped up in Tony to ask how she was feeling. And in fairness, her mother never ailed anything. But looking closely, her normal bright blue eyes seemed dull and the dark circles she fought to keep at bay with endless creams seemed to suddenly be so much darker, as if she wasn't sleeping properly. A sense of impending doom flooded through her. "What is it?"

"I've found a lump in my breast."

"No?" Kym suddenly felt sick.

"I'm afraid so, love."

"Have you seen a doctor?"

"Yes, I have. And I've had a biopsy taken."

"When? Why didn't you say when I came home yesterday?"

"Because you were too upset about your friend going missing. And there's nothing we can do until we get the results anyway."

"I can't believe it." With her own trembling hands, she grabbed her mother's, "This is awful, Mum. When will you get to know?"

"Soon, I hope. Doctor Hill said he'll ring me when he hears from the hospital. We can't do anything until we know what we're dealing with."

"Do you think it might be a cyst or something?"

"I don't know to be honest. I'm hoping it is, but much as I want it to be that, it doesn't feel like one."

Kym leant forward for a hug. Her mum wasn't a huggy type of person at all, but this time, she wrapped her arms around her and Kym settled into her neck and despite not wanting to cry, she couldn't stop herself. Her mother was only in her early forties. It couldn't be anything sinister, it just couldn't. Those sorts of things happened to others, not her mum.

"How's Dad?" she sniffed, pulling away, "I thought he was quiet yesterday."

"Yes, well he's worried, which is only to be expected. Anyway, it might be nothing. Let's be positive and hope that's the case."

"I can't go back to Harlow Wood tomorrow. I want to be here with you."

"There's no need for that. I might not even hear this week. These things take time. I'll let you know as soon as there is anything to tell."

"God, Mum, this is awful," she said reaching for a tissue and wiping her eyes.

"Look, whatever it is, we'll deal with it," her mum said, lifting Kym's hand and bringing it to her lips. "Now then, I'm going to make a cup of tea and have a chocolate digestive. Do you fancy one?"

"Yeah, course," she said blowing her nose. A biscuit was the last thing she wanted.

"And after that, you can give your friends a ring and get yourself out tonight. No sense in moping round here."

"I'm not sure . . ."

"Nonsense. You need to be with your friends. Show Tony you aren't waiting round for him to ring."

Tony had suddenly paled into insignificance. She couldn't think about him right now. Not with this news. Her mother was much more important and she needed to focus her energy on her.

She couldn't have cancer – she just couldn't.

23.

Louise

Arriving back at Harlow Wood from a weekend at home, her mum pulled up in the car park, applied the handbrake and switched off the engine. "Gosh, there's loads of police about," she said.

Louise followed her gaze, "Let's hope they've found Vanya."

"I wouldn't get your hopes up, love. From what you've told me, Vanya doesn't sound like the type of girl to just disappear."

"No, she isn't. She's a lovely person, inside and out. She'd be concerned about worrying us all. I know she wouldn't take off and not tell anyone, I just know she wouldn't."

"So, there's only one thing to conclude. And that's the reason I'm worried sick about you coming back here. Part of me wants you home where I know you'll be safe."

"I'll be fine, Mum," Louise reassured, "you mustn't worry. It's a busy hospital and I'm always with people."

"Well, make sure you are. Don't whatever you do go wandering off on your own, especially away from the hospital. Promise me."

"I promise." Louise leaned forward and hugged her mum, "I'll see you on Friday."

"Alright, watch what you're doing. I know you're worried about your friend, but I've seen a change in you these past two weeks. I think this training will be good for you."

"I think so too. I'll get my stuff out of the boot, so don't drive off."

"I won't. Remember what I've said, be careful. Don't get into a car or go off with anyone. And ring me if you're worried about anything."

"Will do." Louise opened the car door, "You take care too. Love you."

"Love you too, darling."

Louise grabbed her holdall and tapped on the boot to indicate to her mum it was okay for her to go. She stood and waved as her mother drove out of the car park and along the road out of Harlow Wood. There were no tears this time, unlike the first day when her mum and sister had left her. The sadness was still there, but that was more for her mum no longer having her dad. They'd loved each other so much and had done everything together, and even though her mum made light of being on her own, Louise knew it was a struggle. But, it was early days still, so it was bound to take time. And she knew her dad has been right to encourage her to train as a nurse and she would do it for him. The words read out at his funeral stayed with her, *Those we love don't go away, they walk beside us every day*.

She made her way to the nurses' home clutching her holdall and clicked *IN* on the board next to her name. She saw Kym wasn't back yet. After climbing the stairs, and letting herself into her room, she dumped her stuff on the bed, grabbed a mug and coffee from her bedside locker, and made her way to the kitchen. She was hoping to see someone to find out if there was any news.

Simon and Guy were sitting at the table, drinking from cans with Susan and Marie from their intake sat with mugs of coffee in front of them.

"Hi," she said, relieved to see someone, "Any news about Vanya?"

"None we know about," Simon said, "but I've only just got back."

"I came back yesterday," Guy said, "but no news as far as I know. The police have been interviewing male staff this weekend. Well, any that were working, the rest they're going to do tomorrow."

"It's all so stressful, isn't it?" Susan said, "I was glad to get home for the weekend after Friday with that police inspector interviewing us all."

"Yeah," Marie joined in, "and I've had grief from my mum and dad worried about me coming back here. I've had to promise all sorts. If I listened to them, I'd be locked in my room and only come out for meals and school."

Louise sighed, "My mum's a bit like that too, but like I said to her, there are plenty of us around, we're rarely on our own."

"That didn't stop Vanya disappearing though, did it?" Simon said cynically.

"No, but you know what I mean. Why did you come back yesterday?" she asked Guy as she filled the kettle.

"Grief from the old man. I couldn't stick it any longer, so drove back here."

"Aw, that's a shame you being here on your own. What have you been doing?"

"Three guesses," Simon grinned, crushing his can.

Louise rolled her eyes, "Does it start with an R and end in a Y?"

"Spot on," Guy said tossing his Coca Cola can into the bin, followed by Simon's. "Who'd want to be round here when the Rushley's only down the road? This place was crawling with police."

"It still is," she said taking a seat at the table and stirring her coffee. "When you said the police were interviewing male staff, do you mean just questioning?"

"Yeah, just informally, like they did with us on Friday. They haven't got any suspects or anything, not as far as I know anyway. I was drinking last night with Lloyd the gardener and Sutty."

"What makes you want to drink with the gardener?" Louise asked sipping her coffee. Lloyd, to her, hardly looked the type to be a socialiser. She found him to be a bit weird if she was honest. He was always around as they made their way to and from the school of nursing. Yes, he always seemed to be doing some gardening task or other, but it seemed strange he was there every day.

"Why not, he's a good laugh."

"But he's much older than you."

Guy laughed. "When you're buying beer, it doesn't matter what age you are."

"But you're young in comparison to him. It just seems odd that he'd even want to drink with you."

"That's cause you're female, it's not odd to us, is it, mate?" he asked Simon.

181

"Nah, not at all. When I'm home, I go for a drink in the Legion with my old man and stand with his mates. I like hearing the old stories."

"Me too," Guy said. "Last night wasn't a great night though, everyone's twitchy about Vanya and having to explain their whereabouts on Wednesday evening."

"God it's awful, isn't it?" Louise said taking another sip of her coffee, "I was just saying to my mum, Vanya wouldn't have just walked away, something awful has happened."

"Yeah, you're right," Simon agreed. "I hate all this questioning though, they seem to have the ability to make you feel guilty about something when you've done nothing."

"That'll be your guilty past," Guy joked kicking him under the table, "frightened your misdemeanours will come back to bite you."

"Yeah, right," Simon grinned, "you too mate, I bet."

Louise drank the last of her coffee and checked her watch. Kym's train should be in Nottingham by now. Then she'd get the 66 bus to Harlow Wood.

Marie and Susan got up and rinsed their cups in the sink. "We're off to unpack before supper. See you in the dining room later, yeah?"

"Yeah," Louise nodded, "I might go unpack my stuff and walk down to the bus stop to meet Kym. See you both later."

As the girls went out the kitchen door, Guy stood up, "You shouldn't be going anywhere on your own right now, I'll come with you if you like?"

"I'm only going down the path towards the bus stop. I'm not going in the woods or anything. Anyway, from the look of things when we just drove in, there are loads of police around."

"That's true. But you need to be careful," Guy warned, "I'm happy to come with you to meet Kym."

"There's no need, honestly."

Simon chipped in, "Remember Nick Feeney's house is down the bottom, if you are worried."

"Yeah, course. But like I say, I'm not venturing far. I just want a bit of fresh air."

"Busy weekend?" Guy's asked with a cheeky grin.

"Not like you're thinking," she smiled back, "no hangover or anything. I did catch up with some friends for a drink last night which was nice. We went on to a local disco. It seemed better than staying in and worrying about Vanya all the time."

"You did right. Sutty told me that they're going to do an appeal on TV tomorrow night with her parents."

"Who is Sutty?" she frowned.

"The bloke that brings the heated dinner trolleys round to each ward and plugs them in. You'll have seen him the day you did your placement."

She hadn't. The only male she'd seen on the ward was Nick Feeney. There might have been others, but it was him that held her attention the whole day, not some man bringing the meals.

"Right," she stood up and moved towards the sink to wash her mug, "I'll catch you both at supper then."

"Yeah, will do."

The lads followed her out of the kitchen together and headed downstairs while she carried on to her room. They'd all lost a bit of their sparkle. Vanya missing had upset them all.

The wind whistled through the branches of the trees as Louise, wrapped in her corduroy jacket, made her way down the drive towards the entrance to Harlow Wood. It was a long winding walk on the gravel footpath. Many of the tall and proud trees along the way must be hundreds of years old. They'd shed their mixed autumn leaves which were scattered on the soil like a colourful carpet.

She sat down on the low brick wall near the huge metal entrance sign to Harlow Wood. The bus stop that Kym would arrive at was on the other side of the road. She wasn't entirely sure which bus she'd be on, but it didn't matter. She had nothing else to do but wait. The fresh air was better than sitting in her room which, even though she'd brightened it up with some pictures on the walls and a cheese plant on the windowsill, was still bland. But at least she no longer had a dripping tap. Thankfully Mr McGee had fixed that.

Her eyes were drawn towards Nick Feeney's house which was close to where she was sitting. It was rendered cream that had gone dirty with age, and the windowsills were painted a deep blue colour with pretty lace nets at the window so nobody could see in. The bay windows faced the road so the nets would be a must. She wondered what he was doing right at that minute. Could he see her? Would he even be bothered about her sitting there? She willed him to come out, having fantasised about him all weekend. Even going out with her mates hadn't taken her mind off him. She glanced at her watch. Although she sincerely was there to meet Kym from the bus stop, she also had to be honest with herself that she had an ulterior motive. And the gods must have been smiling down on her, as the next time she glanced towards the house, Nick Feeney was striding towards her, looking rugged and gorgeous in his thick cabled jumper, jeans and wellington boots which made him look incredibly sexy. Watching him walk, it was hard to believe he was a male nurse. He looked like a manual worker.

"Hello," he said as he got closer. Her eyes were drawn to his inviting lips as he asked, "Are you waiting for someone?"

"Hi," she gave him her best smile. "Yeah, I'm waiting for my friend Kym, who sits next to me in class, to come back from Nottingham. Her bus is due soon."

"I see. I did wonder. I was just raking up some leaves round the corner of the house and spotted you." His eyes twinkled as he tilted his head on the side, "Didn't your mother ever tell you you'll get piles sitting on a cold wall?"

She widened her eyes, surprised at his playfulness. "Not sitting on a wall, she might have mentioned sitting on a cold step though."

"Ah, you've got me. I'm not much good on old wives' tales, I knew it was something like that." His cheeky smile mesmerised her. For a second their eyes locked. He seemed almost flirty. Did he feel something? No, she dismissed quickly. He couldn't. He was married. It was her overactive imagination.

His expression became more serious. "Don't venture outside of the grounds, whatever you do, will you? Not currently anyway, with the searches going on in the woods."

"I won't go any further than this wall, I promise. I've been home this weekend so haven't heard anything. Do you know if the police have any clues?"

"I'm afraid I don't," he shook his head, "I was questioned the same as every other male working this weekend, but for now I think they're stumped. We all are."

"I can't help but feel something terrible has happened. I haven't known Vanya long, but she's the nicest person. She wouldn't want everyone worrying. I can't imagine what her mum and dad must be going through."

"Absolutely. It doesn't bear thinking about, it's having an effect on everyone. Staff are becoming really jumpy. It's a terrible state of affairs."

"It is. I haven't slept properly all weekend. My mother's been worried sick about me returning."

"That's understandable. But we'll take care of you, I promise you that."

She immediately pictured herself in his arms, taking care of her. It was a nice feeling. If only . . .

"It's always been such a safe hospital," he continued, "Let's hope it's brought to a conclusion sooner rather than later. They need to find her."

He must have seen the sadness in her eyes as he came and stood closer. "Hey, you sure you're alright? You have more than enough on currently with losing your dad, without this."

He'd remembered that day in the woods when he'd lent her his handkerchief and they'd walked back together.

"I'm okay. I just want her to be found. One of the lads said her parents are doing an appeal on TV tomorrow night."

"Yes, so I heard."

"I hope something comes of it."

The double-decker bus stopping at the bus stop out on the road halted their conversation. Louise saw Kym getting off with Zoe alongside. Kym wouldn't be happy having to travel back alongside Zoe. Not that it would be obvious. She was too nice to let it show.

"Ah, here's Kym now," Louise said, wishing she hadn't arrived and she could spend longer with Nick.

"I'll leave you to it," he said with a smile that touched her heart. "I'm teaching you on Tuesday and you're on the ward again Wednesday, so I'll see you then."

Her heart ached. Tuesday seemed ages away.

She gave her best smile, "Great! I'll see you Tuesday."

"And remember what I said, don't venture off anywhere on your own."

He cared and she loved that. Did he have any idea how she felt about him? She felt herself blushing. "I won't," she quickly said, hoping he hadn't noticed.

He walked away towards his house. She waved at Kym and Zoe as they crossed the road.

"This is quite a welcome," Kym said with a smile, but it didn't quite reach her eyes.

Zoe was looking towards Mr Feeney's house, "Was that Mr Feeney talking to you?"

"Yeah. He was warning me not to go anywhere on my own. Were you both on the same train?" Louise asked, changing the subject.

Zoe shook her head, "No. We bumped into each other at the bus station."

"That's good then that you both had company." She purposely didn't catch Kym's eye, knowing full well she wouldn't be struck on travelling with Zoe. Neither of them were that keen on her.

"Any news?" Kym asked.

"I'm afraid not, no. Apparently, Vanya's parents are doing a TV appeal tomorrow night."

"Who told you?" Zoe asked as they started to make their way up the hill towards North House, her and Kym each carrying a case.

"I saw the lads earlier; apparently, Guy came back yesterday, so he's in the know."

Zoe scowled, "Why did he come back yesterday?"

"Problems at home by the sound of things."

"So, what's he been doing on his own?"

"I've no idea, you'll have to ask him yourself. I'm more worried about Vanya than anything Guy might be doing."

"Course. Sorry." Zoe had the grace to look sheepish, "We all are."

"How have your weekends been?" Louise asked.

"Dire," Zoe grunted, "I'll probably stay here next weekend myself now, it was a bore being at home."

"Right." Louise couldn't be bothered to ask any further, she was more interested in Kym as she didn't look her usual bright self. She seemed heavy footed and almost distant.

"How was your weekend?" she asked.

"Not brilliant," Kym said, "I'll tell you about it later. How was yours?"

"Okay. A girlie Friday night with my mum and sister around the TV with popcorn and chocolate. On Saturday I had a shopping day with my mum and was out with friends on Saturday night. Daft as it seems, I wanted to get back. I was praying there'd be some news."

"Yeah, me too. It's just so awful."

"Can I help either of you with your case?" she asked looking directly at Kym.

"Thanks," Zoe said reaching towards her with her case, "I brought a load of stuff back for my room, that's why it's so heavy."

24.

Harlow Wood was saturated with cops, which the new intake couldn't fail to see as they returned from their weekend at home. The quiet room of the hospital where relatives could sit for a period of reflection had been turned into a hub for the police operation. There were more officers carrying out fingertip searches of the woods for missing Vanya. But they wouldn't find her. He wasn't stupid enough to discard her body anywhere near the place. He was meticulous with every piece of evidence that could link him to her. He didn't make mistakes – he'd killed too often before and knew all the pitfalls.

Most blokes had fond memories of the first time they had sex as a teenager, or the first virgin they screwed – but not him. His thrill had been the first kill.

The situation at home became intolerable once he and his brother reached working age. Their father still ruled with a rod of iron, although he stopped hitting them with a belt. His eyes displayed more wariness as he and his brother grew into adulthood. No doubt scared what he might get back. Not necessarily from his brother who was mild, but definitely from him. Despite this, he maintained his cruel streak and made them hand over almost all of their weekly wages. He said it wasn't just for their food, but towards the fuel bills and paying Mrs Baxter as a housekeeper. Not that he'd be paying her much, not monetary anyway. So, even though he and his brother had been old enough to leave home, they couldn't support themselves. He'd tried to look through the old man's documents to find out if he did actually own the house they lived in, or if he had a mortgage, but his father had anything of significance locked up in his writing bureau and only he carried the key.

The situation came to a head one night, following a violent smack across his head for challenging. It had stunned him. It felt like his whole brain vibrated. He retaliated instinctively by hitting his father back equally hard, if not harder, which knocked him off his chair and to the ground. His father had been reeling in anger as he slowly got to his feet. Uncertain what the old bastard might do next, he swiftly opened the cutlery drawer and grabbed the biggest knife. With a shaky hand, he pointed it towards him.

"You hit either of us one more time, and you'll be sorry." Despite his gut trembling with fear – he trembled with another emotion. Power. Seeing his father's uncertainty excited him. The old man wasn't frightened as such, but certainly seemed concerned that his eldest had turned on him, having never done so before.

His brother looked on in horror, but his father must have read something in his threatening eyes as he retreated. "You better find somewhere else to live," he spat, and turned to his brother who was watching them both closely, "both of you. I want you out of this house by the end of the week."

And that was it. No, *look for somewhere else and when you find it, leave*. It was a simple command to be gone.

He'd dreamt for years about what he wanted to do to his father. He'd plan and plot in his head, well into the early hours, of how he'd kill him. Planning energised his mundane life. He became fixated on exterminating the old bastard, and getting away with it. As he matured, it became more a question of when. And his father sealed his own fate that day by giving them both notice to leave.

In preparation for eventually doing something, he'd been delving into Mrs Baxter's sleeping pills for some months, taking a few out each of the pots so she wouldn't miss them. Thursday night was her bingo night. So that was the night he decided to kill the old man. But he had to get his brother out of the way. He was too weak to be involved. So, he'd made up a fictitious errand for him to do. He'd told him he'd purchased a pushbike from Hamilton Street, which was about three miles away. He'd given him the bus fare and a fabricated address and asked him to go on the bus and ride the bike back for him. He'd come up with an excuse he had to work late. Once his brother had left the house and Mrs Baxter had gone to bingo, his father had headed for his shed which was usual for him. He knew why. He'd searched the place and found a drawer full of magazines with naked women in them. It disgusted him thinking of the old man pawing over the pages, no doubt touching himself up while doing so. That was why the old git had boarded up the shed window years ago – so him and his brother couldn't see him fawning over the pages with his hand around his dick.

He'd taken the old man a coffee laced with Mrs Baxter's sleeping tablets to him in the shed. The question on his mind had been, would he drink it? They weren't on speaking terms. But the stupid idiot must have thought he was creeping round by way of an apology as he took it from him and closed the shed door. Earlier on in the day, he'd placed some plastic tubs filled with petrol in the shed and hidden them out of sight under one of the tables. There were heaps of dust sheets so he'd used them to cover the tubs.

His heart was pounding as he carefully wedged a piece of wood under the door latch so it couldn't be opened from the inside. The old man was going nowhere.

He waited forty minutes, enough time for the bastard to drink the coffee, and then made his move. He peered in the small gap at the back of the shed where the wood had warped. Sure enough, the old man was flat out in his chair with his eyes tightly shut and his mouth gaping.

He lit up a cigarette and placed it underneath the shed where he'd made a hole under the wooden boards and covered it with the dust sheets. Then he legged it back to the house as fast as he could and ran to the front door. All was calm though as he made his way out of the front gate. Mr Parker from next door was holding onto his dog and closing his front gate when they heard the WHUMPHHH of an explosion.

They'd both ran into the house, through the hall and into the kitchen to be faced with the shed in the garden looking like an almighty bonfire.

"Keep back," Mr Parker had barked, "where's your father?"

"I don't know . . . in there I think."

"Ring 999, quickly."

By the time the fire engine arrived, there was no longer a shed. The firemen doused the flames and he was taken next door where Mrs Parker made him some sweet tea. She asked where his brother was and he explained he'd gone on an errand. She kept the front room curtains open so she could grab him when he got back.

The police asked the boys questions; his brother was terrified and quiet, while he was ecstatic and quiet. The evil old bastard was dead. Halleluiah. His brother must have sensed something as he'd never to this day asked why he'd sent him to the other side of town for a pushbike that didn't exist.

The Parkers looked after them until Mrs Baxter returned from bingo. Eventually, after the police and firemen had finished examining what was left and took his father's remains away, they were able to return to the house.

The inquest months later found the cause of death was accidental. He'd been anxious about them finding the sleeping pills in his system, but nothing was ever said.

Mrs Baxter stayed on for a short while but eventually went to live with her sister in Torquay. The house had to be sold as they couldn't afford to pay for the mortgage and upkeep. But then the most amazing piece of luck came his way. Angela Morris, one of the pretty cashiers at work was after a lodger as her mother had died suddenly. She was most sympathetic to what had happened to him. As he was in need of a roof over his head and could pay regular rent, she'd offered that he could lodge at hers. But she wasn't keen on having his brother. However, the thought of two sets of money coming in must have been the decider for her as she agreed that he could rent there too, but would have to sleep in the loft as there were only two bedrooms. He quickly swapped rooms and took the loft when he realised it was directly above Angela's bedroom and his life completely changed. She became a significant influence on his life. It was fair to say she changed it completely.

He started to cough. It was becoming more frequent as the days progressed. He reached for a tissue at the side of his bed and coughed a second time into it. A deep-red splattering of blood was bright on the white tissue. The cancer was growing. Time was running out. How much longer did he have?

Long enough he hoped, so he could kill again. He'd known once he started, he wouldn't be able to stop. The question he was toying with was – which of the pretty new students would be next?

25.

Kym

The main sitting room in North House was packed with student nurses and a couple of trainee doctors from the ground floor. Those without TV's in their rooms had gathered to see the television appeal about Vanya. Kym squeezed on the sofa with Zoe and Louise, their conversation subdued. And even though Kym was desperately upset about Vanya, she was worried sick about her mother, as well as being gutted about Tony. During breaks that day, she'd confided in Louise about what had been going on with him. Kym had expected her to berate Tony for his behaviour, but she hadn't. She'd just listened impartially. Guy had asked a couple of times if she was okay, but she brushed him off with a *I'm fine* smile. He'd most likely be on Tony's side if she told him and say it probably was a prank and to give him a second chance. She didn't know what to do.

The room fell silent as the newsreader announced the disappearance of their friend. Inspector Porteous, looking much plumper on the TV, explained it was totally out of character for Vanya to simply disappear. She was happy and didn't appear to have any problems affecting her. He went on to say she'd recently started her orthopaedic nurse training and was looking forward to the future. Kym's eyes filled with tears as she watched the distress on Vanya's parents' faces. They pleaded that if their daughter was watching, to get in touch. It was desperately upsetting. She swallowed away the lump in her throat and noticed that some of the girls weren't able to hold back their tears. Louise seemed to be struggling, blowing her nose as she stared at the screen, and Zoe was half watching and fiddling with her nails. It was unlikely Zoe would be upset. Each day it was becoming more obvious that she lacked any sort of empathy.

The lounge door opened, breaking the spell of the television. Simon's head popped round. "Kym, phone."

She quickly jumped up as the others were chatting, squeezing past the numerous outstretched legs. Was it her mum with news? Or was it Tony who knew she'd be back at Harlow Wood now? She hadn't spoken to him all weekend. Once her mother told her about her breast lump, she couldn't face hearing his voice.

Kym followed Simon along the corridor towards the stairs. "Is it my mum?"

"No. Sounds like your boyfriend."

"Oh." She felt both relieved and disappointed at once. Even though she knew that news of her mum's prognosis was due any day, she was living in a perpetual state of pretend, telling herself that *no news was good news*.

Simon went down stairs ahead of her.

"The police appeal's just been on about Vanya," she told him.

"Yeah, I saw it. Guy brought a portable TV from home, so we watched it in his room."

"Ah, right. It's so awful, isn't it? Some of the girls are really upset."

"I know. It's a bloody mess."

She paused at the phone, "Catch you later," she said and he nodded, carrying on down the corridor.

She lifted the receiver from the small table it was resting on. "Hello."

"At last . . . what's taken you so long?"

Her tummy didn't clench in an excited way like it normally did at hearing Tony's voice.

"I was in the lounge watching TV." Explaining what had happened seemed somehow easier than talking about the two of them. "One of the girls from our set has disappeared. There's been an appeal on TV tonight, that's where I've been, upstairs watching."

"What do you mean, disappeared? You can't just disappear."

"Well, missing then. She's not been seen since last Wednesday night when she left the ward after her shift."

"Has she gone off with a bloke or something?"

"No, I don't think it's anything like that. It's looking more likely something sinister has happened. Her parents are frantic."

"God yeah, that's awful."

"Everyone's really nervous."

"I bet. You be careful, then. Make sure you're with someone all the time."

"I will."

"Is the nurses' home secure?"

"As far as I can see it is. The main door is locked at night and our rooms are locked. And the matron is doing regular patrols along the corridors and in the sitting room, particularly at night."

"Have you got one of those peep holes so you can see who's at your door if anyone knocks?"

"No."

"Maybe you need to ask who it is then before you open the door to anyone."

"Yeah, I will. There's loads of police around at the moment, too, so I think we're all okay."

There was a long pause which she wasn't going to fill. He was the one that had caused all the trouble between them.

"It's great to hear you," he lowered his voice, "I've missed you. I hated that you wouldn't speak to me at the weekend. Your mother's gloating though; I can hear it in her voice."

"Yeah, well you deserve it."

"Have you told her?"

"Only that we've fallen out. But what if I had told her? *I'm* upset," she emphasised. "Anyway, this isn't about her." Her poor mum had enough on right now, she couldn't face him berating her.

"I know it isn't. But I've said I'm sorry. And I promise I haven't been with anyone."

"So you keep saying, but I don't believe you."

"Where does that leave us, then?" Irritation had crept into his voice, "I can't keep fannying around like this all the time."

"What's that supposed to mean?"

He sighed loudly. "Me ringing and you ignoring me." The soft voice was back, "I want things to go back to how they were. I've only got two more weekends at home. Can we see each other this coming one and try and sort it out face-to-face?"

It was her time to heave a sigh.

"If you don't want to, then say so now," he said sharply, "we're either together or not."

She didn't answer, not entirely sure what she wanted.

"Look," he let out a long breath, "I'm coming home Friday. I'll be on the same train as usual. Come to the station to meet me like normal. If you don't . . . then I'll get the message."

"Okay."

"Only okay? Is that all you can say?"

"It's all I can manage. I know you think the world revolves around you, but I've got other stuff going on right now."

"Like what? There's nothing you can do about your missing friend. No point in taking all that on. Leave the worrying to the police and her family."

She wanted to say something about her mum but it didn't feel right. Not yet. It could still be nothing, and at the end of the day, he wasn't struck on her anyway, so he was hardly going to be that sympathetic.

One of the second year students appeared and loitered a few feet from her. It was evident she was waiting to use the phone, even though she stood a respectful distance back. There was a plastic head bubble around the phone which gave a degree of privacy, but you could still hear.

"Look, I'm going to have to go. Someone's waiting to use the phone."

"So, I'll see you Friday, yeah? We can sort this out Kym, just be there?"

"Okay. See you then. Bye."

She put the phone down. Would she be there? Was he even worth it? Once a cheat, always a cheat – she believed that. He'd been with someone else and all the protesting in the world wouldn't change her mind about it. It was now about whether she could forgive him.

Kym stepped away from the phone and smiled at the nurse waiting. "Sorry."

"Hey, no probs. You'd think they'd have more than one phone, wouldn't you?"

"You would, yeah."

"No news then about the girl from your set that's missing. I just saw the appeal. How can someone just disappear like that?"

Kym shook her head, "I don't know, it's awful."

"It is. My father's been warning me to be careful," she rolled her eyes, "it's him I've got to ring now to tell him I'm okay."

"He's right, we need to be." She spotted Guy coming out of his room, "Anyway, I'll let you use the phone. See you later."

She moved aside to speak to Guy as he came along the corridor, looking good in a fashionable blue sweatshirt and jeans. His cheeky grin lifted her spirits; in complete contrast to Tony dampening them.

"Where are you off to?" she asked.

"Looking for you, actually."

"Me?"

"Yeah," he pulled a face, "I need an ear."

201

"Isn't Simon around?"

"He's too busy working his way round any available nurse that'll have him, so he won't get my dilemma. It's a female ear I need."

She laughed. "Okay, I'll go get us a drink and you can tell me what's up."

"Not for me, I've got a beer in my room."

"In your room?" she widened her eyes, "you want me to come there?"

"We can leave the door open if you like."

"We better," she grinned, "we don't want to give Mrs McGee an excuse to throw us off the course."

Guy's room was surprisingly tidy. It was bigger than hers upstairs. There was a huge poster of Farrah Fawcett Majors on one wall and a poster that looked a bit weird, some sort of contemporary art. There was also a record player and a TV. He still had the light blue quilt cover they'd been given but his bed was made neatly which he sat on. She took a seat at his desk, and swivelled it round towards him. He'd left the door slightly ajar which she felt better about. Her eyes drifted towards his sink, it amused her to see he'd got some cans stood in cold water.

"So, what is it?" she asked, resting her mug of coffee on the desk.

"It's about going home at the weekend," he took a sip from the can of lager he had on his bedside table, "I'm going to be seeing Heather."

"Yeah?" She knew that was his girlfriend but he rarely spoke about her.

He took a deep breath in. "I'm not entirely sure I want to."

"Why? Has something happened between you?"

"No. The opposite really, things are fine. She's really excited about me coming home."

"What's the problem, then?"

"Erm . . ." he screwed his face up, "I'm nowhere near as excited about seeing her as she is about seeing me."

"You mean you don't feel the same way?"

"Something like that, yeah."

"Maybe once you see her things will be okay?"

"What if it isn't, though? Is it kinder to finish it between us so she can meet someone else? There's no point in her waiting around for me, is there?"

"No, I guess not if you don't want her to. What's changed, though?"

Was it Zoe? Were they in a relationship now? It wasn't really any of her business, he'd say if he wanted her to know.

"Nothing . . . well, I just feel differently since starting this course. Don't you?"

"Not really. I like the independence, and nursing's what I want to do. But I'm the same person." She couldn't resist, "Do you like someone else, is that it?"

He brushed some fluff off his jeans, as if he was avoiding eye contact.

"Maybe."

Just as she thought, something was going on with him and Zoe.

"Then you'll have to tell her. You can't leave her hanging on if you're seeing someone else."

"I'm not seeing anyone else," the eye contact was back, "I wouldn't do that."

"Good. It's best to be honest."

She must have looked sad as his expression seemed concerned. "Are you okay? Was your weekend good? Your boyfriend was home, wasn't he?"

"Yeah, he was, but we fell out."

"I thought you didn't look yourself today."

"That was him on the phone just now."

"Have you made up?"

"Not yet, no. It's not just that though." Should she tell him? Yes, it felt right. She cleared her throat, "My mum's got a breast lump and we're waiting for the results of a biopsy."

"God Kym, that's a worry." He moved to the bottom of the bed and reached for her hand. "What a shit time to fall out with your boyfriend, you need him right now."

Her breathing was becoming more difficult and a sob caught in her throat.

"Hey," he pulled her towards the bed next to him and wrapped his arms around her.

She nestled into his neck and the tears flowed. "I just wish I could be with her," she sobbed, "especially when she gets her results . . . you know, if it is bad news."

Did he kiss her head? She wasn't quite sure. "You can be," he said softly.

"How?" she sniffed, "they won't let me miss school."

"You don't need to. I could take you home to see her after school."

"What?" she pulled her head back and looked into his warm hazel eyes, "All the way to Cleethorpes? It's over 80 miles."

"So?"

"It's too far in one evening."

"Says who?"

"You're mad," a grin escaped through the tears, "you can't take me there and back in an evening."

"Why not? I like driving."

"You're serious, aren't you?"

"Dead serious. And remember, not all breast lumps are sinister. She might be lucky."

"Yeah, I suppose so. But I have the feeling she sort of knows its bad news. And I want to see her if it is."

"Then you're going to. As soon as you know, we'll go after school."

She grabbed a tissue from her pocket and dried her eyes. He was such a nice person and a really good friend. Zoe was lucky if she was going to get him. Her tummy tightened. She'd never liked the thought of him and Zoe together – he was too nice for the likes of her.

But, at the end of the day, it was nothing to do with her.

26.

Louise

Louise was on her second shift on Ward 7. Making her way to the ward that morning for the early start was a poignant reminder of the week earlier when she'd walked with Vanya and left her at the adjacent ward. There still wasn't any news about how she'd mysteriously disappeared and since that day, everything had changed. The shine seemed to have gone off Harlow Wood. Mrs McGee probably felt the need to *step up* by her constant presence in and around North House. Possibly she felt that being visible offered reassurance, but most of them, certainly in Louise's group, didn't appreciate it and gave her a wide berth. But anxiety was running high amongst them all and they travelled around the hospital in no less than pairs.

That morning, after arriving on shift, the early staff had congregated in the office for the report from the night staff. Louise was sat quite a distance from Mr Feeney at his desk, but she could smell him. It was a delicious blend of lemon and lime. All clean and invigorating.

After they'd listened to an assessment of each patient and made notes accordingly in their pocket notebooks, Mr Feeney looked directly at her.

"Nurse Allard," he said, "if you could shadow Nurse Gibson today for your shift. She's coming to the end of her training here at Harlow Wood, so is quite experienced. I've got to do a ward round this morning with the consultant, Mr Stevens at nine, but after that, I'd like to show you how to do a dressing using aseptic technique."

Relief gushed through her. When he said shadow Jackie Gibson for the shift, she thought that meant she wasn't going to spend any time with him. The previous day in school, he'd been engaging and animated teaching them about the digestive system, but she hadn't got any special smiles from him. Maybe it was wishful thinking he singled her out and didn't smile at everyone else the same way. But she liked to think he did. Yet yesterday, he'd seemed slightly more formal.

"Thank you," she said with a smile.

She headed off with Jackie to the linen cupboard and her colleague grabbed a stainless steel trolley to stack the linen on for bed making. "What's he like?" Jackie rolled her eyes, "I can quite easily show you how to do aseptic technique. Why he has to show you personally, I don't know." She handed her a pile of folded white sheets and pale blue counterpanes which Louise duly stacked on the top and bottom of the trolley. "There's nothing to it anyway," she passed a handful of pillowcases, "they make out in school it's a huge thing, but it's dead easy."

"Is it? We've been shown it and we practiced on each other, but I guess it's much more difficult on a real patient?" Louise followed Jackie as she walked towards the first female bay.

"Not that much different, honestly. Morning, ladies," Jackie greeted as they entered the bay of six female patients, "I've got a new nurse working with me this morning. This is Nurse Allard."

The ladies nodded welcomingly to her. Apart from two who appeared to still be asleep. Louise acknowledged those looking at her with a smile, "Good morning."

One of the patients sitting closest to the window had skeletal traction attached to her leg, the advantages of which had been explained to Louise the previous week by Mr Feeney and she could remember it verbatim. It was used to combat deformity and useful when the union of the bones due to fracture, could be fragmented. She'd read up about it too as he'd suggested and hoped he might ask her about it and be impressed by her knowledge.

"Is this your first ward?" a patient asked.

"Yes, I'm just here for a day. I was here last week too. I did a late shift then."

"Ah, I wasn't though," the middle-aged lady scowled at her leg hoisted slightly off the bed and attached to a pulley and weights, "I only came in at the weekend."

"Right," Jackie interrupted, "We'll give out bowls to those that are confined to bed so they can make a start washing themselves and then we can help them with the bits they can't manage and put fresh sheets on their beds for them. So that's," she reeled off four patients' names and pointed, "then we'll bed bath Mrs Sellers and Mrs Banks." Those were the two ladies that were asleep.

"Draw the curtains around the bed, strip all the bedding off apart from one sheet so the patient can cover themselves." Jackie pulled the invisible shelf out from the end of the bed, "Place the bedding on there for when we make them. Okay?"

"Yes, fine," Louise nodded.

"Come on then, let's make a start. Don't be too quick though," she winked, "as we'll only have to help in the bay next door. They have the heavier patients, so it's going to take longer for them to get everyone washed."

Louise was enjoying working with Jackie. Despite her suggesting they took their time, she efficiently went around the patients. Louise kept up though, delighted to be carrying out actual nursing tasks.

Edna, one of the auxiliary nurses Louise had met the previous week, came into the bay as her and Jackie were making a bed.

"Can I pinch a couple of pillowslips off your trolley?" she asked.

"Course you can," Jackie said, "I noticed there weren't many in the cupboard this morning."

"Yeah, I've rung supplies. They're on their way round with them as we speak." Edna grabbed a handful. "Cheers."

Louise and Jackie diligently worked in unison as they hoisted the sheet to the top of the bed, making sure they did the envelope corners at the bottom.

"We'll miss Edna when she's gone," Jackie said straightening out a crease.

"Where's she going?"

"Retiring, after twenty years."

"Gosh, that's a long time," Louise reached for the counterpane, "has she been on this ward all that time?"

"No, they haven't been built that long. But she has since it opened. Mr Feeney has a real soft spot for her. And she's like a mother hen around him. We will miss her. She's lovely with the patients. We're doing a collection to try and get her some garden furniture. She's no idea though, so mum's the word. Hey, you should come to her retirement do."

Louise shook her head, "I don't think so. I don't really know her. I only met her for the first time last week."

"So? Everyone's invited. We need to give her a good send off. There's a list in the office, just put your name on that and come."

"I'm not sure. Maybe whoever has organised it won't want to include me?"

"Don't be daft. Come. If you fancy it, that is? It'll be a great night. You have to put a fiver in, that's to cover the buffet and at least one drink I think. Oh, and you might want to give to Edna's collection." She lowered her voice, "Personally, I can't think of anything worse as a retirement present than garden furniture, but they've asked her husband and it's what he suggested."

Louise was hesitant, "I'd better check though, if it's okay for me to come. Who do I ask?"

"Staff Nurse Gilmore's organising it. Here's Mr Feeney now. Let's ask him."

"Mr Feeney, I'm just telling Nurse Allard that anyone who's worked with Edna is welcome to attend her retirement do, aren't they?"

"They are indeed." His smile was back, Louise's heart seemed to miss a beat as he looked directly at her. "We want to give her the best send-off we can. We'll miss her, that's for sure. Anyway, after you two have finished your bay, can you offer a hand next door as they have the heavier patients this morning?"

He walked off with his usual swagger she found so attractive.

"See, I told you."

"What, that we'd have to go next door?"

"No! That anyone's welcome. It'll be a great night."

"Will Mr Feeney be there?" Louise asked nonchalantly, pushing the shelf back under the bed and following Jackie who was leading the way to the next bed, dragging the linen skip on wheels.

"Course he will. He'll be doing the send-off speech. It's his ward she's been working on all these years, after all. Don't worry about him though, he's much more relaxed out of work. He's actually quite a laugh."

"Oh, right. It sounds like a good night then."

"It will be, so before we get cracking in the bay next door, go put your name down. You can give your fiver anytime."

Louise made her way towards the office with a renewed spring in her step. The day was good anyway, but it just got so much better.

Louise was delighted to watch Mr Feeney as he demonstrated the use of aseptic technique on a patient's leg with skeletal traction. Mrs Arnold, in her sixties, had fractured her tibia and fibula and was on a form of traction to rest the limb and aid healing of the bones. He'd explained that around where the metal pins enter the bone, they get all crusty so have to be cleaned each day to prevent infection.

Jackie had opened the sterile equipment he needed onto a trolley at the side of the bed and he demonstrated the process of not contaminating the wound. Although it had been explained and shown to Louise in school, Nick Feeney demonstrating it was so much better. She got the concept of cross contamination. And as dextrous as he was, she loved seeing his interaction with the patient – he was so kind and gentle. Her admiration accelerated just watching him.

"There you go, Mrs Arnold, good as new," he smiled as he taped the dressing firmly in place around the pins going into the bone.

"That has cooled it down and stopped it itching," she smiled, "thank you."

"You're very welcome. Nurse Gibson," he said discarding his gloves on the trolley, "would you mind clearing the trolley for me and showing Nurse Allard where and how to dispose of everything."

"Of course," Jackie nodded, already starting to wheel the trolley to the clinical area while Louise opened the curtains around the patient.

"This afternoon Nurse Allard, I'd like you to chat to Mrs Arnold about her accident, and then read her notes in the office during visiting time when it's quiet. It'll give you an understanding of how she's ended up on traction. Is that okay?"

"Yes, fine."

"Right, I'll leave you to it and go organise the lunch rota."

She made her way to the clinical room. Would he be coming to lunch with them? She said a silent prayer he would.

"Ah, look who's here," Jackie grinned, closing the clinical room door. Louise followed her gaze to a chap plugging in the patients' lunch trolley on the corridor.

"Hi, Jackie," he grinned and looked towards Louise, "I don't think we've met before. I'm Sutty. I work in the kitchens preparing the food, loading up the servers and then bringing the meals round to the wards."

"I'm Louise. I've heard about you from Simon and Guy in our set."

"Oh, yeah, great company they are down at the Rushley. So, you're just starting your training?"

"Yes, this is only my second day on the ward."

"I'm sure you'll like it. You do Jackie, don't you?"

"I do, yeah, it's a great ward."

"When do you leave us?"

"Five more weeks, then I'm going to Sheffield to do my general training."

"That's great then as I've got some good news hot off the press. The committee have announced we're having a nightdress and pyjama party in a couple of weeks in the main hall. There's a disco and food by all accounts."

Jackie scowled, "Nightdress and pyjama party? I'm not sure I fancy that."

"Whyever not? It'll be a laugh," Sutty grinned," I think it's a great idea."

"I bet you do," Jackie replied, sarcasm evident in her voice. "Don't get your hopes up we'll all be scantily clad in negligees if that's what you're thinking. We'll be wearing dressing gowns."

"You can't dance in those though," he laughed making his way back down the ward. "You'll have to take them off sometime."

Jackie shook her head, "What's he like?"

"He seems a good laugh."

"Oh, he is that. But watch him though, he's an opportunist. He's just broken up with his girlfriend so he's on the lookout. Maybe give him a wide berth . . . if you don't fancy him that is. He's nice enough if you do."

"Oh, God no. I'm not interested."

"Are you already with someone?"

"Erm . . . not really."

"Oh, I get it. You don't want to be tied down?"

"Yeah, something like that."

She felt the heat rise in her face. She'd love to be tied down. Preferably with the gorgeous charge nurse only a few feet away.

"I'll just go tell Mr Feeney that the lunch trolley's here," Jackie said. "I'm sure you already know, the senior member of staff dishes the meals and we take them out. You might have to feed Mrs Greaves in bed 1, she'll need a hand."

"Okay, that's fine. I'll enjoy helping her."

27.

The nightly recollection of squeezing the life out of Vanya made him high and the compelling urge to repeat the whole process was now a constant. And while he was confident they'd never find her body as the cesspit he'd dumped her in was miles away, there were still plenty of police around Harlow Wood. Like everyone else at the hospital, he'd had to answer their questions but easily managed to evade suspicion. It was never in any doubt.

A coughing fit overtook him and he reached for a tissue. The spots of blood were becoming heavier. His limbs were tired, and he guessed the cancer was spreading into his bones. Time was running out. And he desperately wanted another kill before it did. It was a risk, but he was past caring. One more high before his own life ended was an absolute must. However, the heat was on at Harlow Wood. Dare he try another nurse? The police were lessening in numbers, that was evident. Maybe he'd give it a few more days. A wave of excitement gushed through him at the thought of killing again. The question was, who? It was the young, nubile ones, with their lovely pink flesh, tiny waists and pert tits he liked. He just wanted to stroke their delicate skin. The two pretty friends excited him. Louise, with the sad eyes, now seemed brighter of late – it was as if she'd passed that mantel to her mate, Kym. She seemed morose now, mooching around the place. But she had that lanky slap-head following her around all the time, so maybe he'd give her a miss. She was a beauty though, there was no doubt about that. But Louise was pretty enough and he'd had his eye on her from the beginning. Her or Vanya. He'd gone for Vanya in the end, but Louise was now in pole position.

His thoughts drifted to his beautiful Angela and how his life changed once he and his brother moved in with her. Angela was special, he knew that from when he first met her at work. She was kind, like his late mother. She'd even accompanied him to his father's inquest and held his hand as they listened to the coroner summing up that the old bastard had mistakenly stored petrol in the shed, possibly for use with a lawn mower, and unwisely continued to smoke in the enclosed area.

He played on Angela's sympathy while his brother went into a shell, preferring to work, occasionally have a couple of pints, and sleep. He'd bought himself a portable TV which he watched in his room. That suited him, he was then free of the burden of looking out for his brother and instead, thrived around Angela. It was almost as if he'd been asleep as a teenager; he certainly hadn't participated in normal activities that young men did. But meeting her, a switch had flicked and woke him up to the beauty of women. His endeavours to take the loft room paid off handsomely as he skilfully managed to make a peep hole directly above Angela's bedroom, easily hidden in the light fitting of her room. It was unlikely she would ever get anywhere near the ceiling height, she was hardly the type to be changing light bulbs. She'd ask him, he was sure of it. But the hole wasn't obvious anyway. It was heavily disguised with a floorboard over the top if anyone did ever look.

He'd carefully removed the floorboard each time he wanted to watch Angela, which he liked to do during her most private time. He would lie on the floor of the loft and watch her get undressed at night and put on her pyjamas. She had a lovely body and was neat and tidy. There was a sink in the corner of her bedroom and he would watch while she shaved her legs, and sit at the kidney-shaped dressing table to apply her blue eyeshadow and mascara. Angela wore plenty of makeup. She didn't need it but it fascinated him watching how she applied it. She would use heated curling tongs to wave her hair, which she did nicely at the front, but appeared to struggle with the back. Often it looked flat in complete contrast to the curls around her face. He had an overwhelming urge to help her but that would give the game away. So he'd watch her, having to suppress the desire to ask if he could help.

One particular evening, while Angela was waiting for her friend to call to go to the cinema, she was looking at her reflection in the mirror over the fireplace. The flowered miniskirt she was wearing, showed off her shapely legs and the sheer white top showed off the outline of her pert breasts. He liked that he could see her lace bra he'd watched her put on earlier.

She kept running her fingers through the waves of her hair, as if to check they were symmetrical each side of her face.

He went for it. "The back of your hair isn't quite right."

"What's wrong with it?" She put her hand to her hair, fluffing it with her fingers.

"It's flat." He got up from the settee. "Do you want me to fix it?"

She widened her eyes, "Can you do hair?"

"Course I can. I used to do my mother's for her," he lied. He'd watched her through the peephole often enough – how hard could it be? His brother didn't even look up from the newspaper he was reading. He'd know the truth, though.

"It does need a bit more curl," she pulled a face, "but I haven't got time to heat my tongs up."

"They might still be hot. Do you want me to go get them? Er . . . whereabouts are they?"

"On my dressing table," she checked her watch, "be quick, then. Elaine'll be knocking soon, we don't want to miss the start of the film."

And so it began. He'd help with her hair regularly. It got to a point that he'd go into her room when she shouted and she'd have the curling tongs heated up all ready and he'd style it for her. Initially just the back, but then he progressed and she liked him doing it all.

"You've got a real knack," she told him one day standing in front of the mirror and turning her head from side to side, "you should be a hairdresser."

He'd smiled at that. If his old man had ever heard any sort of talk like that, he'd be spewing out disparaging rhetoric. But thanks to his tenacity, he was pushing up daisies now. And although he hadn't realised at the time how fortuitous killing the old bastard had been – he knew now. It had brought him close to Angela. From styling her hair, he started to iron her clothes and help her choose what to wear when she went out. They became close through their mutual love of all things feminine and pretty. Not in a sexual way, more a brother and sister way. He wasn't one bit interested in screwing Angela. Sex was for animals and he wanted no part of that.

He turned over in his bed and pulled the covers up. Reminiscing made his gut ache, swamping him with emptiness he'd never been able to dismiss, no matter how hard he tried. But right now, he needed to plan. His fingers itched to run them through another girl's hair and to plait it, just like he used to do Angela's. He wanted to savour those solitary moments when his victim lay defensively in front of him, naked with all her femininity on display.

In his mind, Vanya's naked body turned into that of Louise, his fingers gently caressing her, inhaling her feminine scent. Louise's eyes widening as she woke up. His hands around her neck. Squeezing tight.

Yes. Such a thrill. Such an incredible thrill. Louise was the one.

But it had to be soon.

Time was running out for him.

28.

Kym

During lunch break, Kym tapped on Matron's door and waited. Seconds later, it was opened by Mrs McGee. "Yes, what is it?"

"Oh, hi. Erm . . . I've had some bad news and I'm going to have to travel home today after school to see my mother. I won't be back until late so would it be possible to have a key to the front door of North House please? I know it'll be locked by the time I get back."

"What's happened?" Matron frowned, "Why have you got to go home?"

Kym had hoped she wouldn't have to explain. Not when she was barely holding it together. Her mother's GP had confirmed a diagnosis, and according to her dad, she was too upset to speak on the phone and hear Kym's voice. So, despite her dad's protests, she was going home. Nothing would keep her at Harlow Wood, especially not now Guy had offered to take her. She needed to see her mum.

"My mother has been diagnosed with breast cancer," Kym swallowed, "and we're all terribly upset. I want to go and see her." Mrs McGee was staring intensely. Her smudged mascara eyes appeared irritated, making Kym regret not letting Guy call for the key. He had offered but he was doing more than enough facilitating the trip home.

"I'm sorry to hear that," Mrs McGee said, not looking sorry at all. "Where do you live?"

"Cleethorpes."

Her pencilled brows drew together. "Isn't Cleethorpes a bit far to be travelling there and back in a day, let alone an evening? Can you even get a train back tonight?"

"It is quite a journey, but Guy . . . from our intake," she reminded her, "has offered to drive me."

"Yes, I know who Guy is." She sighed heavily, "Wait here."

Kym stared at the partly closed door puzzled as to why Mrs McGee appeared uncaring. Wasn't her role to support? It was only a door key she was asking for, why should it bother her? Footsteps coming down the corridor made her turn. Mr McGee was heading towards her in a boiler suit, heavily stained with paint and wearing a flat cap.

"Hi," she gave the best smile she could as he reached her. He wasn't a hugely tall man, and quite thin. The aroma of cigarette smoke as he got close probably accounted for his skinniness. She'd read smoking was an appetite suppressant.

"Hello," he said, "have you knocked?" he nodded towards the partially closed door with Matron written on it.

"Oh, it's okay, Mrs McGee knows I'm here. She's just gone to get me a late night key to get into the nurses' home."

"I see. Going out on the razzle are we?" He grinned, exposing a missing upper tooth.

She shook her head, "No, nothing like that . . ."

Mrs McGee opened the door clutching the key. When she saw her husband, she opened it wider and glared at him, as if she wanted rid. Her expression as far as Kym could make out, indicated that he made himself scarce. And he clearly understood as he nodded and went inside as Mrs McGee pulled the door to as if to prevent her looking inside.

"Here you are," she handed the key to her, "make sure that Mr Logan sees you safely to your room when you return," she widened her tiny eyes, "and I mean just to the door. We can't be too careful, especially right now."

"I will."

"And bring it back to me tomorrow."

"Of course. Thank you."

* * *

After finishing school for the day, Guy manoeuvred the car out of the hospital gates onto the main road. Although Kym was upset about her mum and didn't feel like talking, she realised they couldn't drive such a distance without saying something. It wasn't fair on Guy.

"It'll take us about two hours or thereabouts," she said.

"Two hours! I don't think so."

"Well, that's how long it takes my dad."

"Yeah, well I'm not your dad. We'll easily be there in ninety minutes."

"We can't be. It's eighty miles or so."

"Yeah, I know. So, ninety minutes, tops."

"I want to get there in one piece you know," she said as they passed Portland College on the Nottingham road.

"And you will. Your dad will take two hours as he'll drive like mine. Strict upholders of the highway code."

"And you're not?"

"Course I am. I just know that fourth gear is not just there for when the other ones wear out."

She rolled her eyes. "Honestly, what are you like? Anyway, you're going to have to let me pay something towards your petrol."

"No way," he said, "I don't want paying."

"But it isn't fair."

"I'm not taking any money from you, so you can shut up now."

"I'd feel better if I paid something."

"Look," he sighed, "don't tell any of the others this, I'm only telling you. I have money. My dad gives me an allowance each month. It's from my grandfather's trust fund he put in place for me."

"Really? Lucky you."

"Yeah. But it's not something I say much about, so don't tell anyone."

"No, course I won't. But why the secret?"

"Cause folk treat you differently if they think you're loaded. I know people realise I have a bit of money by looking at the car I drive and my clothes. And that's fine. They just think I've got a wealthy old man. And I like it that way. I like to stand at the bar, paying my way in rounds."

She laughed, "That's the measure is it, rounds of beer at the bar?"

"Yeah, course it is," he grinned, "what else is there? That's how the male brain works. So no more talking about petrol money, okay?"

"Okay." She smiled to herself. What a charmer he was. "Moving on, tell me, how did it go with Heather?"

He pulled a face. "I won't be rushing back home anytime soon."

"So you told her?"

"Yeah, I did." Although he was staring ahead at the road, his expression was sad. Guy was a decent sort so wouldn't want to hurt his girlfriend.

"And how did she take it?"

"Better than I expected, but she doesn't want to give up on us which made it worse."

"How did you leave it?"

"I told her I wanted to make a go of it here at Harlow Wood and didn't want to be travelling home all the time." He kept his eyes on the road, "I think she understood pretty quickly that if I'd truly wanted the relationship to work, then I would have made the effort, so the writing was on the wall really."

"It's such a shame, I feel sorry for her. How long did you say you'd been together?"

"A year. I feel sorry, too. I hate what I've done. But this is better than stringing her along when I don't feel the same. I'd have had to tell her eventually."

"Yeah, you're right."

"Anyway, enough about me. I want to know how things are with you and Tony?"

She looked out of the window at the side of her. "Not brilliant," she sighed.

"You've not made up, then?"

"Not really, no . . . I haven't forgiven him yet."

"Yet?" He glanced sideways at her, "So, there's a possibility you might."

"I honestly don't know," she shrugged. "I met him at the station on Friday and we went for a drink. We talked a bit but ended up arguing. I know he's been having sex with someone else however much he denies it."

Guy screwed his face up and tentatively asked, "Is there any way he could be telling the truth?"

"I want to believe that but I don't, not deep down. He doesn't want us to finish, but I want a boyfriend I can trust. So, nothing was sorted and I've left it for now."

"When are you both off together again?"

"This coming weekend, it's his last at home. He joins a ship then and will be away for a couple of months."

"Where's he going to?"

"Surveillance around Gibraltar. He finds out more this week."

"You're going to have to make a decision before he goes, then?"

"Yeah, I suppose so. Maybe I should take a leaf out of your book and be single for a while."

"Maybe you should. I can highly recommend it."

"What . . . when it's only been two days?"

"Yep, it feels that good," he winked.

Her tummy flipped. There he was again with the wink she found so attractive.

29.

Louise

It was just after four o'clock as Louise entered the hospital, heading to Mr Duffield's office. They'd been talking in school about putting some posters up about Vanya as things had gone quiet. Louise felt they needed to do something and Mrs Beaumont had suggested she asked the nursing officer before doing anything.

When she reached the office displaying a brass Nursing Officer plate, she tapped on the door and waited to be asked to come in.

"Hi," she smiled at Mr Duffield sitting behind his desk, "sorry to bother you."

"Come in, Nurse Allard," he stood up, "please, take a seat." He indicated to the chair the opposite side of the desk. "You're not bothering me at all. What can I do for you?"

"Thank you." She took the seat. "We've been speaking in school today about putting some posters up with a picture of Vanya on to see if it might jog someone's memory that may have seen her. Mrs Beaumont suggested running it by you first of all."

"I see." He paused for a moment, as if he was thinking. While he did, she noted the untidiness of the office, the shelves were packed to capacity and his desk looked chaotic.

"It's a balance we need to have," he cleared his throat, "while we are all concerned around the hospital regarding the plight of Vanya and being the focus of media attention, we need to be mindful of the public that have to visit relatives in the hospital and attend the outpatients department. Harlow Wood is a safe place, it always has been. And as serious as Vanya's disappearance is, I don't want people to be afraid to visit or attend for appointments."

"I do understand," she replied, even though she didn't. As far as she was concerned, the most important thing was finding Vanya. Who cared what the public thought. Someone might know something and a poster could jog their memory.

"That said," he continued, "I want to help. Vanya was . . . *is* one of ours, if I can put it that way, and we need to do everything we can to find her. Where were you thinking of putting posters up?"

The expectant expression on his face was odd. He was staring at her as if he was doing her a huge favour. Maybe it was her overactive imagination. She'd heard the talk about him, but Kym said he'd been really nice with her.

"I thought maybe outpatients and in the visitors' cafe."

"Yes," again he paused, as if thinking things through. "I'm not sure about outpatients though, but I'm happy with the visitors' canteen. And maybe the bus stops would be good outside the entrance to the hospital."

"Oh, yes," she agreed, "I hadn't thought of that. Could I ask if there's anywhere in the hospital we could get the posters laminated or something. I'm happy to design them but they'll just get wet."

"No problem. Come and see me again when you've done them and I can sort it for you."

"That's a great help, thank you."

She attempted to stand up.

"Before you dash off," he said, "tell me, how are things going on the ward? I didn't get to see you this week. Mrs Valance being off sick is giving me double the work so I'm unable to get round the wards quite as much as I'd like."

She eased herself back into her seat. "Mr Feeney has been really good. He showed me aseptic technique on some Steinman's pins and I've been researching a patient about how she sustained her fractures and her treatment plan. I've really enjoyed it."

"Good. I'm pleased to hear it. I'll try and catch up with you next week when you're on placement and you can tell me all about the patient you're talking about. Maybe she could be your first assessment?"

"Yes. Thank you. Anyway, I'll not hold you up any longer." This time she stood up and made her way to the door. He beat her to it and opened it for her.

"You're not holding me up at all. I'm here for all the students . . . anytime."

She nodded, eager to get away. For some reason, she wasn't entirely comfortable with him.

"Thank you so much for your help."

"Not a problem."

She quickly exited the office. Mr Duffield was creepy. When she had the posters ready, she was going to take

228

Kym or someone with her. She couldn't fathom it out, but he somehow had the ability to make her feel uncomfortable without doing anything remotely inappropriate. Maybe it was the thickness of his glasses and his greasy dark hair she was sure came out of a bottle. And even though he had been attentive as he listened to her, it felt almost as if he had another agenda. Like they were on two different pages. Was she just being paranoid with everything that was going on?

She made her way along the corridor back to the nurses' home deep in thought about what to wear for Edna's retirement party at the Rushley. She wanted to look the best she could to try and catch Nick Feeney's eye. The event was upstairs in the function room and Jackie had offered to take her. Her black dress which was cut really short and showed off her legs would be a good choice, but she was also toying with a pair of dressy, cropped trousers and a sheer top that would show the outline of her bra.

As she came through the main area of the hospital and passed the reception area, she became aware of someone coming up behind her. Lloyd the gardener caught her up.

"Hello Louise."

"Hello." His use of her name surprised her. She wasn't aware she'd told him it. She'd always been polite when she saw him, but he wasn't someone she was friendly with. Particularly not now when they all needed to be alert. She carried on walking with him at her side, "Are you just finishing for the day?" she asked, making an effort to be polite.

"Soon. I've just got to clear my gear away and lock up. Are you going to Edna's retirement party tonight?"

"Yes."

Was he going? Did gardeners get invited to staff member's retirement parties?

"Me too. I'll see you there, then. You're going with someone I take it?"

"Sorry?"

"You've got someone to go with. You girls need to be careful since Vanya's disappearance."

"Oh, I see. Yes, I'm going with someone."

"Good. Strange business all of it, don't you think?"

"Absolutely."

"She was a nice girl," he carried on, "tiny with a big smile."

"Yes." Was? She *is* a nice girl. Before she could say any more, they reached the hospital exit that would take her up the hill to North House.

He held the door open for her. "See you later then," he said as he veered right.

"Will do," she replied.

* * *

"Hi," Jackie greeted Louise as she walked towards the entrance of South House where Jackie had her room.

"I'm not late am I?" Louise asked.

"No. Not at all. I thought I'd save you having to climb the stairs to my room." Jackie fumbled in her handbag for her car keys as they started to walk towards the car park. "You look nice."

Louise had carefully applied her makeup, curled her hair into soft waves with heated curling tongs, and gone for the short black dress hoping it might tempt Nick Feeney. The truth was, she was only going to Edna's retirement because of him.

"Thank you," she smiled at Jackie. "You do too. I love your top."

"It's only a cheap one from Chelsea Girl. It was in the sale. It's actually not my size, but it was all they had and I do love the colour."

"It suits you." She meant it. The vibrant red was striking with her colleague's long blonde hair.

Each step they took as they headed for the car park was tentative as they were both wearing stiletto heels.

"I've made a bit of an extra effort tonight," Jackie said. "I've got my eye on Stephen Williams, the staff nurse on ward 1. Have you met him?"

"No, I've haven't met him as such but I've seen him around. He looks nice."

"Yeah. We almost got together once at Tiffany's in Nottingham, but he had a girlfriend so he sort of pulled away at the last minute. He's finished with her now, so as far as I can tell, the coast's clear."

"You do right to go for it, then. He's quite good looking."

"He is. I think so anyway. Everyone that does a placement on ward 1 says he's a fantastic staff nurse and really helpful with the students."

"That's good then. Shows he's decent. I don't think we do ward 1 until our second year."

"No, you don't. It's because it's a high dependency unit so they want the students to have experience."

"That makes sense. Did you like it on the ward when you did it?"

"I loved it. Stephen wasn't there then, though. I want to work in that sort of discipline when I'm qualified. I like the thought of intensive care nursing."

They reached the car park and approached a red Volkswagen Beetle. "Here we are." Jackie opened the driver's door, got inside and reached across to open the door for Louise.

"What are those lads like in your intake?" Jackie asked, adjusting the rearview mirror and putting the key in the ignition. "I can't remember what they're called?"

"Simon and Guy. They're both great. Simon seems to be working his way round the student nurses," she laughed, "I don't somehow think he's one for anything permanent though."

"Yes, I heard that," Jackie smiled as she started the ignition, "What about the other one?"

"Guy's really nice. I don't think he's in the same camp as Simon, though. He's actually got a girlfriend at home."

Jackie raised her eyebrows, "When has that ever stopped anyone? From what I've gathered from my two years here, long distance relationships don't last. The thing is, many of the nurses are only seventeen when they get here and mature so much during the two years. Even though I was twenty when I started, I know I have."

"Yeah, I bet. I'm not bothered about a boyfriend to be honest while I'm here. I just want to get my qualification and then go and do my general training without any complications."

The idiot Andy Moore who forced himself on her at the school leaver's party was still raw in her mind. It had put her off relationships, until recently that is. Nick Feeney was on her mind constantly and thinking of him at night in her room reminded her she was no longer dead from the waist down.

"I get that," Jackie said turning out of Harlow Wood towards Mansfield, "but remember, a bit of fun along the way can't be that bad."

Louise laughed, "You're right. So, I'll be rooting for you tonight then with Stephen."

"That's good then," Jackie smiled, checking her mirror. "Oh, I forgot to mention, I said I'd pick Sutty up on the way. Hope that's okay?"

"Course it is. It's good of you to offer me a lift."

"Don't be daft. I was going anyway so another passenger, or two even, makes no difference."

"Yeah, but you probably could have hitched a ride with someone else, maybe?"

"Nah, I was never going to do that. I like to drive."

"Well, thanks anyway. Hey, I saw Lloyd the gardener earlier; he says he's coming tonight. I thought it was a bit weird the gardener coming to someone's retirement do."

"Oh, he comes to everything. I think he's a bit lonely."

"Hasn't he got a wife?"

"No, apparently not. He lives with his brother in Mansfield. I think Harlow Wood's his life. That and the Rushley. He seems to like his hats as well. I don't know if you've noticed, but he's always wearing a different one. I think he sees it as a talking point."

"Yeah, he does seem to. And today he called me by my name which I haven't told him."

"He'll have asked someone." Jackie indicated and turned left, "he prides himself on knowing all the nurses. He's harmless though so don't be worrying."

"Okay."

A memory flashed up of Vanya saying he'd bored her to death about some plants once. It hurt thinking about what might have happened to her.

Louise followed Jackie and Sutty up the stairs to the private room at the Rushley. She saw Nick Feeney straight away. He was standing by a table of women engaged in conversation with Mr Griffiths, the charge nurse from ward 9. At a glance he looked gorgeous in a white chambray shirt which highlighted his pale skin, and navy blue chino type trousers with an immaculate crease pressed down the front and a brown leather belt. She looked carefully at who was closest to him and recognised straight away they were staff from Harlow Wood. Would his wife be there? That thought was most probably the reason for her gut ache. She'd been feeling tense since seeing Mr Duffield, but it was more than that. Thinking about Nick Feeney and possibly seeing his wife, turned her tummy into knots.

"Right," Louise said, "let me get you a drink, Jackie. It's the least I can do for the lift."

"Aw, thank you. I'll have a lime and soda please."

"What about you, Sutty?"

"I'll get these," he said.

"No, let me. I'd like to buy Jackie one for giving me a lift."

"Me too. You can get the next."

"Okay, I'll do that. Shall I come with you?"

"Yeah, good idea."

"I'll be right back," Louise said to Jackie.

There was a few at the bar waiting to be served. Sutty was chatting to everyone he came into contact with while he waited to be served. It was plain to see he was popular with a cheeky charm about him that drew people in. Louise surreptitiously gazed around the venue while they waited at the bar, her focus on one man. He'd moved on to another group and in his animated way, he was holding their attention. It didn't appear his wife was with him, not that she'd know what she looked like. It seemed very much like those he was mixing with were Harlow Wood staff.

Once Sutty had been served, they returned to where Jackie was standing with Tracey, another auxiliary from their ward. She was in her early twenties which was unusual for an auxiliary, most of them, as far as Louise could see, were elderly. Or they seemed so to her. Her mum was forever reminding her that forty wasn't old when she'd implied it was.

"Hi, Tracey," Louise greeted her. "You look nice."

"I'll second that," Sutty said, eyeing Tracey up and down in an obvious way."

"You think anything in a skirt and breathing looks nice, Sutty," Tracey said sarcastically, which made them laugh.

"What's wrong with that? Be worried when men stop looking."

Tracey rolled her eyes playfully. "I'll bear that in mind then."

Sutty grinned, "On that note, I better get circulating and sharing myself around. I don't want any women to miss out."

Jackie joined in. "Gosh yes, you must. We don't want any broken hearts, not tonight. Catch you later," she winked at him as he headed towards a group of staff from the kitchens. Louise noticed Lloyd was with them too, minus a hat that evening.

"Hey," Tracey looked at Louise, "I love your hair down."

"Thank you," Louise said, "it's great not to have to pin it up."

Would Nick think she looked nice?

"Are you two going to join us?" Tracey pointed to the table she must have been sitting at. "We're over there."

"Shall we?" Jackie asked Louise.

"Sure." Louise knew most of them from the ward. There weren't enough seats though, but she was happy to stand. She had a better viewpoint and didn't want to get sandwiched in the back in case Nick came over.

"Can everyone hitch round?" Tracey asked those sitting on the booth's curved seats.

"It's okay. I'm fine standing up," Louise said, leaning against the adjacent wall, "I've got a bit of a niggly tummy and it seems to get worse if I sit down."

"It's not appendicitis, is it?" Tracey asked, perching on the end seat.

"God, no, nothing like that. In fact it's eased off slightly so I'm not sure what it was."

Jackie's expression was full of concern. "Tell me if you need to leave early and I'll drive you back to Harlow Wood."

"Don't be daft. I wouldn't spoil your night. If I was feeling that bad, I'd get a taxi back. But I'm not, so let's just enjoy ourselves. I'm fine, honestly." She raised her glass, "Cheers everyone."

The evening was tortuous for Louise, she really didn't want to be there. She chatted to the girls, laughing when appropriate, so to anyone watching, they'd think she was having a great time. But she wasn't – it was all for show. It was a dull evening as far as she was concerned. The highlight to most of them seemed to be the buffet, while to her, pub food made her cautious. There was something about food left standing that made her question the cleanliness of the kitchens in pubs. So, while they were eating what appeared to be soggy sandwiches from paper plates, Louise excused herself and headed outside for a few minutes to get some air. She daren't venture from the entrance, as much as she'd have liked to look round the garden, she was still anxious about Vanya's disappearance and had promised her mother she'd be careful. So, she stood staring at the sky and thinking about her dad. It was still raw and she missed him every day.

After returning upstairs and back through the door to the venue, her heart rate quickened. Nick Feeney was standing at their table. His charm was obvious even from afar – whatever he was saying the nurses were throwing their heads back and laughing.

He turned to her as she approached the table. "Hi, Louise. Are you having a good time?"

He'd called her by her Christian name, she liked that.

"Yes, I am thank you . . ." she wasn't sure if she was supposed to call him Mr Feeney.

"It's Nick out of work."

Nick. It suited him. When she was home at the weekend, she'd looked the name up in a book her mother had of boys and girls names. It was old but described Nick, the abbreviation of Nicholas to mean *victory of the people* according to its Greek origin. Warmth gushed through her. That would be Nick Feeney, all masculine and a sure winner.

Tracey chipped in. "Louise has made an effort to come, she wasn't well earlier."

"Oh," concern showed in his brown eyes, "what's the matter?"

"Nothing much, just a bit of a tummy ache, that's all."

"Well, don't stick around too long tonight, you're probably better off in bed."

His words invoked an instant image of her in bed with him. She felt herself blushing.

"I'm fine, honestly."

"If you're not, as soon as I've done the presentation and said a few words about Edna, I'll be leaving. I'm on an early tomorrow and as if that isn't hard enough after a night out, I have to see a member of the night staff before she goes off duty, so I'll need to be there doubly early. If you want a lift back to Harlow Wood, yell out."

"That's kind. I'll see how I go."

Her tummy ache was going to get one hundred percent worse, certainly in her head. Being alone with him in a car felt like all prayers had been answered. Would his wife be waiting for him, or working?

"Are you drinking?" he asked.

"Nothing alcoholic. My tummy doesn't feel I can cope with it."

"You do right then. Anyway, excuse me. I just want to make sure everything is ready for the presentation. I'll come and find you before I leave to see how you're feeling."

"Thank you. I appreciate that."

And then he was gone. Her heart was pounding. She'd never felt such an attraction to anyone before. And even though he was married, she was sure he felt something too.

Or was that wishful thinking?

30.

It was early evening when he got into his car and drove away from Harlow Wood, heading towards Mansfield town centre. He found driving relaxing; it was never a chore to him. As he worked his way through the gears and accelerated, the question whirling around in his head was how much longer would he be able to drive his car? On a daily basis, at the forefront of his mind, was his life beginning to slip away. Outwardly, he appeared exactly the same, but internally he was failing. He'd noticed that he was losing weight, not excessively but he was dropping a few pounds which he was sure was visible only to him, but over the next few weeks, it was only going to get worse. Thoughts about his demise were becoming more pronounced each day and it scared him. Who wouldn't be sacred? And the thought of being a patient in a hospital bed with nurses waiting on him hand and foot, tending to his every need, filled him with horror. He didn't want that. Thoughts of ending his life was gaining momentum and now becoming more than an idea. Going into woods to hang himself would be simple and quick and had far more appeal than hospitalisation.

He paused at a junction checking left and right for traffic before proceeding. Was there an afterlife? He didn't think there possibly could be even though he'd read books speculating otherwise. He wasn't religious in any way, but it felt comforting to believe there was more. But then he'd logically think if there was an afterlife, what would happen to people that had remarried when they'd lost their spouse. Which one did you end up with when you reached the pearly gates? A shudder ran through him. He wouldn't want to particularly meet anyone again, certainly not his old man, nor any of the girls he'd killed. Except for Angela. He'd give anything to see her again. Dear, sweet Angela. She'd meant the world to him. And he knew categorically he'd meant something to her. But that all changed when she met Ricky Hurst.

He recalled a particular conversation they'd had one morning. Angela had come home the previous evening pissed out of her head. He'd been lying awake in his bedroom waiting up for her so he could spy on her getting undressed. But she was later than usual and when he eventually heard her come in the front door, he'd heard an almighty thud. He rushed downstairs – she was in a heap in the hall, totally out of it.

She was only a lightweight, so he picked her up and carried her to her bedroom. There he carefully undressed her. He didn't take her bra and knickers off though, she might not have forgiven him for that. But he'd managed to touch her as he undressed her and stare in awe at her beautiful legs and big tits which were encased in a tight bra, pushing them up. He savoured her ample cleavage. Despite being comatose, he daren't touch her breasts directly, even though he would have loved to see her nipples up close. But his eyes never left her feminine body laid out in front of him wearing just her pretty pink bra and pants. How he'd have loved to take those last flimsy bits off and see her in all her glory.

"Night, night beautiful," he'd whispered, as he pulled the covers over her and kissed the top of her head.

The following morning, she'd been mortified. "I can't believe I got so drunk you had to undress me and to put me to bed," she said, slurping the second cup of coffee he'd given her after feasting on the bacon and egg he'd fried, "but thanks to you, I'm starting to come round a bit now."

"That's good," he said handing her two Anadin and a tumbler of water. "Take these, they'll help too."

"You're so good," she said throwing the two tablets down and swallowing them, "I don't know what I've done in life to deserve you. Most blokes would have taken advantage of me in that state, but not you." She reached across and squeezed his hand, "You truly are the best friend any woman could have. Thank you."

"You're welcome. You've been good to me also, remember. We'd have had nowhere to go if it wasn't for you taking my brother and me in." He looked warmly at her, "I'll never forget that kindness."

"Don't be daft. You've paid me back hundreds of times. When I think of all you do for me, I can't bear the thought of losing you."

Unease flowed through him. "Why would you lose me?" he asked, removing her plate and placing it on the draining board next to him.

"When I meet someone and get married." She reached in her dressing gown pocket for a tissue and blew her nose.

"Is that what you're looking to do?" he said nonchalantly.

"Of course. Isn't every girl?"

"I guess so. I've just never thought of you married really."

"Haven't you? Well you better do, 'cause that's what I want to be. And to have children, I want those. But I need to meet the right man first," she rolled her eyes, "and there doesn't appear to be an abundance of those around."

He moved towards the sink and started to run some water to wash the dishes. He had to turn away so she wouldn't see the pain on his face. It had to be etched all over it as he hated the way the conversation was going. She couldn't get married. That was the last thing he could cope with. Angela was a major part of his life. He couldn't lose her. It crushed him to think he might. He quickly made his mind up that if anything should happen and she became serious with anyone, he'd have to take care of it. Nobody was going to steal her from him.

Reality kicked back in. He'd been immersed in his thoughts, and unconsciously driven into a seedier part of Mansfield. There were two young women on a corner, touting their services. It was evident exactly what was on offer looking at their miniskirts which barely covered their backsides, and tight blouses displaying their ample wares. No coats of course despite it being a bitterly cold night and drizzling with rain. A thick coat would hamper any visuals for a prospective client. They were worthless sluts. If he strangled one of them, they'd hardly be missed. He'd be doing society a favour. The trouble was, they weren't the females he liked – it was the innocent ones. Young and pretty like Angela.

He took a left turn away from the slappers. The urge for another kill was overwhelming. But there was too much heat at Harlow Wood right now. Louise Allard was going to be his swansong, but not for a few more days. Right now, he was going for a random one. He was nowhere near as prepared as he'd been with Vanya, but the urge was too strong, particularly as he'd already spotted in the mirror, a young girl that fitted the bill for just what he had in mind, patiently waiting at a bus stop. She was only young, maybe about eighteen. Her blonde hair was long, he noticed, as it hung down her back, almost to her waist over her leather short jacket. His fingers itched to run through it and plait it nicely before he strangled her. She had long legs displayed beautifully in a checked miniskirt and leather boots reaching up to her knees. Her large, hooped earrings and fingerless gloves, gave her an edgy look. He liked that. All young and pretty, and stood on her own. And the rain coming down faster was surely going to be in his favour? He quickly decided to turn the car and drove around the block, returning back to the bus stop.

He applied the handbrake and with the engine still running, wound the window down.

"Excuse me. I'm trying to find the way to," he glanced down at the piece of blank paper in his hand, "Harlow Wood. Is it round here do you know?"

The young girl took a step towards his car, she was a little beauty, but more so up close. She leaned in.

"You're not far. It's sort of more or less on this road," she pointed, "you can't miss it. It's about, er . . . two miles away. No more than that."

"That's brilliant, thank you. I'm on my way to visit my brother. He's been admitted there with a back injury. I just got the call today from his wife." He glanced at his watch, "I'd best make tracks to get there. So, I keep on this road you say?"

"Yes, that's right. You can't miss it."

He raised an eyebrow, "Is your bus heading in that direction?"

"Yes, it is, but my stop's a bit before Harlow Wood. I sometimes walk home on a nice day but my dad insists on me taking the bus if it's late."

"Quite right, too. I'm the same with my daughters. I worry about them all the time. Once a parent, always a parent, I guess." He smiled. "I've just had a thought; can I offer you a lift? It's an awful night stood out here in the rain, and it sounds like I'm passing your stop."

Hesitation passed across the girl's face. But he could tell the warmth of the car was enticing her. That's why he'd left the engine running and the heater on full blast.

"I quite understand if you don't want to," he quickly added. "I'd better be getting off myself or I'll miss visiting time."

"If you're sure," she smiled, "I'd love a lift."

"Of course I am. Hop in."

He reached across and opened the car door for her and watched as she eased herself into the passenger seat.

"Thank you," she said wiping drops of rain off her face with her fingertips, "it's very kind of you. I've no idea where the bus is tonight. It must have been delayed."

"Not at all," he said, putting the car into gear and making an exaggerated show of looking in the mirror, while surreptitiously glancing at her slender thighs as she tried to ease her sodden miniskirt down to cover more of them.

She'd do nicely.

Thank you God for bus delays.

31.

Louise

Her tummy ache supposedly worsened throughout the course of the evening, giving Louise the ideal opportunity to accept Nick's offer of a lift back to Harlow Wood. During the drive, he led their conversation, talking about Edna's time on the ward, how pleased she'd been with the gifts they'd given her, and that he was going to miss her cheerful face each day. Louise wasn't sure if it was wishful thinking, but it seemed to her like there was an undercurrent neither of them spoke about. He certainly didn't refer to her so-called tummy discomfort she'd made out had progressively got worse to Jackie, and she didn't either. It was as if he knew.

It had stopped raining, and the confines of the car almost made for a romantic end to the evening with the blackness of the sky and the stars twinkling under the glow of the half moon. She stole a glance at his profile as he concentrated on accelerating to overtake a van – she could almost pretend they were a couple, and the thought of him dropping her off at North House made her feel bereft. But as he turned into the entrance to Harlow Wood, he surprised her by turning right and manoeuvring the car through the gates of the gamekeeper's cottage and coming to a stop outside the back door to his house. He switched off the ignition and turned towards her. "I've wanted to have a word with you in private, but as you'll know already, it's difficult here with it being such a small community. So, I thought my house seems the best place to do it. But I'm conscious you might feel uncomfortable coming inside and that's the last thing I'd want. So, if you do, please say. I can have the conversation here and then walk you to the nurses' home."

"I'm not uncomfortable at all, but what is it you want to talk to me about?"

"I'll tell you when we get inside."

"What about your wife? Won't she think it strange me coming in?"

"She isn't here," he said, opening the car door and getting out.

She followed him into a small porchway and into the kitchen where he flicked on a light.

"Can I get you a drink? A tea or coffee maybe? Or a glass of something else?"

"Thank you, some water would be nice."

"Coming up. You go through to the lounge, it's to the right. Make yourself comfortable."

Louise headed to the cosy lounge with her tummy now genuinely in a turmoil. She never expected this. Was he interested in her? Her heart rate quickened. He must be. If not, why was she even in his house?

She took a seat on the floral settee and scrutinised her surroundings. The room appeared immaculate, and why wouldn't it be? This was Mr Perfectionist, after all. His huge bookcase had the books lined up perfectly according to size; the cushions on the sofa and chairs all looked like they were standing to attention. The windowsills were devoid of any clutter, and the fireplace tiles gleamed. Was his wife house-proud, or was the tidiness purely down to him?

"Here we go," he placed a tumbler of iced water on the table next to her and appeared to be clutching a gin and tonic judging by the type of glass with lemon and ice floating in it.

"Cheers," he said, holding his glass up as he sat on the armchair opposite.

She lifted her water, not entirely sure what to do. It all seemed surreal.

"You'll be wondering why I've invited you in," he said, placing his glass down on the small table at the side of him.

She widened her eyes. "I am a bit, yes."

"Course you are." He took a deep breath in, "Okay, Louise, I need to put my cards on the table." His warm hazel eyes looked directly into hers. "You're an extremely attractive young woman. I've felt that since I first saw you. And I think you feel something for me." He put his hand up, "Don't say anything, I'm struggling a bit here because I'm your tutor and a married man. But before I go any further, I need to let you know my wife and I are separated."

"Oh, I'm sorry to hear that." She wasn't sorry, not one bit. She couldn't believe what she was hearing. Aware that her cheeks were burning fiercely, she took a big gulp of the iced water.

"It happens," he shrugged. "We've tried to make it work, but sadly it isn't meant to be."

"Where is she now?"

"She's residing at the hospital she works at, Mansfield General. She's met someone there."

"Oh."

"Yes, it's not good, but I think it's for the best. I'm telling you this in confidence, I don't share my private life with anyone at the hospital."

"No, of course not. I wouldn't speak about anything so personal."

"Thank you. I appreciate that. We will eventually be divorcing, which brings me back to you." He reached for his glass and the seconds it took for him to take a sip, seemed to take for ever. What was coming next?

He cleared his throat. "Even if I wanted something to happen between us, it couldn't for a number of reasons, the primary one being that I'm your tutor. I could lose my job. And I've worked hard to achieve what I have and I can't wreck that."

Her tummy plummeted. The euphoria she'd experienced moments earlier, dipped. She took another gulp of the iced water. "And the other reasons?" she asked, staring intently into his tormented eyes. He'd always been so vibrant and confident, yet now he was hesitant and obviously uncomfortable.

He lifted a hand, closing his fingers and leaving just his thumb up, "Being your tutor is number one," he raised his forefinger, "I'm married, that's two."

"Separated though," she chipped in.

"Nevertheless, still married." Next was his middle finger, "Number three, I'm a lot older than you."

"How old are you?" she asked, as if she cared.

"Thirty-two. And the fourth, which might not seem much to a young person, but I live my life in a principled way with integrity and honour. I can't start messing around with one of my students when I'm almost old enough to be her father. Affairs, casual sex, or whatever we want to call it, isn't me. And it wouldn't be fair on you, either."

Her eyes never left his face. She wasn't vastly experienced with men, and everything he said was true. They shouldn't even be sat in his house together. It was totally inappropriate. But she wanted to be with him – wanted to feel his arms around her – wanted to kiss him. And wanted to obliterate the memory of the awful assault she'd experienced.

"So," his expression was pained, "you must understand that nothing can happen between us. Not now . . . not ever. By the time you've finished this course, you'll have moved on anyway. That's why I wanted to have this conversation," his voice softened, "I've seen the way you look at me, and I am flattered, but we need to nip it in the bud, now . . . before it's too late." He reached for his drink, taking a large mouthful.

Tears pricked her eyes but she was determined not to start blubbering. How immature would that look? She swallowed down the lump in her throat, "Everything you say is true, but I want to be with you. We can keep it to ourselves. I wouldn't say a word."

"But it wouldn't be fair on you, Louise. You deserve better than this."

"I don't want better. I want to be with you."

He shook his head vigorously. "No," he said firmly, "I'm too old for you and old enough to know better. I chose my path years ago, you're just embarking on yours."

"So what happens now?" she hoped her eyes displayed how upset she was.

He looked at his watch, "I'll walk you back to the nurses' home and leave you at the door. Have you got a late-night key to get in?"

She did have, but she wasn't going to tell him that. She wanted more time with him.

"No."

His eyes said he didn't believe her.

"Okay, I'll get one from reception and let you in. And you need to stop looking at me like you are doing. It's for the best. You'll thank me one day for this. And remember, you have your placement on the ward with me to get through. I'm trying to make that easier for you."

"You're talking all the time about you, but I have feelings too. I..." she hesitated, images of the assault flooding her mind. She lowered her gaze to the floor, her heart racing. She felt sick.

"Louise? What is it?"

Should she tell him? *Could* she?

"I'm sorry if I've upset you," he said.

"Not you," she said, "it's just . . ."

"Please, tell me. Perhaps I can help."

She raised her gaze to meet his and her heart ached for him. He was always so . . . caring.

"Well . . . it was about eleven months ago, I was at a party and I was . . . I ended up having sex with a boy against my will."

"What?" he frowned, "he forced himself on you?"

"Yes."

"Christ. Did you go to the police?"

"No. I felt it was partly my fault, things just got out of hand. And it's in the past now. But what it's done, or had done, was spoil things for me. I've steered clear of boys and . . . relationships since then. I even saw a counsellor before I came here which helped. My mum thought it was to do with my dad dying, and some of it was. But she's helped me deal with the . . . attack . . . rape, or whatever it's called."

He got up and came to sit beside her on the sofa. Warmth flooded through her as he took her hand. "I'm so sorry you've had to go through that. I can only imagine how painful that must be."

"It was. And still is. But that changed when I met you." She struggled to find the right words. She wasn't used to expressing herself. All she knew was she wanted to be with him.

"I feel stupid," she screwed her face up, "because I haven't got the right words, I don't know what to say. All I know is, I want to experience something good, and nice. An intimacy that's special and not dirty. And I want that to be with you," she begged, pleading with her eyes . . . "I'm not bothered about the rest."

He stroked the side of her face. "You're so lovely. How anyone could hurt you like that, I don't know. You should be cared for and made to feel special, because you are. You're a beautiful young woman. I knew it that day when we were in the woods together. I wanted to wrap my arms around you then and take away all the pain I could see in your eyes."

A tear escaped down her cheek. She wanted him to take it all away – the attack, her dad's death, the stupid anxiety about germs necessitating cleaning stuff all the time. In a voice, shaking with emotion, she whispered, "Can't you do that now?"

His thumb caught the tear, his breath seemed to catch before his lips moved closer to her face causing her heart to race as if she was running a marathon. But she was perfectly still. She parted her lips in anticipation as he moved his gently to touch hers. She tasted the lemon of his drink on his lips, light pressure initially, until it increased, causing her stomach to knot as it fluttered with insecurity. He pulled her in and wrapped his arms around her, causing her whole body to tingle. His warm frame radiated heat as his mouth became hungrier. She kissed him back. It was intense, like nothing she'd experienced before. Their heads moved simultaneously as his tongue met hers. Despite her eyes clenched tightly shut, she sneaked a guilty peek just to make sure he wasn't a product of her imagination, like at night when she dreamt about him kissing her. Heat rose from her stomach to her chest. It was as if time had stopped, right there. And nobody else existed.

Only the two of them.

32.

"You've gone wrong," the young blonde girl sitting at the side of him said, turning her head towards the back window of the car, "it's not down here, it's straight on the main road, back that way," she nodded her head.

"Oh, is it? I'd better turn the car around. Keep a lookout for a turning."

"How about there on the left," she pointed.

He drove straight past.

She turned to him with a puzzled look on her face.

"It was too muddy. I don't want to reverse and get the car stuck, that's the last thing we need."

She glanced at her wristwatch, "I don't know what time visiting is, but you're probably going to miss it if we don't turn back soon."

"Yes, it seems so."

"Look," she said, "it's stopped raining. I can walk from here."

"No need for that," he said, "we'll get there in the end."

"Can't you do a three point turn?" she asked. He sensed the change in her tone. As if an element of panic had started to sink in.

"Yes, I suppose I could. That seems sensible." He slowed the car down and brought it to a halt. He turned off the ignition.

"What are you doing?"

It registered then. There in her beautiful hazel eyes, he saw it. Fear.

Without saying a word, he reached at the side of his seat for the weapon to stun her.

"What's going on?" the pitch of her voice was raised, "I want to get . . ." Her face froze. She'd seen the claw hammer in his hand.

Her scared eyes followed the hammer as he held it out over the dashboard, but before she could speak again, he swung it with as much force as he could muster, the dull thud smacking into her forehead. Initially it appeared she was stunned, as if the blow had no impact – so he hit her again. She slumped. Blood began seeping down the side of her face.

His breathing was heavy. Had he killed her? He hoped not. He wanted his hands round her neck to strangle the last breath out of her. She was still, her eyes were bulging open. He reached across her to the glove compartment and retrieved a carrier bag for the hammer, and grabbed a rag to catch the blood seeping down her neck, before starting the engine. Prior to moving away, he reached for a blanket off the back seat and wrapped it around her with just her hair poking out, as if she was asleep next to him. Not that there was anyone around to notice. The road was deserted.

He put the car in gear, let the handbrake off and moved away. For what he had in mind, he needed privacy. Anyone could drive past on the road.

Eventually, he followed a dirt track until he found a place to pull up in the woods. He cut the engine but put the internal light on. He checked her breathing. Shit, she wasn't breathing at all. The blows must have killed her. He'd not been able to judge it properly in the confines of the car. He closed her fearful eyes, he didn't want her looking at him. He touched her face. She was still warm. He reached into the glove compartment again and found a knife. He sliced the front of her top open, and then her bra. She had pert little breasts, just how he liked them. He pulled her top aside to expose them more fully and peered at her nipples. He was in complete ecstasy, stroking her young flesh. She was absolutely perfect. Just beautiful. He ran his fingers through her hair, avoiding the side where the blood had congealed. It was so pretty. He started to gather it in his hands and brought it to his nose. It smelled of rain. Despite the stickiness, he separated it and gently braided it exactly how he liked it. Like Angela's.

It was a bit of a struggle to get her miniskirt lifted back and her knickers down, but the sight of her pale and slender thighs was a beautiful reward. He stroked his fingers up her thighs, touching her warm centre, revelling in the scent of her. Maybe he could move her to the back seat, strip her completely, caress every inch of her young body.

The inside of the car suddenly lit up causing his heart to thump. He turned to see headlights coming down the deserted road. Despite being cold, sweat formed on his forehead. His car was tucked away from the main road, so not visible, but he still turned the interior light off and held his breath, silently praying the car would carry on past. It didn't. It veered off the road and onto the dirt track, close to where he was parked. Although he was confident he couldn't be seen, he knew the engine when he started it, would alert the occupant that someone was in the vicinity.

Anxiousness flooded through him. He'd been too casual.

He covered the young girl completely with the blanket, picked up the claw hammer and, as quietly as he was able, opened the car door and closed it slowly and silently after he got out. The ground was soft from the recent rainfall, and as he tentatively made his way nearer the parked vehicle, the twigs underneath his feet crackled, causing him to slow his movement. He didn't think they'd hear him, certainly not from inside the car, nevertheless he was cautious. It would be disastrous if he was discovered. It'd be the end of everything.

He cautiously hid behind a damp old oak tree and from his viewpoint, while he couldn't see exactly what was going on, judging by the steamed-up windows and rocking movement of the car, he could guess. Should he make a dash for it while they were too busy to spot his car and number plate?

Speed was of the essence. He returned to the car, opened the side door, tossing the blanket covering the girl onto the back seat, before dragging her partially clothed body onto the wet grass.

Without a backward glance, he got back into the car and started the ignition, quickly reversing onto the main road with the lights off. He drove steadily so as not to alert the occupants of the car. No doubt they were too busy to be looking anyway.

He cursed himself as he came out of the woods. He'd been sloppy not planning properly. He'd wanted to take her to his secret place. And he could have done. But they'd disturbed him and he'd panicked and hastily dumped her body. Now it would soon be found.

He slapped the steering wheel in frustration. His temples throbbed. For only the second time since he'd been killing, he'd made a mistake that could lead to his capture. The previous time resulted in him currently working at Harlow Wood and living his life under a pseudonym. He hated thinking about his previous mistake.

He'd slipped up big time by killing the only person in his life that he truly loved.

33.

Kym

Kym rushed to the front door of her home in Cleethorpes knowing it was Guy ringing the doorbell. He'd dropped her off and had taken himself off to the seafront for fish and chips. Despite telling him he didn't have to do that, Kym was grateful he'd insisted. He'd said she needed time alone with her parents and they'd feel awkward if he was there initially.

When she'd first arrived home that evening, her mum and dad had cried with her at the cancer diagnosis. But her parents were pragmatic people and had decided they were going to pay privately to have the operation done quickly and they'd got a date for the following week. Her mother was to have a mastectomy and radiotherapy afterwards. There were tears, hugs and reassurance for them all as they talked about the injustice of it, and once they'd dried their tears, her mum and dad seemed a little more relaxed, as if the future wasn't quite so gloomy. And Kym felt better, even though she was under no illusion about what was ahead. But the three of them were close and would support each other through the following months.

Once the tears were dry, her mother insisted on them eating, and dished up a supper of quiche, salad and new potatoes which she'd prepared earlier. Although Kym was still anxious, she was less so and managed to eat. It was the first meal in a while she'd been able to stomach. During their meal, her mother had berated her for letting Guy go off, but Kym explained that he would do exactly as he wanted, there'd be no budging him once he made his mind up. And she was grateful they'd had the time alone, but was soon clock watching when it got near eight when he said he'd be back.

"Hello, you," she smiled opening the door at exactly 8 pm, "come in. My mum is dying to meet my knight in shining armour."

"Is that what I am?" Guy grinned, stepping inside and wiping his feet on the doormat.

"Well, that's what she thinks you are."

"That's good then. And you?"

"I think you're . . . kind, supportive and," she closed the door, "you drive too fast."

He laughed. "Oh, right, two out of three – not too bad then. I'll try and improve."

She took him through to the lounge. "Here he is. Guy, this is my mum."

Guy reached his hand out, "Pleased to meet you, Mrs Sullivan."

"Please," she smiled, "it's Dorothy, and this is my husband, Ron. No need for any formality here."

He took her dad's hand, "Nice to meet you, Ron."

"You too, son," her dad smiled, "Have a seat. Would you like a drink? I know you can't have beer with driving, but a cold drink, or some tea . . . coffee?"

"I've made a carrot cake if you can manage a slice?" her mother interjected.

"He's had fish and chips, Mum," Kym said, keen to get off now she'd seen her mother was okay. "He'll be full, I bet." Kym looked expectantly at him as if to say, let's get off now.

"I think I've a bit of room left for cake," Guy rubbed his tummy playfully, "and tea would be great, Mr . . . Ron."

"Just a couple of minutes, you make yourself comfy," her mother said, disappearing into the kitchen.

Kym was about to go and help.

"Sit down, love," her dad whispered, "let her keep busy. She's been baking to take her mind off things. I'll go give her a hand."

"Oh, right, course." She was relieved Guy had stayed now. He looked at her with a knowing smile. He'd guessed as much.

"We better have this and get off," Kym said, keeping her voice low.

"No rush. We have that late-night key, it doesn't matter what time we get back."

"No, I know. But it's a long way for you to drive, especially as you've done it once."

"It's fine. Stop stressing. And make sure you go to sleep, cause if you think it was quick coming here, it'll be even faster on the way back."

"What! I hope not. You can't go any quicker. Seriously, I mean it, I don't want you speeding."

"Would I? The roads will be quieter, that's what I meant."

"Did you?" she rolled her eyes.

"Sure did. Now relax. And enjoy some of your mum's cake. I know I will."

"Do you even like carrot cake?" she frowned.

"Love it," he grinned.

Kym's eyes opened as the car came to a standstill. She looked out of the window onto the car park at Harlow Wood.

"Sorry," she sat upright, "I was flat out."

"Yeah, I know. I had to put up with you snoring," Guy grinned pulling on the handbrake and cutting the ignition.

"I don't snore, thank you very much," she laughed, opening her car door.

"You do. But at least it's a sweet feminine noise and not like a bloke."

"I should hope not," she sniggered as they walked out of the car park and made their way to North House. Everywhere was deathly quiet and pitch-black with only the light from the moon guiding them.

"Thank you for taking me. I'm so pleased I got to see Mum."

"I told you I'd take you. It wasn't a problem."

"Still, you didn't have to."

"I know I didn't. I wanted to."

"Well, I am grateful. And I'll be seeing them at the weekend again."

"Yeah. They are nice people. I liked them."

"They are. And they loved you, I could tell. What's Dad like showing you his model train set. Honestly."

"I thought it was great. You're lucky, he seems a great dad. And your Mum's a nice lady, too."

"She is. And typical of her, when I went to say goodbye, she was giving me the look."

"What look's that?"

"The one that tells me you're a good catch, and I should snap you up, marry you and have three children with you."

"These mums talk a lot of sense."

"Stop it," she tapped him playfully.

Within minutes she was using the key to open the main door to North House. Guy altered their status on the wall to *IN*. "I'll come up with you," he said.

"Thanks. It seems a bit eerie I must say."

Guy followed her upstairs and once outside her room, she reached in her bag for her key.

"Thank you again for taking me." For some bizarre reason, tears were perilously close again. Most probably due to his kindness and her mother's plight.

"What is it?" His eyes were full or concern.

She swallowed. "Nothing."

"Come here." Guy put his arms around her and pulled her closely towards his chest. His hold felt tight, as if he'd never let her go. She wrapped her arms around him, barely reaching his shoulders. His chest was warm, and she relished his rich musky smell. With his strong arms holding her, she was sure she could hear his heart beating as rhythmically as hers.

She didn't break away. She didn't want to. It felt right and she wanted to hang onto him for a few minutes more before the spell was broken.

34.

Louise

Louise had barely slept and there was still an hour before she needed to be up to get showered, ready for school. The reason for her insomnia was Nick Feeney and the intimacy they'd shared hours earlier. It was almost as if her chest would burst, she was so happy. Staring up at the cracked ceiling, warmth flooded through her as she thought about when they could next make love. She'd relived every minute in her mind, hour after hour during the night, thinking about their first passionate kiss.

"This is so wrong," he said, his voice full of torment.

"No, it's not wrong at all. I really want this," she'd begged, "please."

And he'd delivered pleasure like she'd never felt before. Laid on his sofa, he'd kissed every inch of her, caressed her so gently, told her she was beautiful as he'd kissed his way down her stomach. She'd opened her legs for him and his glorious tongue had explored her most intimate places and brought her to orgasm before finally he'd sheathed himself and thrust inside her. They'd moved together as one. Never had she experienced anything as beautiful as his sensational mouth nipping and biting, and them both moving rhythmically together, resulting in her climaxing again almost simultaneously with him.

He'd held her tightly afterwards and she'd leaned in, not wanting their intimacy to end. But it had to. He'd gently told her she'd got to return to the nurses' home. She searched for regret in his eyes, but there didn't appear to be any. And once they were dressed, he wrapped her in his arms and told her again how beautiful she was. There was no mention of anything further between them, and she didn't want to break the spell by asking.

They'd walked slowly up the drive towards North House with a respectable space between them. To any observer it might seem odd, a tutor walking a student to the nurses' home, but if anyone did spot them together and asked, she'd explain she was feeling queasy and he'd kindly offered her a lift back, left his car at home and walked with her as she wanted some air. It all sounded feasible. And, everyone thought he was married anyway, so they'd think his wife was waiting at their house at the bottom of the drive, so it would be unlikely he'd be doing anything inappropriate.

As they walked along, the moon guiding their way and the wind whistling through the avenue of oak trees, he'd chatted about his hobby of photography and how he'd always loved the outdoors. It was all something and nothing. She knew it was to try and somehow get things back on a normal footing – as if they ever could be after what they'd shared. And she'd owned up to the fact she did have a late-night key, so he wouldn't need to get one from reception. He'd smirked at that. He'd known all along.

"Right, Louise," he winked as they paused at the entrance to North House, "I hope you feel better tomorrow."

"Yes, I hope so too. Thank you for the lift home, which really was kind of you."

"Not at all. If you aren't feeling well tomorrow, do let Mrs McGee know."

"Oh, yes, I will, but I'm sure I'll be fine. Actually, I'm feeling on top of the world right now."

He'd smiled at that. "Me too," he said quietly. "I'll see you on the ward. It's Monday next week, isn't it?"

"Yes, and Tuesday, we have two days ward duty."

"That's right. Well, I'll see you then. Sweet dreams."

"Thanks, Nick," she said, knowing full well she'd be dreaming of him.

And then he was gone. She let herself into North House and peered from the doorway as he made his way down the path to his home. Her heart was busting. The attraction she'd felt had moved up a gear – she was now one hundred percent in love with him.

An hour later, having carefully applied her makeup, she selected a white shirt and an edgy blue waistcoat that complemented her fitted jeans and boots. She opened her wardrobe door and stared at herself in the full-length mirror on the inside, pleased with the way she looked. She prayed Nick would too. She was sure to bump into him somewhere in the hospital, and he most probably would be looking out for her. She hoped so. With a mouthful of toothpaste, she called 'come in' to whoever was knocking on the door.

"Morning," Kym said poking her head around the door, "you about ready?"

"Yeah," Louise dried her mouth on a towel, "you okay, you look a bit pale?"

"You're never going to believe this," Kym said as Louise reached on her desk for some text books and piled them into her rucksack, "I've just heard on the local radio that another girl disappeared last night. Not far from here."

Louise stopped what she was doing. "Oh, God, no."

"Yeah. There are search teams out looking for her now."

"I thought I heard a helicopter earlier."

"It's been going round since first thing. I've been watching out of my window."

"Bloody hell, it's like Vanya all over again. It's getting really scary now."

"I know," Kym screwed her face up, "it's too much of a coincidence for two girls to disappear."

"Yeah, it is. It feels really creepy, doesn't it? I still haven't come to terms with Vanya being missing. I've got the posters in my bag ready to take to Mr Duffield. I was going to ask if you'd come with me sometime today to take them to him. I went on my own last time to ask, but he freaked me out a bit. I find him weird."

"No probs, I'll come. He doesn't bother me, even though he is odd looking."

"Isn't he just? Anyway, if we can get them up in the patients' canteen and at the bus stops, you never know, someone might come forward."

"What about the rest of the hospital, like the outpatients department?"

"I wanted to put one there, but Duffield said no."

"Why?"

"Said it might worry the visiting patients."

"Oh, for God's sake, it's been all over the news anyway."

"Yeah, I know. But that's what he said."

"Okay. Not much we can do about it. We'll go after school, shall we? Come on, let's get to breakfast and see if we can find out any more about this missing girl."

"Hang on, before we do," Louise checked her watch, "sit down a sec. We've got a couple of minutes."

"Is everything okay?" Kym took a seat at the desk chair and swivelled it round to face Louise who sat on the bed.

"Yeah, everything's fine. Well, more than fine actually."

Kym peered into her eyes, "Is it something to do with last night?"

"Yep," Louise grinned, bursting to tell someone. "Nick Feeney brought me back, well, to his house, and . . . we had sex."

Kym's mouth dropped open. "No!" she stuttered in disbelief, "I can't believe it. He's married."

"Not any more. Well, technically he is, but he's separated. I told him I wouldn't say a word as he could lose his job, but I'm beside myself and I know you won't say anything. It was fantastic between us."

Kym frowned, "I hope he wasn't just using you for a quickie, you know, if he's separated, maybe he just . . ."

"No way was it just a quickie," Louise said, "the way he kissed and caressed me, well, I've been awake half the night thinking about him."

"God, Louise, you need to be careful. You could end up being thrown off the course. And he could lose his job. He's our tutor."

"Nobody's going to find out."

"Still, it shouldn't be happening. Was it just a one-off?"

"God, I hope not. I really care for him and I think he feels the same, although he is a bit hesitant about us."

"I bet he is. So what happens now?"

"I honestly don't know. But I do know that I want more. He's amazing, Kym. Just amazing!"

A tap on the door stopped them saying any more.

"It's me Louise," Zoe called, "are you coming to breakfast?"

Louise opened the door. "Kym's here. We were just coming." She turned to pick up her rucksack. "I must say I'm starving," she winked at Kym as she got up from the chair.

Louise, Kym and Zoe collected their breakfasts from the serving hatch and took seats in the dining room at one of the large dining tables next to Marie and Helen from their intake who looked almost finished. Simon followed behind, "Room for a small one?" he said, plonking himself down at the table.

"No Guy?" Louise asked, reaching to the middle of the table for utensils.

"He's on the phone getting grief from someone. Said to go ahead."

"Who's giving him grief at this time of the morning, I wonder?" Kym asked.

"Probably his old man. I think it's a daily occurrence to get him back to medical school."

"Oh dear, that must be hard."

"Yeah. Hey, changing the subject, I've just walked up with Rosanna Smith from South House. Her boyfriend's in the police and he says there's a girl gone missing last night, just down the road from here."

"Yeah," Louise buttered a slice of toast, "Kym just said. It's all getting scary now. I wonder if they'll tell us more when we get to school today?"

Simon nodded to a table in the corner where Mr Duffield was sitting with Mr McGee. "You could go over and ask those two if they know anything? I'd go myself but Mr Duffield doesn't like male nurses."

"That's a good idea," Zoe urged, "I can't help wondering if this is all linked to Vanya."

"It must be," Simon took a drink of his orange juice, "it's too much of a coincidence two young girls disappearing without a trace."

"How do you know this one's young?" Zoe asked.

"I don't. I'm just guessing. You don't hear of older women being abducted, do you? It's always the young ones."

"Hey," Louise reached in her bag, "I've just thought. I could go over and give Mr Duffield the posters I've done about Vanya," she turned to Kym, "save us going later."

"Good idea," Kym said.

"I'll go over then. Don't go to school without me though, will you?"

"No, we'll wait."

Louise stopped at the table Mr Duffield was sitting at with Mr McGee. "Sorry to disturb you both."

"Not at all, Nurse Allard, what can we do for you?" Mr Duffield gave one of his sly smiles. She inwardly shuddered; she really didn't like the man.

"I've done the posters," she said and handed four to him.

He glanced at the top one. "These are really good," he passed one to Mr McGee. "Nurse Allard thought it might jog someone's memory if we put a poster up about the missing nurse. I've suggested putting them in the patients' canteen and at the bus stops."

"It's a good poster," Mr McGee agreed.

"Thank you. Mrs Beaumont had a photo of Vanya from the school records and photocopied it. I just wrote the text."

"I think it's an excellent idea," Mr McGee smiled, displaying a missing tooth. "I could put them up at the bus stops if you'd like. Knock a small nail in to hold them in place."

"That'd be great. I did wonder how I was going to do it. I wasn't sure exactly how long Sellotape would stick for, once it started raining."

"I'll see this one is put up in the patients' canteen," Mr Duffield said.

"Great. There's a fourth one I did just in case, but I'm not sure what to do with that."

"How about next to the public telephone?"

"Oh, yes, that's a good idea."

"Right, leave them with me. And Mr McGee will do the others."

"Brilliant." She hesitated not sure whether to ask about the so-called missing girl. But she could feel the others' eyes boring into her back.

"Was there anything else?" Mr Duffield peered through his glasses.

"Yes . . . erm . . . we've been hearing that a girl has gone missing from near here, we just wondered if you knew anything."

"I'm afraid I don't. I only know the same as you, which was on the radio. If there is anything to tell us, no doubt Inspector Porteous will pay us a visit. I'd imagine he may be involved with searching for this other missing girl. But if we hear anything official, then we'd do updates for everyone as we did before. But for now, we just carry on as normal, as hard as that might be for those of you that were close to Nurse Mann."

"Yes, we are finding it difficult. Anyway, thank you for sorting the posters out."

"My pleasure. We all need to do our bit. Now," Mr Duffield stood up, "if you'll excuse me."

"Oh, yes, sorry for keeping you. I must dash off myself. We're due in school."

Mr McGee stood too. "If there was anything to update you on, Mrs McGee would call a meeting for the nurses, I'm sure."

"Thank you," Louise made her way back to the others at the table.

"Anything?" Simon asked.

"Nothing. They know as much as we do. Mr McGee said if there was anything to report, Mrs McGee would speak to us like before."

Simon screwed his face up, "On that joyful note, we better be making a move."

As they gathered together their bags, Simon asked Kym, "How did it go with your mum last night?"

"What's the matter with your mother?" Zoe chipped in.

While Louise half listened to Kym explaining about her mother's upcoming surgery, her eyes were frantically searching the adjacent coffee lounge for Nick. He'd said at the retirement party, he was going to the ward early to catch one of the night staff before she went off duty. She desperately needed to see him. A thought struck her. Maybe she could pop to the ward later, on the pretence of putting a request in the off duty request book which hung in the office. It was her mum's birthday the following month so she could legitimately request it as a day off. It couldn't do any harm and if she timed it right, she'd see him. He often worked until about five.

As she followed the others out of the dining room and headed towards the school of nursing, her senses seemed heightened somehow, as if she wanted to run, jump, scream, or do something. Anything than to sit through a boring academic lesson with Mrs Beaumont revisiting fractures and how to restore and maintain alignment of bone with traction in the afternoon.

All she wanted was to see Nick, to reassure herself it was real between the two of them. And to make love again, of course. Her heart raced at the very thought.

35.

Kym

The day in school had dragged. Kym's mind wasn't on academic work. She tried to concentrate but felt they'd exhausted fractured bones to death. Thankfully, after Friday, they only had two days on the ward placement the following week, three days in school, and then it was their final weekend off. After that, they were full-time on the wards for eight weeks.

Much as she'd have liked to get Louise on her own to talk further about the bombshell that she'd dropped that morning, there hadn't been an opportunity to. There always seemed to be someone else around. It was evident to her if nobody else, that Louise was on a complete high. She'd got it bad, that was for sure. Most of the lesson she'd spent gazing out of the window in a dreamy state. Even Mrs Beaumont had pulled her up for her lack of attention – if only she knew. Although Kym acknowledged to herself it wasn't anything to do with her, she wished Louise hadn't told her. She was dreading coming into contact with Nick Feeney again, knowing about their intimacy.

She'd wanted to speak to Guy at lunch also, and she had tried, but everyone was around so it was hard to. It was kind of him to take her all the way to Cleethorpes, meet her parents and then drive back to Harlow Wood.

It felt to her that he'd gone over and above friendship and she'd have liked to thank him again. Last night she'd been too emotional to mutter anything much, particularly after their hug.

Today, he seemed his usual cheerful self, seemingly his father had 'been on his case' that morning he'd told them at coffee break. It appeared he had an associate who was a senior principle at Leeds medical school and he could pull a few strings to get him in. Kym wondered if Guy was considering it, as it was becoming obvious to them all that he was exceptionally bright and could easily become a doctor, and possibly more in the future. But she couldn't ask him anything as Zoe was stuck to him like a lovesick limpet, not allowing anyone near them. And he didn't seem adverse to it. It appeared to Kym, he lapped it up.

As Mrs Beaumont called an end to the lessons for the day, her, Louise and Zoe exited the classroom together, with Simon and Guy following behind.

"Anyone for the Rushley, tonight?" Guy asked as they made their way along the corridor.

Simon playfully put his hand up, "I'm in."

"Me too," Zoe joined in, "I reckon we could all do with a drink to take our minds off this second girl going missing. This place is really starting to freak me out."

"Yeah," Simon said, "funny nobody knows anything."

"I don't think anyone genuinely does," Kym said, holding the door for them all to walk through to the outside gardens, "like Mr Duffield said to Louise, the police will only inform them and us if there's something to tell."

The door closed behind them and they made their way through the gardens with a few mobile patients and their relatives sitting on the benches. "Anyway," Kym said, "I'll pass on the Rushley tonight. I need to do some studying for Friday's exam."

"Me too," Louise said, turning her head towards the newer part of the hospital. It was evident to Kym that Louise had been scanning the rest areas of the hospital at breaks and lunchtime for Nick Feeney, but to no avail. He didn't appear to be around.

As they continued through the gardens towards the main hospital, Lloyd was pruning a privet bush right next to their pathway. It always seemed to Kym as though he was waiting for them to finish school each afternoon, although he hadn't been around quite so much lately.

"Hiya mate," Guy greeted him, "where've you been hiding? It's ages since we've seen you in the Rushley."

"I was signed off work. Bad chest infection."

"You're okay now?"

"Yeah, getting back into it." He gave a grin, "I've got to, in order to make myself available for the nightdress and pyjama party next week."

"Oh, yeah, I'd forgotten about it. It's Thursday, isn't it?"

"Yep. Are you girls coming?" Lloyd looked expectantly at her, Louise and Zoe, "it's for a good cause. It's a fund raiser for a girl in Mansfield to get some equipment to assist her mobility."

"Yes, I was reading about it," Kym said, "it's really sad for the little girl. I'm hoping to be there."

"Yep, me too," Louise added, "but just in normal clothes, I might put my dressing gown over them though, but that's about it."

Simon rolled his eyes and grinned at Lloyd, "You always get one. Zoe won't need asking though, she's always up for a good night."

Zoe nudged him in the arm, "Cheeky."

"Might see you before then, Lloyd, at the Rushley," Guy said, "we'll be there tonight if you're up for it?"

"Better not as I'm just finishing my medication. But I'll be done by the party next week, so I'll be able to have a good drink. They have a bar and everything."

"Sounds good," Guy nodded, "see you then."

They carried on walking towards the hospital. "He still doesn't look that well, does he?" Kym kept her voice low.

"Nah, he doesn't, he looks anaemic to me," Guy said. "Maybe he should have taken longer off."

"Yeah," Simon interjected, "but he hasn't got anyone at home to look after him. He lives with his brother and he'll be out at work all day. Besides that, he lives and breathes Harlow Wood, so he wouldn't want to be off a day longer than he had to."

As they walked into the hospital, Louise said she needed to pop to the ward to make an off duty request which Kym knew was code for going to see Nick Feeney. The rest of them made their way towards the hospital exit and the pathway to North House. Zoe gave a groan at Matron who was making her way down the path towards them. "Oh God, look who's coming. I hope nobody has been leaving the front door of North House open," she sniggered.

Mrs McGee approached them all with a fierce look on her face. They all stopped.

"Nurse Sullivan," she scowled at Kym, "a male visitor has turned up at reception asking for you. I've taken him in the patients' canteen and told him to stay there until I found you."

"A visitor?" Kym frowned.

"Yes. Say's his name is Tony."

Kym widened her eyes, "Tony?"

"That's what he said he was called," Mrs McGee said firmly.

"Thank you. I have no idea why he's come here. I didn't even realise he knew where Harlow Wood was."

"Well, clearly he does. And may I remind you that we don't encourage boyfriends here, so if you could explain that to him before you send him on his way it would be helpful. And do not for one minute think you'll be entertaining him in the nurses' home."

"No, I wouldn't."

"I'm pleased to hear it," she said and turned away in the direction of South House, tottering along in black patient shoes with a block heel.

Simon laughed, "You do realise she'll have you labelled as a fallen woman entertaining a man here at Harlow Wood."

"I know. What's she like?"

"She obviously can't remember what it's like to be young," Zoe sneered.

"She probably never has been," Simon laughed, "bet she's always looked like that."

"I better go," Kym said, turning back towards the hospital. She glanced at Guy. Almost as if she had to apologise, which was stupid. She wasn't going out with him. Yes, he'd been kind taking her home to see her mum and they had shared a hug, but no more than that. And Zoe had been all over him that day, so much so she'd barely spoken to him. Yet his brown normally vibrant eyes, looked sad. But the moment was lost by Zoe nudging him and asking what time they were off to the Rushley.

Kym made her way along the corridor towards the patients' canteen. What on earth had possessed Tony to come to Harlow Wood?

Tony was sitting at a table by the window of the canteen when she walked through the door. Her heart no longer leapt like it used to at the sight of him. As she walked towards him, she could see he'd bought himself a can of Cola and was munching away on a Mars Bar.

"Hi," he stood up and she felt obliged to go into his open arms for a hug.

"What are you doing here?" she asked, breaking away and taking the seat opposite him.

"I wanted to see you before I sailed. Do you want a drink?" he nodded towards the counter.

"No, I'm fine. I didn't know you even knew where Harlow Wood was."

"I didn't. Tom, one of my mates, lives in Nottingham, he told me. I'm stopping at his tonight and then we're leaving tomorrow for Portsmouth. We sail for Gibraltar on Saturday."

"So, why have you come here?" she frowned.

"Why do you think?" His eyes she'd once found so attractive stared intently at her. "You won't see me in Cleethorpes, which I'm guessing is down to your mother."

"Don't start about my mother."

"Why not? She's never liked me. I know she puts the boot in."

"Not right now, she doesn't. She's not well . . ." Kym swallowed, it hurt explaining about her mum, especially as he didn't like her. "She's going for surgery next week."

"What's up with her?" he nonchalantly put the last bite of the Mars Bar into his mouth and screwed up the wrapper.

"It doesn't matter. What does matter right now is, she's the focus of my attention. So, you're right, I didn't want to see you in Cleethorpes, I wanted to spend some time with her."

"Okay, I get that. But what about us, all the plans we made? Are they over now? Is that it?"

"I think it is, yeah. Look," she sighed, "I always knew it was never going to be easy with our careers, but you've hurt me. I hate the thought of you going with someone else."

"I haven't." Irritation crept into his voice, "I keep telling you that."

She blew a breath out, it was as tiresome to her as it was to him. "I know you do. But the trouble is, I don't believe you."

"Oh, for fuck's sake, I told you what that was. I've never been with anyone. I can't keep going over this time and time again. It was a prank. They've done it tons of times to matelots going on leave. A few hold you down while one of them does it."

"It's disgusting. And however many times you tell me, I'm not convinced. It sounds to me like something you lot think is a great excuse if you have been with someone. Tell the girlfriend that, she'll believe it."

"I'm telling you the truth." He reached for her hand, "I'm not giving up, Kym. I want us to be together."

Her insides clenched. Tony wasn't what she wanted. She knew that deep down. It wasn't just that he'd been unfaithful, it was more she'd changed. She didn't want him any longer – it was like the end of an era. They had been happy and in love, but not anymore. It was time to move on now and go their separate ways. Sad as it was, it was over between them. And even though she didn't want him, tears pricked her eyes at the finality of it all.

"What?" he said softly, "Tell me."

Out of the corner of her eye, she became aware of Guy coming through the door into the canteen. He must have come on purpose. Simon was lagging behind as he made his way to their table. She sniffed her tears away.

"You okay, Kym?" Guy asked.

Tony turned his head. "We're having a private conversation here if you don't mind."

"Yep, I can see that. I'm just checking she's alright, mate."

"Well, she is, so why don't you fuck . . . "

"Stop it," Kym said firmly, "I'm fine Guy, leave us would you."

Tony moved his eyes to look up at Guy standing beside them, and then back at her. "Oh, I get it," he shook his head from side to side, "all this crap about what I've done. Now I see exactly why I've been bombed out."

"It's not like that."

Tony quickly stood up and pushed his chair out with his leg. And totally surprising them all, he swung his arm back and thumped Guy in the face with so much force, he tumbled backwards, crashing into a table behind him and ending up on the floor. A woman screamed. Simon pushed his arm against Tony's chest, stopping him from doing anything else as Guy scrambled to his feet.

Tony's eyes burned with anger as he glared at her. He pushed Simon's arm away, and picked up his jacket from the back of the chair. Without a word, he headed for the door.

Guy had eased himself onto a chair, and reached for a serviette from the dispenser on the table to catch the blood dripping from his nose.

Kym rushed over. "Are you okay? I'm so sorry."

"Not half as sorry as me," Guy dabbed his nose, "I reckon he's broken it."

"Let me look," she eased the serviette away. "I don't think so. It looks the same shape. I can't believe he did that."

"Me neither. Guess he didn't like me?"

She couldn't help but grin, "No, I don't think he did."

"Is it over between you?" his uncertain eyes stared directly into hers which were equally so. Something had shifted between them.

"Yep," she nodded, "it pretty much looks like it."

Had the uncertainty turned to relief? Dare she believe he was genuinely interested in her? He'd finished with his own girlfriend, but there was still Zoe. Something was going on between the two of them, she was sure of it.

Guy's eyes moved toward the canteen door opening. She followed his gaze. Mr Duffield made his way towards them with a thunderous expression. A member of staff must have rushed to his office to tell him about the altercation.

"Get yourself cleaned up, Mr Logan, and then to my office," he snapped.

36.

He'd had a major meltdown since the previous night when he'd dumped the young girl's body in the woods, his only slight comfort being that when she was eventually found, there wouldn't be anything to link her to him. He'd worn gloves the whole time, disposed of the blanket and claw hammer and deep-cleaned his car. Nevertheless, it had been a stupid mistake to dump her, but he hadn't been thinking straight of late. He'd read that cancer rapidly spreads though the body via the lymph nodes and could often cause metastases in the brain, which he suspected was most probably happening to him. That and nausea which was something new. He hoped the horrible sick feeling was more to do with the drop in adrenaline levels, rather than the cancer, but he suspected it was the latter.

That morning at breakfast, he'd just about managed to drink a cup of tea which was more to do with keeping up appearances than wanting it. He remembered a previous time when he'd experienced sudden and severe sickness. It was the night he'd killed Angela. He hadn't meant to, it had been a terrible accident. He'd loved her, she was everything to him. But she'd taken up with Ricky Hurst who'd become a regular at the house, and how he'd hated him. He just didn't get why Angela chose him to be her boyfriend. Not when he didn't have a single thing going for him. He was short, stocky, lived on cans of beer and, as far as he could see, his pleasure in life, apart from taking Angela to the pub or occasionally the cinema, was sitting in front of the television. Yet Angela seemed to adore him. From his peephole upstairs, he watched as she lay naked underneath Ricky, moaning and groaning as if she enjoyed him pawing over her. He'd be riled into a frenzy of hatred watching him slobbering over her breasts and sucking hard on her nipples. Surely she was pretending to enjoy it? And even worse was when he went down on her. She screamed, Ricky, Ricky, Ricky over and over again and he hated hearing her call his name. He couldn't stop watching them, though, night after night. It was almost an addiction. Angela was so beautiful naked, her figure was all woman, but nothing incensed him more than Ricky's dirty bloody manual worker's hands, groping her most intimate places. He had to turn away rather than watch his fat arse moving about as he thrust in and out of her. As far as he was concerned, she must have been faking enjoyment just to please him. Sex was for animals after all.

Of late, he hadn't been able to get Angela out of his mind. Whether that was because of his own imminent demise, or that killing her was the biggest mistake of his life, he didn't know. All he knew was that he'd slipped up big time the previous night with the girl he'd picked up, and maybe it was some sort of divine comeuppance.

A way to bring warmth to his cold body, which he'd deduced must be due to the cancer ravaging it, was thinking about dear sweet Angela. Talk about being in the wrong place at the wrong time. He'd come to the conclusion he had no choice but to get rid of Ricky

Hurst just as he had done his father. Angela deserved better than him. He started to track his movements, which wasn't difficult. Most nights he was in with Angela. He drove round to her house in his Fiat 128 and parked it at the corner of the street near a couple of garages.

The night he decided Ricky was going to die, he'd taken a hacksaw, crawled underneath the car and nicked one of the brake pipes, which would allow a discharge of the brake fluid slowly on his journey home that night. He usually travelled home work evenings which took about twenty-two minutes on several long and winding country roads. His heart rate quickened and gave him a feeling of elation as he purposely sabotaged the car. With a bit of luck, during Ricky's drive home that evening, the brakes would fail and he'd be history. Then Angela would be all his again.

That fateful night was etched on his brain. After tampering with the brake pipe, he nipped to the local pub, the White Heart and stayed until last orders. As he made his way home along the rows of terraced houses, the indoor lights hidden behind closed curtains, he felt euphoric. Soon Ricky would be gone, then things would go back to normal with Angela. Yes, she'd be upset, but he'd be her shoulder to cry on. He'd make himself indispensable to her.

He arrived home just after eleven and hung his coat up on the hall stand. He guessed they'd hear that night sometime about Ricky's demise, if not then, certainly in the morning. He walked into the lounge expecting to find his brother watching TV, but sitting directly opposite on the sofa, was Ricky. He cursed under his breath, usually he'd have headed off by now, or he might be in bed with Angela. The adjacent chair was vacant, so she didn't appear to be there.

"Hi," he stood in the doorway, "what you watching?"

"Midnight Cowboy with Jon Voight. It's pretty good. It's not been on long if you want to watch it."

"No, I'm fine. I'll go to bed. Where's Angela?" he injected a casual tone in his voice.

"She got a phone call. Her aunt . . . think it's her late mother's sister, has been rushed into hospital with a suspected heart attack."

"Oh, God, how awful," his heart hammered against his ribs, "how's she got to hospital?"

"In my car. I offered to drive her, but she didn't know how long she'd be. I told her I'd stay over tonight and wait till she gets back, just in case . . . you know, it might not be good news."

"Yeah, sounds sensible. Let's hope she's okay."

He closed the door behind himself, the beat of his heart hammering inside his head.

Please God, not Angela. He couldn't lose his dear Angela . . . he just couldn't.

In his loft bedroom that fateful night he waited, and sure enough, the police had arrived in the early hours and informed them that Angela had been killed in a road traffic accident. She'd lost control of the car on a bend and crashed full on into an oncoming vehicle. It was the first time in his life he'd known emotional pain. He'd cared for her so much as a dear friend. He loved the way she looked, how she smiled, how she carried herself, her kindness, her laugh, everything about her. The pain was so great, he wondered how he was going to go on. And there was the worry that he could be found out, although initially he wasn't even bothered about that. A life-time in jail was no worse than losing Angela.

The driver she'd hit head-on, survived but with life-changing injuries. He thought the car would be a write-off, therefore unlikely that the accident investigative team would be able to tell the brakes had been tampered with, but nevertheless, it had been an anxious time.

The day of the funeral, he'd been distraught but had to moderate it. He'd sat with his brother in the church for the service and had to stand at the graveside as they lowered her coffin into the ground. Her grieving relatives had held each other upright, crying silently. Ricky had howled while he, beside his brother kept a dignified silence even though he was screaming inside.

"What happens now?" his brother asked, "Where are we going to live?"

They had no choice but to find somewhere else to reside. They'd viewed a small flat which was all they could afford. It was basic but adequate. However, it wasn't long before the cops started sniffing round about the brake pipe. He'd managed to evade their questions initially, but he felt it was just a question of time. He realised he needed to move away, sooner rather than later. And because of the police inquiries, he had to develop a new identity, not only for himself, but for his brother too. There was no question of him staying behind. Even though he worked and mixed with men and women, his brother was largely dependent on him. It didn't take much to deduce their father's behaviour had caused it. He wasn't confident to go out in the world and maybe take a wife. That was never going to happen.

Six months after losing Angela, he'd found a beautiful young girl and strangled the life out of her. But unlike before when he'd killed his father, and then inadvertently killed Angela, this was for a different reason. It was the lure of beauty that attracted him. He wanted to see the young woman naked, to plait their hair, just as he had done with Angela, and then stroke their feminine white skin. He hadn't ever done that with Angela, he'd been content to watch from his peephole at her beauty, but killing young girls gave him the opportunity. And if he tried hard enough with each one, he could pretend it was his darling's flesh he was caressing.

Both he and his brother flitted around the country, undertaking a series of jobs using their new pseudonym. He'd even undertaken training. It was a revelation to discover that as well as being able to follow instruction, he was fairly bright. His brother never asked about the actual killings, therefore he hadn't volunteered any information. But he knew. He had to. He was just content to be led. And his brother had come up trumps caring for him when he came home from hospital having undergone a major, life-changing operation. For that he was grateful and he vowed he'd repay that kindness by always taking care of him.

Eventually, he'd settled on a post at Harlow Wood. He'd had to be creative with previous work experiences and had paid for forged references in his false name.

And for a while, he stopped killing. But the urge raised its head eventually – it always did.

A bout of coughing overcame him. He placed a handkerchief over his mouth to catch the spots of blood. After a sip of water, he closed the book he supposedly reading and stood up. Next week it was the nightdress and pyjama charity event at Harlow Wood. He was ready. That was when he would strike again. One more kill. He was weaker now so it would be the last. And it was going to be Louise, the girl who once looked painfully sad, but now seemed to have a spring in her step.

Not for much longer though.

37.

Kym

Kym had to stop looking at herself in the full-length mirror. She couldn't change again, it was only a nightdress and pyjama party after all. She unlocked her door, and directly opposite, Zoe was leant against the wall in Louise's room, while Louise had her wardrobe door open and she was looking at herself in the mirror.

"Gosh, you two look amazing," Kym said, genuinely meaning it. Unlike her, they'd made much more of an effort.

Zoe was dressed in a blue and white striped nightshirt which, unless she was mistaken, had been altered in length – she was fairly certain they didn't come that short. Not that she'd ever bought a nightshirt, but she knew they were made to cover legs. Louise was in pretty, pale blue pyjamas with white piping around the short sleeves and small lapel.

"I thought you said the other day you weren't wearing pyjamas?" Kym frowned at Louise.

"Who did I say that to?"

"Lloyd, when we were coming through the gardens after school last week. You said the most you'd be doing is putting on a dressing gown over your clothes."

"Oh, yes, I did say that," Louise rolled her eyes, "maybe I wasn't so keen then, but I saw this pair when I went home at the weekend and couldn't resist them. They were cheap from C&A."

"They are pretty and the blue really suits you. Your nightshirt is a nice colour too, Zoe. Is it new, too?"

"Yeah it is. The stuff I sleep in isn't suitable, it's old and bobbly."

Kym looked down at her pink polka dot pyjamas, "I feel a bit scruffy next to you both, I haven't bought anything new."

"Well, they look new enough," Louise said, "and that colour suits you too."

"Thank you. In fairness, they aren't that old, and my dressing gown was new to come here. They're not too sheer are they?" Kym asked.

"Don't be daft. It's a nightdress and pyjama party, the stuff will be light. You've got a crop top on underneath haven't you?"

"God, yeah, and my knickers."

"Well then, what are you worrying about?"

"I dunno, really. I can't say I've ever been to a nightdress and pyjama party before. It's hard to know the erm . . . protocol, if that's the right word."

"Who cares," Zoe smirked, "it'll be a laugh. The main thing is to enjoy ourselves, I know I will."

"Have you got a dressing gown, Zoe?" Louise asked.

"No. I'm going like this."

"Well, I'm wearing mine," Louise reached to the back of the door for her silky cream one. She put it on and made a bow around her waist with the tie.

"What about slippers?" Kym said, her eyes drawn to Zoe's crimson toenails peeping out of her fluffy-heeled mules which looked expensive.

Louise looked down at her feet encased in towelling flip-flop mules. "It's not raining so we'll be okay walking down the footpath to the hospital." She turned to Zoe, "You're lucky, you've got a heel, mine are flat and I hate being so short. Are yours new?"

"Yeah, everything is I'm wearing. You don't know who is going to turn up at a nightdress and pyjama party," Zoe winked.

Kym looked down at her fluffy, grey slippers. They'd have to do. It was all she had.

As Louise locked her door, Kym locked hers. The three of them made their way towards the stairs. "Hey," Louise said, "this is going to sound really weird. Can you believe a pair of my knickers have gone missing?"

A memory flashed in Kym's head causing a chill to run down her spine. A pair of Vanya's knickers had gone missing prior to her disappearance. But they'd both decided at the time she'd left them in the bathroom or something. She'd completely forgotten to ask Vanya if she got them back and until now, hadn't thought any more about it.

Zoe screwed her face up. "How can you lose a pair of knickers? You haven't been fraternising with a male in his room and left them there, have you? You'll have Demis Roussos after you," she playfully warned.

"God, no," Louise shook her head, "nothing like that."

Zoe wouldn't understand the irony of her remark. Louise had been fraternising, as she put it, but it was unlikely she'd left Nick Feeney's house without her knickers.

Kym clicked their names to *OUT* on the board. "How do you know there's a pair missing?" she asked, a nervousness running through her as they exited North House. What if there was a connection to Vanya's disappearance? Surely not? It didn't bear thinking about.

"Because I always have matching and I've lost a pair to my pink set I wore two days ago. I've searched everywhere in my room, and the bathrooms, but they've gone."

"You've got the bra though?" Zoe asked as they went cautiously down the footpath in their slippers.

"Yes, that's what's so odd. Even though I rinse them out and dry them on my radiator, I've still been taking them home to wash properly, and I always pair them up in my laundry bag. I was putting in yesterday's when I noticed just the pink bra on the radiator and no knickers."

Kym had an urge to say something as they made their way into the hospital and along the corridor that would take them to the recreational hall. But she had to stop herself. It would freak Louise out if she did – just like it was currently doing to her, right now. Should she have said anything to Inspector Porteous when she was interviewed after Vanya had gone missing? She inwardly cursed herself. It wasn't something she'd even considered was relevant, she'd completely forgotten about it. Now though, she was full of regret. It was too much of a coincidence. There must be some sort of a connection. Surely two student nurses couldn't both lose their knickers from the nurses' home.

The hall that the party was to be held in was attached to the main hospital, but towards the back of the old part. On a Sunday morning, the hall was utilised by a local vicar who conducted a church service each week. Patients could be taken in wheelchairs from their wards and those bed-bound on traction that wanted to attend, could be wheeled down on their beds by the porters. It was also used as a teaching area for the children on Ward 3 that were in the hospital long-term. Teachers would attend for part of the day to ensure they were receiving some form of education.

A huge red brick wall adjacent to the hall separated it from an outside area which was used for long-term in-patients at Harlow Wood to retrain. It was an occupational therapy outside area Kym recalled Mr Duffield saying on their first day when he'd shown them around. There were old cars allowing them to work on engines, an area set aside for bricklaying, and even a double-decker bus which Louise wasn't sure if the patients got to drive. Mr Duffield had said it was an initiative setup while patients were undergoing pool therapy and physiotherapy, with a view to taking up another occupation should their injuries be such they couldn't go back to their previous jobs.

As Kym walked alongside Louise and Zoe into the hall, Louise's missing knickers were at the forefront of her mind. Did she need to speak to someone or was she being silly? Maybe if she got an opportunity, she could speak to Simon and Guy. The last thing she wanted to do was say something to Louise and have her worrying over nothing.

The loud thumping music as they made their way through the entrance to the hall, distracted Kym temporarily. Lloyd greeted them. He was sitting on a chair with a makeshift small table, taking the entrance fees.

"May I say how lovely you ladies are looking tonight," he grinned, reaching out his hand for the pound notes each of them gave him.

"I like the hat," Zoe laughed at his floppy old-fashioned striped hat with a pompom dangling from it. He looked like something from a Dickens' novel.

"That's good then," Lloyd grinned, "seemingly there's a prize for the best dressed, so I thought I'd make an effort."

"Well, you've certainly done that," Kym said, "and it does suit you. Good luck."

"Thank you. Maybe I'll see you girls for a dance later?" he raised an eyebrow enquiringly.

"We'll have to see how many we have marked on our cards," Zoe joked as they walked away and into the main hall. Once out of his earshot, she whispered, "As if we'd be dancing with him, he's old enough to be our dad. Make sure we give him a wide berth."

Kym was amazed how the room had been transformed by the committee. There were some banners with the little girl's name on, and a festoon of balloons around the hall. An array of coloured balloons were above the dance area held in place by a net which no doubt would be released at some stage during the night.

The lights in the hall were dimmed, but the DJ's podium gave them plenty of light. It was flashing constantly with a range of colours and displayed the name, *The Church Mice*. There were already plenty of people boogying to the catchy tunes on an area that they'd cordoned off as a dance floor. Sutty was the most noticeable, strutting his stuff with a group of second-year nurses. He was certainly throwing himself into it, Kym smirked to herself. Another one to avoid when it came to dancing.

"Shall we go get a drink?" Zoe pointed to the area with two long trestle tables displaying endless assorted bottles. "Not sure whether we'll get anything alcoholic. Looks like Mr Duffield's manning the bar with Charge Nurse Griffiths from your ward, Kym. I can't see either of them giving us mates rates, either."

"They won't charge much, surely?" Kym frowned, "They'll have got everything from a cash and carry I would have thought. You're right about the alcohol though. Mrs McGee put a notice up in the sitting room saying alcohol wouldn't be served to those of us under eighteen. It's not like at the Rushley, they know our ages here."

"Zoe might be right," Louise said, "they're trying to raise as much as they can so you can bet they'll be hiking the drinks up we buy. Shall we have a kitty, do you think?"

Although Louise asked the question, she only appeared to be half listening. Her eyes were scanning the room and Kym knew exactly who she was looking for. And as far as she could see, Nick Feeney wasn't there. Not yet anyway.

"Nah, we don't need a kitty," Zoe dismissed, "long as us three stick together and just buy for us, it'll be fine. So, beers if I can get them, if not Cola?"

"Yeah," Kym nodded, "fine for me."

"Me too," Louise said, her eyes drifting expectantly towards the door.

Once Zoe was out of the way, Kym asked. "Do you think he'll come tonight?"

"I honestly don't know. This has been the worst week of my life. The two days on the ward were awful with him not being there."

"Has anyone said anything more?"

"Only that his wife's father has had a stroke and they've gone to Peterborough. Nobody knows anything, or if they do, they're not saying."

"They could be a while then, particularly if his father-in-law isn't going to recover."

A pained expression passed across Louise's face, "I understand that. But what I don't get is why he's with his wife. He told me it was over between them both. He even said that she'd met someone else."

Kym shrugged. "I guess he's still a big part of her family. I don't know how long they've been married but she must have needed him to lean on when she got the news."

"But where does it leave me?"

"I don't know. Only you know how serious it was between you both."

"It was serious," Louise snapped, "we had sex."

"Yeah, I know you did and I'm not being awful, but maybe you need to consider he might get back with his wife."

Tears filled Louise's eyes, "Oh God, don't say that. I know it's all new, but it feels like I'm in love with him."

Kym didn't get the chance to reply as Zoe returned clutching three plastic cups of Cola. "Not a bloody chance. Duffield said straight away, *'Don't you even try it'*. But I found out he's only doing an hour at the bar and someone else takes over. We'll have to see if we can sweet talk whoever it is to let us have beer. Be nice if it was Sutty, he's clueless and would sell us it, and at mates rates. He'd be trying to impress one of us. But remember with him, anyone would do, so no need to flatter ourselves if he comes on to any of us."

"Well, he needn't bother trying it on with me," Louise said taking a sip of her drink, "I'm not one bit interested. But you're single now Kym," she said, as if she needed reminding.

"And that's the way I want it to stay. I'm not interested in Sutty, not now or ever."

"Me neither," Zoe pulled a face, "not when there are other eligible males around. If you follow my eyes, you'll see a rather special one that's just walked in."

Kym followed her gaze. Guy and Simon were paying Lloyd to gain entry. Simon had gone to town in pyjamas and a towelling dressing gown, Guy less so. He was wearing jeans but appeared to have made a bit of an effort, teaming them up with a burgundy pyjama jacket which looked too big for him, so he'd most probably borrowed it from someone. Even in the darkness she could see the bruising below Guy's eye had now yellowed. She hated Tony hitting him. And more so as Guy had got a warning from Mr Duffield for the altercation in the patients' canteen and seemingly no amount of pleading on his part would budge Mr Duffield. As far as he was concerned, Guy had been fighting. He'd been given another chance, any more misdemeanours and he was out. Kym was gutted for him. She could no longer deny that she found him attractive. But there was always Zoe lurking around him.

"I'll just nip and say hello," Zoe said, "you two coming?"

Louise shook her head, "I'm okay," she said, with an eye still on the door.

"Me too," Kym said, "See you in a bit."

"Come on, Louise," Kym said, "let's dump the drinks and have a dance. It might take your mind off you know who." She dragged her friend by the hand towards the dance floor. And once they started swinging, swaying and clapping with some of the others to their favourite records, they had a laugh and Louise seemed more relaxed. The DJ was lively and seemed to know just the right songs to play to ensure the dance floor was busy. Kym was enjoying herself, it had been a tense time lately worrying about her mum, and while she still had to undergo the surgery the following week, it felt more positive than it had been so she was determined to have a good time.

"Phew," Kym wiped the sweat off her forehead with the back of her hand, "ready for another drink?" she asked Louise after about twenty minutes dancing.

"Yeah, that'd be nice." Kym linked her arm with hers as they made their way towards the drinks area.

"Oh, no," Louise muttered, "look who's at the bar. Any hope of a beer has gone right out of the window."

Kym followed her gaze. Mrs McGee was stood talking to Mr Duffield. While he'd made a bit of an effort with his smoking type jacket over what looked like trousers and a shirt, Mrs McGee appeared to have made no attempt to join in at all. She was wearing a flowery yellow and white dress and her obligatory cardigan, but that was about it. Maybe the white choker-like scarf around her neck was to enhance the outfit, but to Kym, she looked more like a trussed up chicken.

"What do you reckon," Louise pulled a face, "another Cola, or shall we push the boat out and have an orange juice."

"God, decisions, decisions. I think I'll stick with Cola for now. I don't want to mix my drinks," Kym giggled.

As Louise was about to head to the bar, Simon arrived and flung his arms around each of their shoulders. "Now then. Can I get you two beautiful ladies a Simon Buckingham cocktail?"

"That'd be great," Louise grinned, "but I don't know whether you've noticed, hawk-eye Mrs McGee is keeping a watchful eye on proceedings. She knows we're not eighteen."

"Ah, fear not, I have a cunning plan. Follow me."

They walked with him to the drinks area. "Two Colas for the girls, and . . . go on, then, why don't I join them. Don't want to have too much beer so early." Simon smiled pleasantly at Mr Duffield who gave no acknowledgment whatsoever. It did appear that he wasn't keen on the male nurses, as was rumoured.

Once he'd prepared their drinks with ice, he handed them over. Simon led them towards a corner where some of the girls had left their handbags. He reached for a rucksack which Kym knew was the one he took to school each day.

"Allow me to introduce my bar. He crouched down and took a half bottle of vodka from his bag and, with his back to everyone, he poured a generous amount in all the Cola cups.

"Enjoy," he grinned, "plenty more where that came from. Just let me know when you need topping up."

Kym laughed at his audacity, and even the increasingly morose Louise did too.

"Cheers," he winked as he took a mouthful of his own.

Kym shuddered at the strength of it but continued to sip it. "I see Zoe's keeping Guy busy," she said nodding to the two of them fooling around on the dance floor. They were making an attempt to sort of jive, not that well by the looks of things. But they were laughing and appeared to be enjoying themselves which made Kym's gut clench.

"They're only dancing and having a laugh," Simon said, "I wouldn't worry if I was you."

"Why should I worry?" she said quickly.

"Just saying, that's all. If you think for one minute that Guy's interested in Zoe, I can tell you categorically, he isn't."

"Really?" Kym took a sip of her drink. What did Simon know that she didn't? "How have you worked that out?"

He tapped his nose. "That's for me to know and you to find out. Instead of fishing around me, why don't you ask him yourself?"

"I can't. He's with Zoe."

"He isn't with Zoe. You just think he is. Why don't you ask him to dance? I tell you what. Follow me and I'll get you another one of my specials and it'll give you Dutch courage. Come on."

Following quite a few of Simon's *specials,* the party appeared to be getting better by the minute. Kym had never spent so much time on a dance floor. Louise had joined in, and maybe it was only evident to her, but it was obvious as the evening wore on, her heart wasn't in it. She was pining for Nick Feeney. In her tipsy stupor, Kym remembered another one of her mother's frequent sayings, *It'll only end in tears.* Kym couldn't help but feel that was apt.

As a boppy little number ended, the DJ announced it was time to slow things down, and said to grab a partner for a slow smoochy number. Kym and Louise had said they were going to get some air and were about to leave the floor, when Guy appeared right in front of her. "Can you take pity on me for a dance?"

"Where has your fan club gone to?" Kym said, slurring her words.

"Had a better offer as far as I can see."

"Poor you. Come on, then," she grinned, "my card's empty right now." She clasped his hand and led him to the corner of the dance area as the lights from the DJ's podium dimmed and the hall became much darker. Whether or not it was the music by her favourite artist, or the excess alcohol that Simon had plied her with, she wasn't sure, but as she eased herself into Guy's arms, she felt warm and content and she knew categorically that she was exactly where she wanted to be. She fitted perfectly into his tall frame and inhaled his shower freshness. With him, she felt safe and protected. Something shifted on the dance floor as they rhythmically swayed to the music, his arms became tighter, and there wasn't a gap between them as she nestled into his neck, not wanting the music to end.

When their heads did move apart, spontaneously at the same time, his silky lips met hers. Not in a sloppy, let's have sex sort of way, but in a gentle, I really like you sort of way. And she did like him, much more than she'd realised or had previously acknowledged to herself. She wanted him, and it was clear he felt the same way. It seemed almost to her that it was just the two of them on the dance floor and nobody else.

The music stopped, and was replaced by a quick, jerky song. The DJ's podium lights came alive as he announced, "Now it's time for a few more up-beat songs folks, and then we'll slow it down again."

Guy took her hand and she was content to let him lead her away from the hall. As they made their way along the corridor, he wrapped his arm around her and she rested her head on his shoulder. All thoughts of anyone but the two of them went out of her mind. She'd had too much to drink, she knew that by how light-headed she felt, but maybe some of that was down to Guy. Tonight, as far as she was concerned, had been a long time coming. She hoped he felt the same. But whatever, she was resolute, there'd be no regrets. She wanted him more than ever.

As they arrived at the nurses' home entrance, instead of heading upstairs to her own room, she was determined to follow him into his.

38.

Louise

Louise had come to the conclusion early on that Nick Feeney wasn't coming. All the time she'd spent getting ready had been wasted. Her insides had been in a turmoil since Monday. After her and Nick made love on the Thursday evening following the retirement party, she hadn't seen him. The weekend at home had dragged endlessly; the only thing keeping her going was that she'd legitimately see him on the following week on her ward placement. But as soon as she'd arrived and gone in the office to report, she knew something was wrong. He was nowhere to be seen. Carol Mason, the senior nurse in Nick's absence, was sitting where he usually did behind the desk.

Louise daren't ask where Nick was. She had to wait until she was making beds with Jackie to casually enquire. And when Jackie explained about his father-in-law having a stroke and him taking off to Peterborough with his wife, Louise had to nip to the toilet to compose herself as she'd felt physically sick. Please no, she'd inwardly screamed in the confines of the toilet, don't let them be back together. The only thing keeping her going all week was telling herself that he maybe was just supporting her and their marriage was definitely over. It had to be. She loved him.

The nightdress and pyjama party had been purgatory. If only Nick had been there. She'd tried her best to join in, but once the DJ put a slow dance on, it had upset her more. Watching the couples on the dance floor together, made her even more distressed. She knew she wouldn't be able to go public with Nick, not yet, but she was prepared to put up with anything just to be with him.

She spotted Kym dancing with Guy. At least they looked like they finally were together. It was obvious to everyone that was meant to be – everyone that is, other than Kym. But Guy had waited patiently for her to split with Tony, and now she had, it didn't look like he was ready to let her go anytime soon. Their lovey-dovey display was too much for Louise. She needed to get out of there and back to her room so she could cry into her pillow for Nick. Surely he would be back next week when she was on the ward full-time. She desperately needed to see him.

Before the dance ended, she crept out of the hall. Her intention had been to head for the corridor to walk through back to the nurses' home.

"Hello." A voice startled her.

Louise turned sharply. "Gosh, you made me jump."

"Sorry, I didn't mean to. Aren't you enjoying the party, you look like you're leaving?"

"It's very good, but I'm a bit tired and calling it a night."

"Right. I wonder, before you do, could you help me? I'm on my way to get a few extra beers and mixers from the boot of my car for the bar. It's just outside. Would you mind giving me a hand? It'll save me doing two trips."

"I could," Louise looked down at her flimsy flat slippers, "but I'm not really dressed for outside."

"Mmm, so I see. I suppose I could go back inside and get someone else . . . but then again, I'm here now. Don't you worry, I'll try and manage."

"It's okay," Louise said, "it isn't raining. I'll help if it's not too many trips back and forth."

"No, not at all. With us both, I think we'll do it in one trip. Thank you. Follow me."

* * *

His lips twitched into a smile as she followed him out to where he'd left his car. An eight foot wall separated them from the hospital, so they couldn't be seen. He'd watched her at the nightdress and pyjama party. The sadness in her eyes was back. It was obvious she was distracted by the way she kept looking around and keeping her gaze on the door.

He knew if he was going to kill her, he had to make his move tonight. Time was running out. That morning, as soon as he got out of bed, things had shifted significantly. It had been the worst day since his diagnosis. He hadn't been able to finish washing before throwing his guts up. And he couldn't keep food down. Pain had begun to radiate down his spine and into his hips. All he seemed to have left was adrenaline for a kill. And that wouldn't last much longer. So, it was now or never.

"I've never been round this part of the hospital," Louise said, "it's a bit eerie."

"Yes, it is, so I don't advise you come round here on your own. Especially not with what has been going on recently. But you're safe with me, I promise."

Nothing was further from the truth. He was familiar with her most intimate smell since he'd stolen her knickers from her room. Pretty pink frilly knickers – he'd been inhaling the gusset all day. His hand touched his pocket – they were still there. He'd put them back in his safe place once he'd killed her.

His heart-rate accelerated. *Stupid, stupid girl.* He licked his lips, dry from having very little to drink all day. Surprisingly, the nausea had subsided and he felt a little of his strength had returned.

Good. He needed all his faculties for the task ahead.

39.

Kym

Once they'd let themselves into the nurses' home, Guy registered them both *IN* on the board. Many were still out. It appeared that Zoe and Louise were still at the party, as they were marked *OUT*.

He led her by the hand towards his room. She didn't hesitate. She knew the rules – if she was caught with him, she'd be off the course, but she didn't care. Alcohol and lust had given her a couldn't-care-less attitude. It was the most natural thing for her to follow him in. No way was she going to do otherwise. Not when she wanted him so much.

He closed the door behind them and pulled her to him. The kissing assault began. She liked his sensual way of kissing. It wasn't rushed, he took his time. It seemed as if both of them wanted to enjoy the new experience rather than rush into anything. As the kissing continued, he gently removed her clothes and she enjoyed him doing so. Again, it was slow, he didn't rush her. Her head was fuzzy from all the vodka, but she knew what she was doing as he eased her down onto the bed. Once she was naked, he lifted the oversized pyjama top off over his head and discarded his trousers and underpants. "You're perfect, Kym," he said pulling her towards him, "I always knew that."

His kisses became more intense with his tongue probing and demanding. And she matched him, loving the newness of him and wanting so much more.

"You're beautiful," he murmured, taking her hand and placing it on his hardness, continuing with his tormenting mouth, gently moving downwards to caress her breasts and to lick and suck on her nipples. Her senses seemed more aroused as she stroked him. Was it the alcohol or him? She didn't care, it was sensational and she loved it.

His tongue moved down to her tummy where he continued the onslaught. "Bring your knees up," he coaxed.

Her legs fell open as his magical mouth moved to lick the insides of her thighs, and his fingers stroked her labia. Her tummy somersaulted and she groaned as his tongue found her most intimate place. Her hands found his hair as he relentlessly licked and sucked, using his fingers to build her pleasure into a frenzy.

"God," she groaned, feeling his hardness pressing against her leg. She wanted him inside her so badly. "God," she said again, gripping his hair, writhing against his face. It was incredible. She couldn't hold back any longer. "Guy," she screamed, as wave after wave gushed down her body, on and on and on. Seconds of ecstasy, but deeply fulfilling.

And still he didn't stop. His mouth carried on back along her tummy, breasts and eventually her own mouth. It was so erotic, tasting herself on him.

"That was lovely," she murmured.

"You're lovely," he said, deepening their kiss. "I loved hearing you shout my name. Do it when you come again."

And she did, minutes later when he'd sheathed, she was lost in the rhythm of him filling her once, then filling her again. Powerful thrusts as he'd moved in and out of her. One minute slow, the next hard and fast. He paused, deep inside her as his dilated pupils studied hers, his lips leaving no part of her face un-kissed. And as his mouth moved down her neck, gently biting just below her ears, it was too much.

He must have sensed she was on the brink again as he urged her, "Come. Come again." He lifted her legs back and changed his angle, thrusting fast, so fast it set her insides on fire and her mind into a spin.

"Oh God," she cried, "that's so . . ."

"Fuck," he said, grunting with every thrust and, like a fountain gushing down, hot pleasure cascaded through her, and she called out his name as she fell down and down. He quickly followed, letting out an almighty roar and calling her name over and over again as he thundered into her.

He gently eased himself away from her and she nestled in, resting her head on his shoulder in the small single bed. The feeling of them both naked thrilled her. She loved the intimacy.

"I knew it would be good between us," he kissed her cheek, "thank God we finally got there."

"It was rather special, wasn't it? Thank you."

"Trust me, the pleasure was all mine," he said, "I've waited a long time for that."

"Have you?" she lifted her head to look into his eyes. "I didn't know that."

"No, I know you didn't. I've been biding my time since the day I first met you."

She grinned and laid back down. Her heart lifted at his words, but Zoe was on her mind. She didn't want to spoil the moment, but she had to know if she was going to be a problem. She had no idea what was really going on between the two of them.

She cleared her throat. "What about you and Zoe?" she asked, almost holding her breath.

It was his turn to move so he could see her. He leant on his elbow, "There is no me and Zoe. She's just a mate on our course . . . what makes you think otherwise?" he frowned.

"Er . . . well, maybe the fact she sticks to you like glue. Nobody else gets a look in."

He grinned, "I'm not sure that's true but if that's the way you see it, from now on I'll make myself only available to you, so we can get to know each other better. How's that sound?"

She kissed him gently. "That sounds wonderful."

He deepened the kiss. "I think we need to start on the getting to know each other better right now."

40.

Kym

It was the morning after the night before. Kym smiled at her reflection in the mirror as she applied her makeup ready for school. What a night it had been with Guy. She still couldn't quite believe it. They were just perfect together. By the time he'd walked her upstairs to her room after their time in bed together, it was almost dawn. He didn't want her to go, but she had to. They'd tiptoed upstairs, doubting Mrs McGee would be on the prowl at that time, but cautious anyway. And once she'd got into her own bed, she'd barely slept.

Excitement made her feel giddy. What a considerate lover he'd been. After the first time, he'd slowed things down and it had been incredibly special between them. He felt it too, she was sure. As she applied a final lashing of mascara and some pink lip-gloss, she was content she looked her best with a brilliant white shirt tucked into her jeans, and a leather tan belt with a large buckle matching her heeled boots. She'd scooped the front part of her hair back in a tie, and used her tongs to curl the loose ends of the surplus, trying to achieve a bit of a wow factor for Guy. The radio was on and she was joining in to a chirpy melody even though she couldn't sing for toffee. She didn't care, she was happy. The news bulletin interrupted her singing. A chap with a monotone voice made reference to Mansfield.

'The body of a young woman was discovered by a dog-walker in Thieves Wood early this morning. We have no more details currently but police are at the scene and we are expecting a statement later today.'

Her excited tummy plummeted. Please God, no. Not Vanya. She quickly stood up, opened her door and tapped on Louise's. No answer. She checked her watch. Louise was cutting it fine for school if she was still in the shower.

She sat back down in her room and left her door ajar so she'd see Louise when she came back. To calm her racing heart, she had to remind herself that there had been a local girl close by that had gone missing. It was awful to want it to be her body they'd discovered, but she couldn't help it. While none of them had any idea what had happened to Vanya, they couldn't contemplate she might be dead. It was too horrible to think about. It was easier to pretend she'd left of her own free will.

Kym heard footsteps approaching. But it was Zoe that appeared, not Louise. "Morning," she paused in the doorway, "You ready for breakfast?"

"I am, but Louise isn't in her room. Did you come back with her last night?"

"No, I thought she'd left with you."

"No. I left with . . ." Kym hesitated, the last thing she wanted was to share anything about her and Guy so soon, especially not with Zoe, "earlier on."

"I got distracted with Francis, the trainee doctor from the ground floor, and came back with him for a . . .

nightcap," she winked. "Maybe Louise got off with someone and spent the night with him? I know Sutty was sniffing round her."

"Mmm, she could have, I suppose," Kym agreed, knowing full well the only person Louise would be spending the night with was Nick Feeney. Did he come back from Peterborough last night and surprise her? Or would Louise have been stupid enough to walk down the drive to his house? Surely not though? Not at night – and she wouldn't know if his wife was there, anyway. Even though Louise didn't want to contemplate they could be back together, she'd know deep-down that might be the case.

More footsteps were coming down the corridor. Kym's heart leapt at the sight of Guy as he paused at her door, his hair still damp from the shower. He was wearing a dark green v-neck jumper over a cream shirt which suited him. Even in a bin bag he'd be gorgeous to her after what they'd shared together.

Before she had a chance to speak, Zoe turned towards him. "Where did you get to last night, you must have left early?"

"Yeah, I did." His vibrant eyes met hers, causing her heart to race a little faster, "Early night and all that," he said.

Zoe scowled, "Not on your own, I bet."

"We're a bit worried about Louise, Guy," Kym said, silently cursing Zoe. She'd so wanted to see him on her own before school. "She's not in her room. And I've heard on the radio this morning a young woman's body has been found in the woods."

"Hey, don't get carried away," concern registered on his face, "it'll be nothing like that."

"That's what I said," Zoe agreed. "She'll have copped off with someone," she gave a sly smirk, "like you did."

"But what if it's Vanya?" Kym continued. The whole conversation was bizarre. Zoe was on a completely different tangent. Her tummy was twisting in knots about their missing friend, while Zoe was fishing about Guy's love life.

"Bloody hell," Guy's eyebrows creased, "Surely not Vanya."

"Maybe we need to inform someone about Louise?" Kym said, looking for his direction. She was clueless what to do. All she knew was, something was definitely wrong.

"We can't do that," Zoe scowled, "what if she was with someone last night? Aren't we better waiting? She might be downstairs now with one of the trainee doctors. Give her a bit of time, she easily could have overslept. We've all done it."

"She won't be," Kym dismissed. She knew categorically that wasn't true. "Something's wrong, I know it is. Even if Louise did go with someone last night, she'd have come back to get ready for school."

Guy turned to Zoe, "Why don't you nip and check the bathrooms, she could be running late."

"Yeah, good idea."

He looked at Kym, "We could nip downstairs and check the *IN OUT* board?"

"Okay." Kym reached for her rucksack.

"Wait for me though," Zoe said as she headed off, "don't go to breakfast without me."

"We won't." Kym turned her attention to Guy. "If the board says *OUT,* maybe we ought to go see Mrs McGee? I'm not sure what to do for the best."

"Maybe," Guy said, "let's see if Zoe finds her first."

He waited until Zoe was out of sight then stepped into her room.

"Morning," he said tenderly, "trust her to be here. I wanted to see you before school on our own."

"Me too," she smiled lovingly at him, desperate to feel his warm arms around her but not daring to get close as the door was wide open. They were still new and secret as far as she was concerned.

"Last night was amazing," he whispered, "I can't tempt you to twag school and repeat the whole thing again, can I?"

"What and have Mrs McGee banging on your door," she laughed, "I don't think so."

"We can't even go out tonight, you're heading home aren't you, for the weekend?"

"Yeah, I want to see Mum before her surgery. What about you?"

"I'm staying here. I can't face the old man. Even my mother's on the case now. One way or another, they'll have me back in med school."

"Will they?" she asked, her tummy suddenly knotting. It was going through a range of emotions that morning. She followed him out of the room and locked the door behind her, suppressing the desire to hold his hand or kiss him.

"Much as I hate to say it," he walked down the stairs in front of her, "the oldies do seem to be right. They said I wouldn't last five minutes here."

She tried to keep her voice light. "You're not thinking of quitting, are you?"

He turned his head to look up at her, "What and leave you?" he winked, "Not a chance."

Relief flooded through her about the two of them, but not for long. When they stopped at the *IN OUT* board, her anxiety reared its head again. Louise was marked *OUT*.

"She's not in the bathrooms," Zoe said, reaching the bottom of the stairs, "now what?"

41.

The pain was becoming unbearable. He sat on the edge of his bed, trying to summon up the strength to wash and dress. He'd bought some over-the-counter analgesia from the chemist, but it no longer touched him. Every muscle throbbed and his whole body ached. The temptation to curl up again in his bed and stay there was at the forefront of his mind. Killing Louise had physically taken its toll, reminding him of his own demise. His intention was to kill himself, he'd come to that decision a while back. Putting a noose around his neck was far more preferable to being arrested. The thought of intimidating prisoners and officials scared the shit out of him. They'd have a field day with him. He'd have to end it all soon. But before he did, he needed a conversation with his brother. Not a confession about the women he'd killed, but the truth about the cancer and how he only had weeks left. Then, when he did hang himself, his brother would understand why.

His brother wasn't the sharpest tool in the box, but he was no dummy either. Whatever job he ever did, he worked hard at. It was his social skills that were lacking. He would call into a pub and have a pint, but always on his own, they never socialised as brothers. They were both completely different. But the one thing that had always been a constant had been his brother's loyalty. Due to his deviant lifestyle, with many moves around the country to avoid detection, his loyal sibling hadn't hesitated to follow him, often leaving jobs he was good at. How he would fare once he died, he didn't know. When he'd had cancer some years previously, his brother had gone over and above his role as a sibling. He'd made sure he was fed nutritious food to assist the healing process, helped him wash, and even dealt with his soiled dressings that initially had to be changed frequently. And he'd gently reassured him when he could barely look at the hideousness the surgeon's knife had left behind. He'd been there for him for all the months it had taken to come to terms with what the cancer had done to him, which had to be nature's cruel revenge for his own heinous behaviour. Life changed dramatically following his surgery. It had to. And now cancer had returned to ravish his body once again, just as he'd always known it would.

The previous night's killing was still on his mind and reinforced to him what he'd always believed. Females were stupid, particularly young ones. It had been a piece of cake enticing Louise to his car. Although she did wonder what was going on when he opened his boot and there weren't any bottles in it. It was then he hit her on the back of the head with the claw hammer he'd hidden up his sleeve. She didn't even squeak, just dropped to the ground. He'd quickly hoisted her lifeless body into the boot. He then had to drive a short way to the place he'd prepared earlier. In the depth of the woods, about four miles away, there was a small disused cabin, close to a pond. It was occasionally used by ramblers to take shelter from the rain, or those wanting to sit quietly and watch the wildlife. The glass on the small window had long ago been smashed, and the other window had no glass at all, it had been replaced by a shutter. On the door was an old wooden plaque with faded letters naming it, *Larry's Lookout,* which he guessed was named after whoever had erected it. He'd visited earlier and sussed it out, preparing it with a blanket so he could strip Louise, caress her naked body and strangle her. He'd chosen the blanket carefully; its dark blue colour would enhance the beauty of Louise's naked form.

Right now, following the previous evening's activities, there was little wonder he was wracked with pain. He put his hand under his pillow and retrieved Louise's pale pink knickers, pressed them to his nose and inhaled her feminine scent. With Louise unconscious in the boot, he'd driven down the dirt track into the woods on dimmed lights and switched them off as he pulled up outside the small cabin. He had the hammer ready to whack her again should she come round, but she was still flat out. She looked so peaceful, curled up in the boot in her silky dressing grown and cute pyjamas. This was going to be an incredible kill.

With a sigh, he laid back on his pillow and closed his eyes, touching Louise's knickers to his chest while summoning every detail of his last kill, determined to relish in it.

A trail of footprints to the door had been evident, but they were from him when he'd visited the place earlier to prepare it. No one else had been near. He lifted Louise's lifeless body from the boot with adrenaline-fuelled ease, kicked open the door and took her inside, laying her down on the blanket. He returned to the car, retrieved the large torch and bin bag from the back seat, remembered to pick up the hammer, then closed the boot and locked the car before stepping back inside the cabin and closing the door behind him. He rested the torch on the floor, which gave him adequate light, and quickly undressed her. He removed the silky, lightweight dressing gown and pretty blue pyjamas. Her cute underwear was matching – pale blue bra and knickers – he liked that. Angela always wore matching underwear.

What a joyful moment it was when he released the clasp on her bra and revealed her breasts, pink nipples so perfect and so hard with the cold. He sighed as he stroked them, caressing the curve of her small breasts.

Such a joy to ease her knickers down, revealing a bush of hair. Such a wonderful moment to ease her legs apart and see her beautiful femininity. Soft to the touch, it brought a tear to his eye.

He'd hurriedly scooped up her clothes and stuffed them in the bin bag. His intention was to burn them later as he always did. He was far too clever to leave any evidence. Though he kept the knickers for now.

Lying naked in front of him, fully exposed, his breath caught in his throat. She was beautiful with her milky white skin. Her breasts were small and perfectly round and her pink nipples stood proud. She had slender hips and a generous amount of pubic hair that he couldn't resist touching again. Such beauty. It was a shame he was going to snuff the life out of her. But he had to. She'd be able to identify him, if he didn't.

He pulled a comb out of his pocket and began to comb her long silky dark hair. He leaned in to smell the fragrance. It smelt summery, like flowers. He pulled it around to her shoulder and began separating the hair into three so he could plait it – just as Angela used to let him do hers. She loved it being in plaits overnight, so she could wear it down for work and it would be all kinky and wavy at the ends. He started to plait the first bunch, left over the centre, then the same with the right. He kept repeating the process until he reached the end of the hair and rested the neat plait down on her chest, nestled between her breasts. Oh, how he loved the memories of doing the same with dear Angela's hair.

He was surprised how long Louise remained unconscious. He maybe had hit her with too much force, perhaps harder than he usually did. Never mind, it gave him more time to absorb her beauty.

He rolled her onto her tummy. Her small but rounded buttocks were just divine, especially under the torchlight. He kneaded them with both hands, leaning in to breathe her womanly scent. She was surely the perfect specimen – perfect for his final kill. He rolled her back over onto her back and used the torch to examine her more closely. While he was absorbing her flat tummy and milky thighs, she started to twitch. And then came the groan. He was used to that – right before he strangled them. He'd wait for them to open their eyes before throttling them. Liked them to realise moments before death, what fools they'd been.

He hoped this one did, although her pupils didn't look quite right when she opened her eyes. One seemed larger than the other. And she didn't appear quite as terrified as they usually were before he snuffed them out. Her eyes seemed almost glazed. But he didn't have time to analyse her state of mind. He needed rid of her. He quickly straddled her and tightened his hands around her slender neck to begin the process of cutting off her oxygen supply. It wouldn't take long to finish her, she looked half dead as it was. But she did begin to wriggle. They always did that. He pinned her down and tightened the pressure around her neck, squeezing the last breath out of her. The wriggling was beginning to lessen.

Bang!

He jumped. *What the fuck was that?*

He was frozen for a moment. Was someone there?

He turned his head at the same time as releasing his hands from around her neck. Nothing was evident in the semi darkness, only the sound of the trees scratching the outer wood of the cabin.

He stood up and walked towards the door where the noise had come from. The hairs on the back of his neck stood to attention. But nobody was there. The noise baffled him, though. He fished in his pocket for a smaller torch he carried with him and moved around the confined area. It was then he spotted a latch had come loose on the tiny window and the wind must have caught the shutter banging it on its hinge. That had been the cause of the bang. Relief flooded through him as he tried to steady his breathing and racing heart. It would have been disastrous to have been caught.

He walked back to the girl and gazed at her lifeless corpse. In death, her nakedness was beautiful. And the plaited hair suited her. Just like it had done dear Angela.

The task was done. His last kill. Now all he had to do was take her where he'd dumped that mate of hers, and head home. He opened the door, bundled her up in the blanket and lifted her up. She was light and easy to carry. He opened the boot and dropped her in before slamming it shut. He'd quickly retrieved the torch and the hammer and the bag of clothes, ensuring no evidence had been left behind.

He got into the driver's seat and started up the engine. He was elated. It was always the same after a kill. Another stupid girl had bitten the dust. He wiped the sweat off his brow with the back of his hand. This one had taken its toll. As he drove away, a sharp pain at the side of his chest gripped him. He took a deep breath in which only added to the discomfort. There'd be no more killings now – she was the last. He gave a sly smile, he might not have strength anymore but he still had his wits about him. Even now, the police were clueless. There was absolutely nothing that could link him to the girls . . . only Harlow Wood. But they employed a lot of staff and who was to say it was an employee that had done the recent killings. It was likely, but not a foregone conclusion. No, they'd never get him. He wasn't the dimwit his old man had called him. He was cunning and clever. Hadn't he outsmarted them all?

As he'd reached the main road, a thought had sprung into his mind. He had to get rid of his stash of knickers. They would be evidence. Shame as he loved having them. They gave him power. He'd hang onto them until the last minute, then he'd burn them. He'd do that before he took his own life.

He checked the bedside clock. It was time to move now, he needed to get to work. One last, deep sniff of Louise's knickers and he eased himself from his bed, stood up and stretched as best he was able. Just a few more days – the time for his demise becoming closer by the minute.

42.

Kym

Kym was sitting in the library in the school of nursing opposite Inspector Porteous and Mrs McGee. Guy was beside her, holding her hand. It had been him and Simon that had insisted once Louise hadn't appeared at breakfast, to go and tell Mrs Beaumont. She was quick to realise how upset Kym was and insisted she stay in the privacy of her office. Guy stayed with her when Mrs Beaumont, after making a phone call, had to go and speak to the class. It was supposed to be their last day before being on the ward full time, and they were going to sit an end of block exam. That was highly unlikely now. Nobody could possibly concentrate.

Minutes earlier, while they were alone, Guy had wrapped an arm around Kym and comforted her when she'd burst into tears.

"I know what it looks like," he soothed, "but we don't know anything for definite."

"Yes, we do," she said wearily. She knew it, and he knew it. Louise wouldn't just disappear, any more than Vanya would. Someone had taken them both. And the police would know it too. Within minutes, sirens could be heard arriving at the hospital. Having previously scaled down their presence, they'd be back in force now another girl had gone missing. They should never have left as far as she was concerned. Poor Louise, she prayed silently that she'd soon be found.

The Inspector cleared his throat. "I'll come straight to the point, Kym," his eyes looked expectantly into hers, "time is of the essence. We know that Louise was at the party last night. What we don't know is what time she left, and if she left with anyone. When was the last time you saw her?"

Guy tightened his grip on her hand in a comforting way. It all felt like déjà vu. Only weeks ago she was being questioned in exactly the same way about Vanya when she'd disappeared.

"I was on the dance floor with her, probably about ten thirty and we were about to get a drink when Guy," she turned and smiled at him, remembering the good that had come out of the previous evening, "asked me to dance. The DJ had dimmed the lights and slowed the music to a smoochy one." She screwed her face up, "I didn't see her after that."

"So, she wasn't there when you came off the dance floor, or did you leave the party after that?"

She swallowed. There was no choice but to say that she went back to Guy's room. And no doubt Mrs McGee, who was intensely focussed on every word she was saying, would have them thrown off the course.

"She left with me," Guy interjected, "we walked back together and went into the kitchen for a coffee. We had a lot to talk about. Kym has recently split with her boyfriend and I have with my girlfriend. We spent a couple of hours talking about whether we wanted to be together and if I should return to medical school." He shrugged, "My parents' wish, not necessarily mine."

"And you didn't see Louise at all, either of you?"

"No," Kym said emphatically. "Once Guy and I had . . . finished talking, I went to my room. But it was late. Louise's room door was closed, as was everyone else's."

"I see. Is there anything you can think of going on in Louise's life that might be relevant to her disappearance?"

She shook her head. "I can't think of anything."

"What about boyfriends? Did she have one?"

"Err . . . no."

"You're sure about that? If there's anything that might be relevant, you need to tell us now." His stare was intense. His eyes never left hers as he continued, "I'm not trying to scare you, but we need to be realistic. Two young women in this area have disappeared, one of whom was murdered, and now we have a third one. There's a pattern here and Louise could be in great danger right now. We need to find her. So, if you know of any man she might be seeing, or anything you think has happened that might be odd or out of place, you need to say."

She took a deep breath in, she had to tell him. It could save Louise's life. "There is one thing. I feel bad now as I should have spoken sooner . . . I just never saw the significance of it."

"What is it?" Mrs McGee's expression was one of irritation. As if she'd somehow been withholding vital evidence. "You need to tell the Inspector," she glared through her beady little eyes.

Kym explained about the evening Vanya had told her a pair of her knickers had gone missing, and more recently, Louise had said a pair had gone from her room.

"What day did Louise tell you this?" the Inspector asked.

"Yesterday. On our way to the nightdress and pyjama party."

"And can you remember how soon after Vanya told you her pants were taken that she went missing?"

Kym shook her head, "I can't. I just remember Vanya and I looking for them in her room and then deciding she must have left them in the bathroom, and possibly someone picked them up and sent them to the hospital laundry. That was the end of it really. I never asked if she'd got them back because she went missing shortly after that. It could have been a day or so before, I'm not entirely sure."

"I see. Well, that has certainly been helpful. Anything else? Do you know if Louise is involved with anyone currently? Has she mentioned a boyfriend, maybe someone new on the scene?"

"Erm . . . there is sort of someone . . . but it's difficult . . . I don't want to get him into trouble."

"This is no time to be thinking of loyalty, Kym," the Inspector said firmly. "We need to speak to this person. Do you have a name for us?"

Kym's heart juddered. It was going to be massive dobbing Nick Feeney in. He was sure to end up losing his job if she disclosed it. And he'd hardly be the type to abduct Louise. There'd be no point when she'd go with him willingly.

"Is he married? Is that what's troubling you?"

"Yes."

"Well, right now," his voice became even more authoritative, "informing on a married man is the least of our worries. You must tell us so we can decide if this man is relevant."

"He could lose his job," she said nervously.

"And your friend could lose her life. Now please, tell me now what you know. I need to speak to this man urgently."

"Tell him, Kym," Guy urged, "you have to."

She took a deep breath in. "Nick Feeney, the charge nurse on ward seven."

There was silence. This would be new information to Mrs McGee and Guy.

"Thank you. I know that must have been hard for you. I'm sure Louise told you that in confidence, but you've done the right thing," the Inspector reassured. "Now, if there isn't anything else."

"Whose body is it that's been found?" Kym blurted out, knowing full well what his answer would be, but she had to ask anyway. "I heard it on the radio this morning."

"I'm afraid I'm not at liberty to discuss that right now," he adjusted something at the side of his knee. Kym remembered him doing the same last time he'd been in school. It must have been some sort of false leg from the knee downwards and he had to fiddle with it to sit and stand. As he was about to stand up, Guy asked. "Would it be possible to have a word . . . in private?"

Mrs Mc Gee was astute enough to realise Guy wanted her out of the way and eased herself out of her chair. "I'll leave you to it," she said and turned towards Kym. "We'll get you a drink, Nurse Sullivan. You're very pale. Hot sweet tea should do it. Come with me."

Kym had an idea what Guy was going to say to the Inspector. He wouldn't have liked telling the lie. She knew that about him. He'd want to clarify they were together in his room and the ramifications of that if Mrs McGee found out. When he'd intervened and made out they'd been in the kitchen together until the early hours, her heart contracted. Her respect for him went up a notch.

She dutifully followed Matron as she led her down the corridor into a small sitting room with a kitchenette which must be used for tutors in the School of Nursing.

"Take a seat," Mrs McGee said, filling the kettle. Her taking charge was just what Kym needed. Such was her concern about Louise, she couldn't think straight. What now? They'd have to inform her mum who was still grieving for Louise's dad. And parents of the students were going to want their offspring out of Harlow Wood. Even her own dad wouldn't want her returning. It was hard enough after Vanya disappeared, but now, she was sure he wouldn't let her come back. And did she even want to return if Louise wasn't there? An added anxiety now also was Guy. She couldn't stay away from him, not after what they'd shared together.

"There you are," Mrs McGee handed her a cup of tea, "drink this, it'll put some colour in your cheeks."

"Thank you." Kym moistened her lips, the need to apologise was at the forefront of her mind. "I feel awful saying about Mr Feeney, I hope he doesn't get into too much trouble."

"That's for his employers to decide," Mrs McGee said. No chance of being absolved. A kind response like, *you had no choice,* would have helped.

"I'm just going to find Mrs Beaumont," Mrs McGee said, walking towards the door. "I'll send Mr Logan in. Judging by the way he was holding your hand, the two of you are a couple now, I take it?"

Kym shrugged, noting her lack of warmth. Had she ever been young? And why did senior staff at Harlow Wood not use Christian names? It seemed archaic to be using surnames all the time. Fine for the patients to address them as Nurse so-and-so, but surely the staff didn't have to resort to it. Yet they all did.

She took a sip of her tea so she didn't have to elaborate about her and Guy. Now the old battle-axe knew, it'd be curtains with regard to any intimacy between them if she did stay at Harlow Wood. Mrs McGee would make it her business to be watching them like a hawk.

Guy was longer than she expected. Kym fidgeted while she waited, thinking up awful scenarios about what might have happened to Louise. She recalled her talking about her mum and sister and the devastation when her dad had died. Please, Kym prayed silently, let her be okay. Her mum and sister are going to be distraught.

When Guy did arrive, he looked relieved she was alone. He took the seat next to her and reached for her hand. "Everyone's gone for coffee. Seemingly when we come back, a policewoman is going to speak to us. It sounds like they are going to have police around the hospital permanently until they apprehend whoever is responsible for all of this. They're setting up meetings with the rest of the staff."

She was barely listening and blurted out, "I can't bring myself to believe that Nick Feeney has anything to do with all this."

"No, me neither. But they'll take him in for questioning, that's for sure."

"And will he definitely lose his job, do you think?"

"Yeah, I expect so. But he shouldn't have been with Louise, he's a tutor, he'd know it was wrong. Has it been going on long?"

"No. Just the once as far as I know. He's gone on compassionate leave currently so I'm sure none of it has anything to do with him. God," she shook her head, "this is awful. What happens after we've listened to the police officer?"

"We can go for the day. Most of us are going home anyway with it being our last weekend before our ward placements."

"I wonder how many of us will actually come back? I reckon some of the second years will be bailing out too. I know for sure my dad will have something to say about this as soon as he finds out." She met his worried eyes, "I can't see him letting me return, somehow."

"He will. He knows how much nursing means to you. And anyway, I've got a plan."

"What sort of plan?"

"Instead of you going on the train, I'll take you home and speak to your dad. I'll tell him we're a couple now and I'll look after you."

Her heart leapt at his use of the term couple, but she still scowled, "And you think my dad will take notice of you? You're forgetting I'm all they've got. You know, the only child and all that."

"Yeah," he smiled lovingly at her, "quite right too. But it's worth a try. You want to come back, don't you?"

She let out a huge sigh. "I don't know anymore. I want to do my nursing, and be with you of course," she quickly added, "but I don't know if I can face it . . . if anything has happened to Louise."

"I know. It is hard. But remember, we don't know anything yet."

"Yeah, we do," Kym said wearily, "she wouldn't just disappear. And Vanya wouldn't have either. Maybe it suited us to believe she had, but now two of them, plus that other girl," she shook her head, "no way. Someone has taken them. And I can't see my dad or my mum wanting me here. They'll be terrified for me."

"Let's see how it goes," he urged. "They might be better once they know I'm with you, so at least let's try that, shall we?"

"Okay, we'll give it a go." She pulled a face, "You'd have to stay in the spare room, Mum and Dad wouldn't let us stay together."

"No, I know that. But there's no need to put your mum to any trouble. Cleethorpes will have B&B's, I'm sure."

"Oh, she'd have none of that, not now we're a . . . couple," she gave a gentle smile, the first one in hours. "It'll keep her busy having you to fuss over. It'll take her mind off her surgery next week."

"Sounds like a plan, then." He stood up and held out his hand, "Let's go see the others and grab a coffee. They're all worried about you."

She eagerly clasped his outstretched hand. Hers fitted perfectly in his. If only her friend was there – Louise would be thrilled that her and Guy were finally together. But for how much longer, she pondered. She had an inkling Guy wasn't going to stay the course. Even though he denied it, she was fairly sure he'd end up going back to med school.

As they left the school of nursing and walked through the gardens, Lloyd was hovering around some bushes, clutching hedge clippers.

"Great night last night," he smiled at them both.

"Yeah, it was, mate," Guy acknowledged, slowing down but not stopping.

It had been only hours earlier that Lloyd had taken her and Louise's entrance fee at the hall door.

She could barely nod – too busy trying to swallow the huge ball forming in her throat.

43.

Louise

Cold. Icy cold, wrapped around her in the darkness. She spluttered, spat out water. *Water.* She was lying in it. A muddy puddle maybe. Her head throbbed. Was she hit by something? Someone? Where was she?

Was she dead?

It was so cold. Her teeth were chattering. One of her arms seemed to be trapped underneath her. Excruciating pain gripped every bone and muscle as she attempted to shuffle away from the water. Pain that seemed to break from her chest, making it hard to breathe.

She was naked. Where were her clothes?

Where was her mum? Was she looking for her? Crying for her?

She tentatively moved her throbbing head around, but her vision was blurred. All she could make out in the darkness were muddy, oppressive walls surrounding her, like some sort of cave. There was the sound of running water, maybe a stream.

Was she even alive?

One last shift away from the water and hot pain spiked through her arm, making her cry out. Maybe she was dying, moving over to the other side. No. She was alive. Had to be. Needed to focus. To breathe.

She tried taking a ragged breath in, then gagged and almost puked at the rancid air that filled her mouth. She might not be dead but something was. Something dead and rotten nearby.

"H-he-help," she said, her teeth still chattering madly. Her voice was weak, her throat sore.

She looked up to what might be a night sky. Or a nightmare. That was it. A dream. A horrible dream. She closed her eyes. Wake up. Wake up! Louise, wake up! My name's Louise, I'm . . . hospital. A ward. A patient. I'm elevating the traction.

Bottles. Something about bottles but there are no bottles.

Whirring. Spinning. Louder. Like a helicopter.

Not a dream. Someone . . . someone touched me. Hands on my backside.

Whirring. Spinning. Quieter now.

"H-help," she said again, louder this time. Gagging again at the stench surrounding her, trying not to look into the shadows. "Mu-Mum. H-help me, Mum."

* * *

It had been a long shift for the rescue team, so when the call came through on the radio that the missing child had been located, Mike yelled his delight.

"Hallelujah," he grinned to his mate Ian, stood by the back of the Land Rover, "they've got him. Sounds like the little fella had fallen asleep in the woods. Poor bugger, he must have been exhausted. It's been almost six hours."

"Thank Christ for that," Ian said. "I wonder where they found him."

"Didn't say exactly. They're just going to let the chopper know to stand down."

"That's a relief. I honestly thought he might have fallen down the ravine," he gestured to the ravine next to them, cordoned off and with intermittent signs indicating its danger to the public.

"Yeah, the fence they've put up isn't much of a deterrent. There's a gap there," he nodded to an area where the fence was missing. "I might call that in. It needs looking at."

"You're right. Not that I think many venture down here. It's too dangerous. But there are tyre tracks so someone has been. Anyway," Ian folded the map he was holding, "all's well that ends well, thank God. We'll be home for supper now, mate. I don't know about you, but I could eat a scabby horse."

"Me too. Come on, let's head back."

Ian paused and cocked his head. "Did you hear that?"

"What?"

"Sounded like someone shouting."

"Nah, I didn't hear anything, must have been the wind."

They both stopped speaking and listened.

"There. Did you hear it?"

"I heard something," Mike frowned.

Ian held onto a post and leapt over the fence towards the edge of the ravine. He got as close as was safe and peered over the edge.

Mike followed. "There'll be no one down there, if that's what you're thinking," he said. "It'll be an animal if anything."

"Do you reckon? Shall I call down and see if we get a response?"

"If you like. Can you do animal noises?" Mike grinned.

Ian put his hands around his mouth and yelled, "Is anyone down there?"

"You're a silly sod," Mike said, "nobody could survive a fall down there."

"Shush, listen . . . I think I heard something."

Ian knelt down to get closer to the edge and peered over. He screwed up his eyes, "All I can see down there is darkness. Get the thermal nocs from the truck would you."

While he waited, he shouted again, "Is anyone down there?"

A weak noise came back. There was definitely something. He wasn't entirely sure, but he thought he saw a slight movement.

Mike returned and handed the night vision binoculars to him. He lifted them to his eyes and focussed deep into the ravine.

"Holy shit. There's someone down there."

"What! Let me look." Mike grabbed the binoculars and took a look himself. Ian was right. He could see a young girl, naked and waving an arm in the air.

"Christ! Ring it in. Get the flying squad back. And fetch the megaphone, would you."

Ian ran back to the truck and returned with the megaphone.

Mike lifted it to his mouth. "Don't try to move," he called. "My name's Mike from Search and Rescue and we're coming for you. Lie still and take some deep breaths. Help is on the way. We're going to get you out very soon, I promise. Just keep still."

* * *

She thought she heard a voice in the distance. It must be her dad. He'd come after all. He'd never let her down. She must let him know where she was. She shouted again as best she could.

The whirring noise was back again. Her head was pounding incessantly. The pain was unbearable. She tried to move but couldn't; the pain in her chest the worst. Her limbs seemed frozen by the relentless cold. The voice kept interrupting, telling her that he was coming for her.

She gagged again on the stink. A few feet away from her, she could make out something. The rotten-flesh smell was rancid. Maybe it was a dead animal, though with her blurred vision, it looked too big. She could just make out some hair. Hair that looked like it was plaited. Flies were buzzing around it and the stench was nauseating.

The whirring noise grew louder, like a chainsaw.

That face – leather face – *his* chainsaw, cutting people up. Mandy, her friend had laughed at her for being scared to walk home in the dark after watching the film, The Texas Chainsaw Massacre. She remembered it

344

vividly, the bodies stacking up. Maybe she was a victim too. Dying slowly, shivering from the cold, hardly able to breathe.

Where was her dad? She thought he was coming for her.

The whirring noise became unbearably loud. She prayed it would stop. It was making her throbbing head much worse. *'Please stop the noise'* she called out.

A blinding light exploded, the chainsaw so loud now. Shadows vanished. Plaited hair shone golden in the light. A shrivelled face stared back at her.

Vanya – the name appeared in her head.

Vanya?

Hands around her throat.

Squeezing.

Those eyes.

Piercing eyes.

44.

Kym

"You have been amazing this weekend," Kym smiled at Guy as the car approached Harlow Wood.

"How amazing?" he grinned.

"Very. You've captured my mum's heart and my dad loves you. You've certainly helped, that's for sure."

"Good. The main thing is, you're coming back to Harlow Wood with me."

"Yeah, and again that's down to you."

"Not just me. Your parents want you to train as a nurse."

"I know. But I'm still not sure how I feel about being back. There's still a dark cloud hanging over everything with Vanya and Louise . . ." she trailed off speaking. The tears were close again. What could she say? Nobody knew what had happened to either of them. They'd heard on the news that the body of the girl found in the woods just outside of Mansfield was that of a local girl who had gone missing on her way home from work. Whether it was related to Vanya and Louise's disappearance, the police wouldn't say. The news bulletins stuck to the same script – investigations were ongoing.

"I know you're worried," Guy said softly, "but like I said, let's take it day by day. We've finished in school, thank God, so now it's time to do what we came here to do. I'm on an early tomorrow on the ward and you're on a late. I'll come and meet you at 8.45 when you finish and walk with you back to North House. Shame we're on opposite shifts really."

"Yeah, it is. It'd be nice to work together."

"It would. But we'll have to make do with our evenings. And I'll stay here on my days off so I can keep an eye on you."

"But what about your parents, won't they be expecting you home?"

"I'm sure they can manage without me. And when I do go home, I'll take you with me. You can meet them."

"Really? That'll be nice."

"Oh yeah," he rolled his eyes, "really nice. They'll love you though, that's the main thing."

"Good. I'm looking forward to meeting them. I want them to know what a special person their son is."

"Good luck with that, then, I'm not sure they'll share your sentiment. All it'll be is," he changed his voice to a deep authoritative one, "how I'm wasting my life, how I should go back to med school and train as a doctor." He winked, "They'll try and get you on their side, you'll see."

"I'm not taking sides. Remember, I'd rather have you here."

He squeezed her hand, "And I'd rather be here."

"That said though, I am realistic. Your mum and dad know you much better than me. I can see your potential so it must be hard for them as they want the best for you."

He pulled into the car park and cut the engine.

"I've got what's best for me sitting right here." He leaned in and kissed her.

She shook her head playfully, "You're such a smoothie, Guy Logan. Has anyone ever told you that?"

"Not exactly been called a smoothie, I've had charming, sophisticated, desirable . . ."

She slapped his arm. "With a head that's getting bigger by the minute."

As Guy locked the car door, Kym stretched her stiff arms in the air, relieved to be out of the car. "Do you think Mrs McGee will have her eye on us, now she knows we're together? You know, nipping into North House more than she usually does to keep a check on us?"

"Is the pope catholic? Course she will. My fear is that she'll move you into South House. I wouldn't put it past her to have you in the room next to hers with a bolt on it."

"Oh, God, I hope not . . ."

Someone called out to them as Guy lifted their bags out of the boot. "It's Simon," Guy said, closing the boot and locking it. "I wonder if he's got any news about Louise."

They hastily made their way towards him.

"Hi," Simon said, "I've just cut through here to see if you were back. I've seen Sutty in the canteen and he reckons they've found a girl and she's alive."

"Who?" Kym's heart raced, "Louise . . . or Vanya?"

"We don't know. I've just been to the incident office the cops have set up, but they won't say anything. I

348

didn't hang around as Duffield's in there, talking to Inspector Porteous."

Guy screwed his face up, "What's he doing here on a Sunday?"

"Dunno, but he's here."

"What about Nick Feeney?" Kym asked, still feeling guilty about dobbing him in. "Do we know anything about him?"

"Only that he's not in his house. So Lloyd says anyway."

"Lloyd?" Kym frowned, "Is he here on a Sunday too? Don't these people have homes to go to?"

"I reckon he sees himself as some sort of amateur detective. And he's only got his brother at home so I think this place is his life. But as for why Duffield's here, God knows. Probably nothing better to do either, I can't imagine he's got anyone keeping the home fires burning."

Kym had to agree. Even though he didn't bother her, she could see why he wasn't liked. His demeanour was odd to say the least, which was strange for someone who had a senior role as a nursing officer. His job was to support, yet half the student nurses didn't like him.

A mixture of hope and dread was running through her veins when she thought about Vanya and Louise, and whichever one it was who had been found, the mental and physical torture they must have gone through. "So," her lips trembled, "we don't know any more than they've found a girl?"

"That's about it. I was just going to my room to put the radio on for any news bulletins."

"I've just thought," Guy said. "Do you reckon it's worth knocking on Mrs McGee's door? See if she can tell us anything?"

"That's not a bad idea," Simon nodded, "shall we nip there now?"

Kym pulled a face, "I wouldn't imagine she'll tell us anything even if she does know. We'll just get a telling off for disturbing her."

"I reckon it's worth a try, though," Guy smiled lovingly at her. "She's more likely to find something out than us."

Although Guy had the right intention, Kym was uncomfortable about disturbing her. South House was her home after all, and it was a Sunday. And if she was truly honest, she didn't want the old battleaxe to see her and Guy together. It might remind her to put restrictions on them and the last thing she wanted was to have to move to South House.

"Come on, let's give it a try," Simon urged, "it can't do any harm. She'll tell us more than the cops, surely?"

"Yeah, I agree," Guy said to Simon. "Can we dump our bags first, though?"

Kym left Guy with Simon and made her way up the stairs to her room. Louise's door firmly closed opposite hers caused her tummy to clench. Was it Louise the police had found? It had to be. Please, she silently prayed. How she missed her friend and had worried about her all weekend. She'd barely slept. Knowing Guy was in the room along the landing hadn't helped either, but her mum and dad would be mortified if she'd set foot in his bedroom. Their one night together had been so lovely, she longed to be intimate with him again.

After leaving her bag on the chair, she went to the sink and splashed some cold water on her face. As she dried it, she peered at herself in the mirror. She didn't look brilliant. The dark circles under her eyes were affirmation there was a lot going on. Her mother's surgery the next day was still at the forefront of her mind. Having Guy there all weekend certainly appeared to take her mind off things. It had been nice to see her smiling and fussing round him. But the worry was still there about the road ahead and cancer. And added to that was her return to Harlow Wood with a killer on the loose. She understood her parents' anxiety, she was scared herself. Without Guy, she may not have even returned. But he'd been positive and reassuring which added to her developing feelings towards him. As she locked her room door, she spotted Zoe at the top of the stairs.

"Kym," she called, making her way towards her, "I've just got back and seen Francis downstairs. He said they've found a girl and she's alive."

"Yeah, Simon told us. I've just put my bag in my room. I'm going with Guy and Simon to see Mrs McGee to see if she can tell us anything more."

"I'll come with you. Wait for me would you while I dump my bag."

While Kym waited at the top of the stairs, she glanced down the corridor towards Zoe's room remembering their first days at Harlow Wood and all the excitement at leaving home for the first time. It had been so nice getting to know everyone and being together in school. Now it was all sad, flat and depressing . . . apart from Guy. Did Zoe know yet about the two of them?

"Hey," Zoe said as she followed Kym down the stairs. "Francis reckons he was sat near two of the police officers having coffee and he heard one of them saying someone's background doesn't check out."

"Who?"

"That's the bit he doesn't know. But it's someone from here by the sound of things. They'll be onto whoever it is right now I reckon."

"Good. Let's hope they arrest him soon."

As they approached Guy's room downstairs, he was perched on his desk talking to Simon sitting on a chair. Kym's heart fluttered and she smiled inwardly at her luck in finding him and him feeling the same way about her. It had all been full-on since Thursday evening. Had it only been three days since the nightdress and pyjama party? That night had been so exciting, until the following morning when they'd discovered Louise was missing.

"Hi, Zoe," Simon smiled, "Good weekend at home?"

"Not really. I got a load of grief from my mum about me coming back." She turned to Kym, "How was your mum and dad?"

"The same. I just told them there'd be lots of police around." She omitted to say that Guy had persuaded them he'd look after her.

"Hey, another thing," Zoe's eyes lit up, "rumour has it that Charge Nurse Griffiths on your ward isn't qualified."

"Who said that?" Kym scowled.

"Francis. Reckons he's been asked why he isn't wearing his SRN badge on his lapel like qualified staff are supposed to."

"Maybe he's lost it," Guy said. "I can't see him not being qualified, he really knows his stuff."

"They'll be looking closely at everyone, though," Zoe's eyes widened, "and he was serving drinks at the nightdress and pyjama party when Louise went missing."

"That doesn't mean anything," Simon dismissed, "Duffield was too, and while I can't stand the bloke, I can't imagine he'd be abducting nurses."

"Yeah but, I was just telling Kym. Francis overheard the police saying someone's background isn't checking out properly. So maybe someone's changed their name or something. I reckon they must be getting close now."

"I'm fairly certain they can rule Mr Griffiths out," Guy scowled, "he seems kosher to me. It could be anyone. People change their names all the time," he shrugged, "it doesn't mean they're killers."

"Well, I've never heard of anyone changing their name, why would you, unless you were up to something?"

"My uncle goes by a different name for work than his personal one," Simon said, "but he's a freelance journalist so I suppose that's more legit. And women do when they get married, remember."

"Yeah, well it's hardly going to be a woman abducting nurses is it?" Zoe scoffed.

"That's true," Simon said, "Come on, let's go and see the delightful Demis Roussos and see if she's as objectionable as she usually is."

As they made their way towards South House, Marie and Lisa from their intake were standing close to the entrance, both smoking cigarettes. Kym could see by their pale faces they were anxious. What a terrible mess it all was. Who could abduct two girls? It was so horrible.

"Hi," Marie said as they approached, "have you heard, they've found a girl and she's alive."

"Yeah, we just heard," Guy said, "any news on who it is?"

Marie shook her head, "No. We were just trying to pluck up courage to knock on Mrs McGee's door." She stubbed her cigarette out on the wall ashtray, "Not that I think she'll tell us anything, but it's worth a try."

"Great minds think alike," Simon said, "we're on our way there too. Let's go together . . . strength in numbers and all that."

The girls stood back and let Simon and Guy knock on Mrs McGee's door. Kym's tummy was jittery, almost convinced now Guy had put the idea in her mind, that she most probably would be moved to keep them both apart. That would be awful when they'd reassured her dad that he would be close by and look after her. Her mum and dad were thrilled to hear that she was now going out with Guy. And she'd been proud too. He was someone rather special. It was a pity that Harlow Wood had turned into such a nightmare.

The door opened. Mrs McGee was wearing a blue velour lounge suit. Her hair was greasy and lank, hanging around her shoulders and looked in need of a good wash and cut. She was still wearing a silk scarf around her neck, even though she was indoors.

"Sorry to disturb you," Simon smiled kindly at her, "we've heard that the police have found a girl."

"Who told you that?"

"Sutty from the kitchen."

"And how does he know?" she scowled.

"We're not sure," Simon shrugged, "we're just frantic to know if it's Louise or maybe Vanya."

"Well, I'm afraid I can't help you. I've not been told anything."

"Is there any way you can find out?" Guy interjected, "we're all pretty worried about our friends. The girls are particularly upset," he nodded towards the four of them stood a few feet away on the corridor.

"Yes, well we all are." Mrs McGee raised her painted-on eyebrows, "However, right now, I'm about to eat," she said firmly. Her expression indicated that nothing was going to get in the way of that. "When I've finished," she continued, "I'll go across to the incident room and see what I can find out."

"And you'll come and let us know?" Guy asked. "We'll go to the dining room for supper and then wait in the kitchen in North House."

Her eyes looked irritated as she took a deep breath in. "I'll see what I can do."

She closed the door.

Simon raised an eyebrow, "No surprises there then. I knew she wouldn't tell us anything. She's as odd as a box of monkeys that one."

355

As they began to walk down the corridor, Marie said, "She didn't seem that surprised to me. I bet she does know, she's just not telling us."

"Yeah, I thought that," Guy said holding the door open for them, "she's been in the know from the beginning with being in the police interviews. She knows more than she's letting on, I'm sure of it."

"You'd think she'd be more compassionate with the job she's in, wouldn't you?" Kym said.

"I reckon compassion's missing from her job description," Simon answered sarcastically, "that and kindness."

45.

Louise

Muffled voices were all around her, and an incessant bleeping. The sound of her mum's familiar voice was reassuring. Although she wasn't able to respond, she liked the soft tone of it. It made her feel calm. Her mum had been talking about holidays they'd been on to Scarborough when she was a child, and mentioned her friends by name and how they had sent their love. She even joked about her sister Karen being in trouble yet again at school. It surprised her how chilled her mum seemed to be about that. It had to be for her benefit as she knew her mum. She'd be cross and have some form of punishment lined up.

"How much longer before she wakes up, do you know?" she heard her mother ask, "it's been days now."

"Don't worry," a pleasant female voice answered. "As the doctor said, she'll wake up in her own time. We're reducing some medication now the swelling has subsided following surgery. She's suffered a significant amount of trauma, so we just need to be patient. I know you're terribly worried, but all her vital signs appear to have stabilised."

"You keep saying that, and I don't mean to sound ungrateful, but I don't find that reassuring. Is the doctor here at the moment? I'd like to speak to him."

"Yes, he'll be here shortly. We all know how difficult this is for you. You're doing ever so well."

"Am I? I don't feel like I am. I just want some answers. I feel so helpless. I want to know who did this to her. I don't know how much more I can take of just sitting here."

Things went quiet. And then the other person spoke again. "Keep on talking to Louise as you are doing, holding her hand and reassuring her. She will come round. The body is miraculous and currently I think it's allowing her the time to rest and heal."

"This isn't helping the police though is it? We need Louise to wake up and tell us who did this to her. It has to be someone she knows. My daughter would not go off with a complete stranger. It has to be someone who works at the hospital. And he may strike again if he isn't caught."

"Of course. We all appreciate how difficult this is for you as her mum, and the police. They want this person caught too. But they may not be able to see her straight away anyway. It's up to the doctors to decide when she is well enough to talk to them. We have no idea currently what Louise will be like when she wakes up. It's going to be a long process. The broken arm and fractured ribs will heal quickly, but the head injury is going to take time. We won't be able to rush anything. We have to be guided by the doctors. So right now, we just need to be patient and keep talking to Louise like you are doing. She'll be able to hear you, I'm sure. Now, let me go and get the domestic to bring you some more tea."

Louise felt the urge to open her eyes. It was a struggle as they had a will of their own and seemed to want to stay closed. But she forced them. As she tried to focus, the incessant bleeping increased.

"Where am I?" she managed to whisper. The bleeping became faster.

"Thank God," she heard her mother say. "You're in the hospital, love. There's been an . . . accident."

"Accident?" Louise swallowed causing her throat to hurt.

"Don't worry about that for now." Her mum's hands were soft as she stroked her forehead and caressed her hair. "The main thing is you're safe. Everything is going to be alright."

The nightmare must have finished. That was good. No more whirring, leather-face, chasing her with his chainsaw. Bright light. Plaited hair . . . then darkness.

Someone was moistening her lips with something cold. It was an effort but she managed to open her eyes again. It was her mum. Did she ever sleep? She always seemed to be there.

"You're alright," her mum reassured, "I'm here."

She felt her soft lips kiss her forehead. It felt nice, comforting.

"Thank goodness you're okay, love. Everything's going to be alright, I know it is. You just need to rest."

"Where am I?" she tried to cough away the lump in her throat.

"You're safe, in the hospital, being looked after. I'm staying here with you, and I'm not going anywhere."

Louise had no comprehension of time. Only that she was waking again and trying to open her eyes. Her vision was clearer than the previous time. A nurse in a uniform was stood with a clipboard at the side of the bed.

"Hello, sleepy head. I'm Elizabeth. I'm looking after you today. The doctor will be coming shortly now you've woken up. We are giving you less medication now so you'll be staying awake much longer each time. You understand you're in the hospital, don't you?"

"I think so," Louise croaked, ". . . my throat feels sore."

"It will do. You've had a tube down there. It'll ease off though. As soon as the doctor has spoken to you and says you can have fluids, I'll get you some cool water."

Louise could see her mother on the chair the other side of her bed. She had a tissue in her hands and was dabbing her eyes.

"I'm okay, Mum," she tried to reassure.

"I know, sweetheart," a warm hand squeezed hers, "you just need to rest now and get better."

"I will." Louise tried to clear her throat, "Did someone say it was an accident or did I dream that?"

"We don't know for certain, love. The police are going to speak to you when the doctors allow them to."

"The police?"

"Yes, to try and find out what happened to you . . . how you had your . . . accident."

Louise shook her head from side to side, trying desperately to clear the fuzziness.

"Can you remember anything?" her mother asked gently.

"No . . ." her eyes were closing of their own accord again, despite her efforts to keep them open, "only being cold . . . and . . . and plaited hair."

"Plaited hair?"

"Shining in the light from above."

"Your hair was plaited when they found you," her mum said, "Did you plait it yourself?"

Did she? She couldn't remember.

"I don't know."

"Can you remember anything else? Can you remember who did this to you?"

Bottles. Bottles that weren't in the boot.

"Something about bottles."

"Bottles?"

Louise sighed and rested her head back. "I can't remember."

"Don't worry," her mum said, squeezing her hand. "Rest now."

46.

As if the police finding the body of the dead girl in the woods wasn't bad enough, they'd now got the one he hadn't finished off properly. How the hell had she survived? Memories of that night were vivid. He had strangled her and she was dead, he was sure of it. But then he remembered the bang of the shutter and he'd thought someone was there, so had rushed to find out what the noise was. She must have somehow got oxygen into her with a final breath. But even so, how the hell had she survived him dropping her into the ravine with the other one? It couldn't be possible – or shouldn't be.

He had to get away now; there wasn't a minute to lose. There was no time to speak to his brother and have the conversation he'd wanted. He'd been putting it off and putting it off. But it wasn't as if he could directly say goodbye anyway, his brother would be sure to stop him taking his life and nobody was going to do that.

Where was his brother anyway?

There was no time to find out. He'd got rope in the car ready, now all he had to do was drive to the woods and find a tree. It all seemed sorted in his head, it was carrying it out that scared the shit out of him. Any choices he'd had were well and truly gone. Time was of the essence now. The cops would be knocking on the door any minute. He opened the kitchen cupboard and reached for the half bottle of Bell's whisky that had barely been touched. Neither he, nor his brother were spirit drinkers. The liquor was going to aggravate his already sickly stomach, rebelling against the cancer on an hourly basis, however, despite that, he unscrewed the top and took a mouthful directly from the bottle. As it slid down his gullet, warmth spread through him. But he ended up gagging in the sink. Still, he put the bottle in his anorak pocket, ready for when he needed it. He'd have to force more down to give him courage to take his own life.

With one last look around the place he'd called home for the last few years, he made his way towards the door, pausing at the hallway mirror to take one last look at himself. Staring back at him was an image of his evil father. He'd never noticed how like him he'd become. Or was he imagining it as he faced his own demise? Either way, there was no time to dwell on that bastard. He quickly closed the door behind him and tightened up his coat to protect his cancer-ravaged bones from the cold. His pace was quick as he headed towards his car. The most prominent thought in his mind was, he didn't want to die, even though he was going to soon anyway from the cancer. It was the thought of speeding the process up that scared him. But there was no way he was going to spend the last few weeks he had left in a jail. That wasn't going to happen. He'd vowed that from the day he sat in the consultant's office and he'd told him about the cancer diagnosis. It had come as no surprise. He'd survived it once before, which caused him significant suffering, but his time was up now, he'd known he couldn't survive a second time.

Considering how ill he felt, even he was surprised how swiftly he was able to walk towards his car, despite the breathlessness. He dreaded anyone stopping him for a chat along the way, so kept his head down. As he approached his car, he became aware of footsteps growing louder the closer they got to him.

"Going somewhere?"

His stomach clenched as he turned around. Inspector Porteous, the man leading the enquiry at Harlow Wood, approached with a uniformed officer alongside him.

"I am actually," he replied assertively. "I have a sick relative that I need to go and see. It's an emergency . . . a heart attack. I have to leave right away."

"Well," the Inspector's face was deadpan, "I'm afraid you can't. Right now, you need to accompany us to the police station. We have some questions we'd like to ask you."

"Can't they wait?" he frowned, "I really want to see my relative before . . . well, you know. I need to get there sooner rather than later."

"I'm sorry but our questions won't wait."

He softened the pitch of his voice. "Surely a few hours won't make any difference? I could come to the station later?"

"I'm afraid not. You need to accompany us now."

"Why the urgency? I don't understand. You're not arresting me, are you?"

"No, but we will do if you don't voluntarily accompany us."

His gut clenched. Just a couple more minutes and he'd have been on his way. Now his past was about to come out. And they'd have an absolute fucking field day.

There was no choice but to accompany them. He could hardly run away, the last five minutes had taken their toll. He barely had the energy to walk anymore, let alone run. A fluttery feeling in his chest made him feel light-headed as he walked alongside them to the parked Ford Granada. This time the empty feeling of sickness he felt in the pit of his stomach was not only down to the cancer – it was the sheer gut-wrenching realisation that he'd been caught and the ramifications of that.

Time was finally up for him.

Inspector Porteous held the car door and the accompanying policeman got in first and shuffled along. He ducked his head to sit alongside him as the Inspector got in the driver's seat and started up the engine.

As the car moved off, an impending sense of doom caused his head to throb relentlessly. He massaged it with his fingertips and silently cursed. He'd been so close to escaping and outmanoeuvring them one final time. If only he'd have left a minute or two earlier. But he'd stopped to look in the damn mirror, which had been pointless. All he'd seen was his old man. It seemed as if the evil bastard was mocking him.

Because now he'd been caught, it was going to be the biggest circus in town.

47.

Kym

Banging on her door woke her.

"Kym, Kym," Guy shouted, "open the door."

As she tossed the sheets back, she glanced at the bedside clock. It was ten minutes past eight. She'd purposely been sleeping in, as she wasn't on her shift until eleven thirty. The previous evening, her, Marie, Lisa, Zoe, Simon and Guy had all been huddled together in Zoe's room which was next to the kitchen, with the door wide open, drinking endless cups of coffee and beer. They waited for Mrs McGee to come and tell them what she'd managed to find out from the incident office, but she never came. Whether it was because she couldn't get any information, or she had and didn't want to share it with them, Kym wasn't sure. Her instincts told her it was the latter though. By 1 a.m. they'd decided to call it a night.

Her heart did a leap as she opened the door to see Guy in his uniform. The white tunic and dark trousers suited him. He looked hot. He was beaming, displaying his perfect set of white teeth.

"It's Louise they've found," he stepped into her room and closed the door behind him, "she's alive."

"Oh, my God!" Kym flew into his arm and he held her tightly. Relief rushed through her. "Thank you,

God," she said to the ceiling before she pulled back, "Is she okay? How do you know?"

"Charge Nurse Griffiths told us at report first thing. I don't know how she is though, I don't think anyone does. She's in the City hospital."

"I can't believe it. I'll have to go and see her . . . as soon as I can."

"Yeah, I'll take you. It's fantastic, isn't it?"

"Brilliant. I wonder if they know who took her?"

"Not sure about that." He screwed up his face, it looked almost painful. "There's also some not so good news. It sounds like they've recovered the remains of someone close to where they found Louise."

Kym's heart plummeted. "Vanya?"

"Highly likely," his expression was pained, "And there's another thing. When I was going to work this morning, a police car was outside South House. It's got me wondering if it's Matron's husband, Mr McGee?"

She put her hand to her mouth. "Mr McGee? Never! He's too quiet. Seems to mind his own business."

"Yeah, but think about it, he has access to the rooms in the nurses' home, with him being an odd-job man. He could have taken the knickers."

"I know, but . . ." she shook her head, "no, it can't be him. I reckon you've got that wrong. Maybe the police were there to speak to Mrs McGee?"

"Could be I suppose," Guy shrugged, "but remember, the quiet ones are often the worst, don't they say?"

"I think you've got this completely wrong, Agatha," Kym gave a wry grin, "you'll have to come up with a

367

better theory than that, I reckon. Anyway, the main thing is, Louise is safe. Thank God."

"Yeah, it's fantastic news," he pulled her back into his arms and held her for a few seconds before pulling away. "And can I just say, as lovely as you look in those cute pyjamas, I think you'd look better with them off."

The feeling of how much he wanted her was pressed against her tummy. Excitement flooded through her as she looked into his vibrant eyes. But it just didn't feel right. Not with Louise in hospital and remains found.

"We can't," she feebly protested as he started nuzzling her neck, "What about Mrs McGee?"

"What about her? She'll think I'm at work as I'm registered out on the board."

"Yeah, well . . . how have you managed to leave the ward anyway?"

"I asked Mr Griffiths," his gorgeous mouth was working its magic on her lips, "if I could come across and let you know about Louise."

"That was nice of him. But he'll expect you back pronto, won't he?"

"I better be quick then," he said and deepened the kiss.

* * *

Excitement flooded through Kym as she made her way down the ward at the City hospital to see her friend. She was grateful to Guy for taking her. He couldn't come in with her though. When she'd telephoned the ward to ask if she could visit, they'd told her that visitors were limited.

A staff nurse directed Kym towards Louise's room. "Not too long for a visit, she gets tired easily."

"I won't stay long. Is her mum here?" Kym asked.

"Not right now. She will be shortly though. And no hugging! Louise has broken ribs."

"Oh. Okay. Thank you."

Kym headed towards Louise's room with a mixture of eager anticipation and trepidation running through her. There was lightness in her chest, but a fluttery feeling in her stomach. How was her friend likely to be? And how exactly should she respond to someone who'd been beaten and left for dead? Guy had told her to be led by Louise. If she didn't want to talk about it, then talk about anything but, however, she might want to say something and if so, be a good friend and listen.

The female police officer sitting outside the room nodded to her she tentatively opened the door. Louise was facing her, looking as pale as the sheets on the bed. There was an intravenous infusion in one arm, and the sling on the other with a monitor attached to her forefinger. Kym wished she could hug her.

She pulled up a chair, then leaned in to kiss her cheek.

"Thank goodness you're okay," she whispered in Louise's ear. She smelled of hospital, all fresh and clean. "You gave us all such a fright."

"It's so good to see you," Louise smiled as Kym sat down, "I've missed you."

"I've missed you too. We all have. How are you? Sorry," she screwed up her face, "bit of a daft question."

"It's okay. I think I'm doing as well as I should be."

"That's good, then. Here," Kym reached for the bag she'd brought with her. "I got you these," she placed some magazines on the locker and a box of Dairy Box chocolates, "if you don't eat them the nurses will."

"Yeah, I'm sure they will. Thank you."

Louise was looking visibly gaunt, with her pretty eyes dull and lifeless, sunken deep into their sockets. Kym couldn't help herself. "God, Louise," she swallowed down the ache in her throat, "I can't believe this has happened to you."

It was hard not to show how shocked she was. Even though her appearance was understandable, seeing her friend looking so frail, upset her. She remembered what Guy had said about remains being found. It could have been Louise. Could have been her. Could have been any of them.

"It has been pretty awful. Look," Louise lifted her hair up above her ear and revealed a shaved area and two puncture marks. "That's where they pierced it, to help reduce the swelling."

"How awful. Is it painful?"

"Not half as bad as when I first had the head injury. I remember that pain was excruciating. I thought my head would burst."

"I'm so sorry you had to go through that." Kym had to stifle the tears that were so close. "What have the doctors said?"

"Just that I've got to stop trying to remember. It's hard to explain, but it's like a dream you've had which you try and recall, it's there somewhere, but you just can't grasp it. It hurts my head if I try to think too much.

Seemingly, it might come back, but I'm told I need to be prepared it might not. There is also a part of me that's maybe blocking it out, so the doctors say."

"Well, that's understandable. I can't even bear to think about what you went through, so I can't imagine how it must be for you."

"One good thing is though, they did tests on me while I was unconscious and it seems I wasn't sexually assaulted . . . you know . . . no evidence to show there'd been penetration. But it's all a complete blank."

Kym winced at the graphic reminder of what her friend had gone through, "That's one good thing."

"Yeah. Oh, and they told me my hair was plaited when they found me. I haven't had plaits since I was about ten, so that's really creepy."

Louise's expression was pitiful, so Kym quickly changed the subject, "How long are you going to be in here for, do you know?"

"Not yet, although they tell me I'm making good progress."

Kym couldn't resist asking, even though she knew the answer really. "Will you be coming back to Harlow Wood, do you think . . . eventually?"

"I'd like to." Louise looked down at her arm in plaster and a sling, "But I can't work with my elbow and wrist fractured, and my broken ribs, so I'll be back-schooled if I do return. My mum doesn't want me to though."

Kym let out a huge sigh. "It's so bloody unfair what happened to you."

"I know. That's what I feel like. But with the best will in the world, if I do well with physio, it's going to take a while to be able to carry out any nursing duties, if I ever get back to them."

"I'm gutted for myself as I'll miss you, but devastated for you. I know how much you wanted to do your training."

"I still do, especially since being in here. The nurses have been fantastic taking care of me and encouraging me. From what the police are saying, I'm lucky to be alive. It's terrible about Vanya," tears started welling up in Louise's eyes and she reached for a tissue from the locker. "Sorry. I'm so emotional, I seem to cry at the slightest thing."

So the remains were definitely Vanya? Kym didn't want to ask.

"Well, you can forgive yourself for that. You have been through something terrible."

"I know," Louise dabbed her eyes. "I wish I could help the police. They must be browned off with me that I can't tell them anything. I try, but I just have no memory. I can remember lots of insignificant stuff, but nothing that could help. Seemingly, I was hit with a severe blow to the head and the police believe I was strangled and thrown down the ravine. They say the culprit would have believed I was dead."

"Bastard. Who would do something so terrible? One thing I've said all along is, you wouldn't have gone off with someone you didn't know. So, I would think the police are right. You must have been hit over the head."

"Yeah, I think that too. I'd have never gone off with anyone. I have a female detective, Lisa that comes each day to update me. They've got someone in for questioning but she can't say who."

Kym shuffled uncomfortably. She still didn't believe for a minute Guy's theory was right. There had to be another explanation.

"What?" Louise's eyes narrowed, "do you know something?"

"Not really. Guy just had an idea that it might be Mrs McGee's husband, you know the odd-job man because he saw a police car directly outside South House. But nobody's sure what's happening. It's a bit like Chinese whispers with everyone adding a bit on here there and everywhere. Anyone wearing trousers and working at Harlow Wood seems to be a suspect according to gossip. Even Charge Nurse Griffiths just because he's not wearing his SRN badge."

"Really? Louise sighed, "The detective told me they're pursuing several lines of enquiry. She did say they had a man helping with enquiries but nobody has been charged yet."

"God knows what's happening, then. The sooner they get him though, the better for Vanya's family as well as that other poor girl in the woods. And you," Kym squeezed her friend's hand, "you need to know, too."

"It will help, yeah, definitely." Louise scowled. "I can't somehow see it's Mr McGee. I can barely remember seeing him to be honest. I reckon he'd be a bit more vivid in my mind if it was him."

"Yeah, I'm with you. He seems a quiet sort of man to me. Keeps himself to himself from what I've seen and others have said. You did go to see him once, to see if he could fix the dripping tap in your room."

"Did I? I can't remember that."

"Yeah, well it would be an insignificant event really, so you're hardly likely to remember with so much happening since then," Kym reassured. "And in any case, it is only Guy suggesting it's him, nobody else has. There's loads of gossip as you can imagine. Half of it's made up, I'm sure."

"I bet. Anyway, enough of all this, it's making my head throb. Tell me about you, any developments with Guy?"

"Funny you should say that," Kym beamed, "he's outside waiting for me. He brought me here."

"And?"

"And . . ." Kym grinned, "we're together now."

"Hallelujah! About time. When did this happen?"

"The night of the nightdress and pyjama party. He's been fantastic since you went missing. He came home to Cleethorpes with me to persuade my dad to let me stay on at Harlow Wood. My dad was frantic after Vanya and then you went missing."

"I bet. So Guy's a bit of a knight in shining armour then?"

"Just a bit."

Louise's eyes twitched, as if she was trying to concentrate. "I'm trying to remember what else was going on with you . . . there's something."

"My mum's surgery?"

"That's it. Has she had it?"

"Yes, and she's doing well. Not sure she's the best patient though. I bet they'll be pleased to discharge her. I know my mum, she'll be telling the nurses how they should be doing things."

"Once a nurse, always a nurse," Louise smiled, "we'll probably be like that one day."

"Do you reckon?"

"I'm sure of it. So, you sound like you're happy with Guy, yet you have a look as if something's wrong. What is it? Am I that frightful to look at?"

"Don't be daft." Kym braced herself. She had to confess to what she'd done. It was preying on her mind and she needed to be honest. She swallowed. "I had to tell the police about you and Nick Feeney."

"Nick Feeney . . . what's he got to do with anything?"

"You can't remember?"

Louise's vacant expression indicated she couldn't.

"They took him in for questioning. You and he . . . had a night together."

Louise was silent for a moment. Kym could see she was trying desperately to think. "Nick Feeney? The tutor and charge nurse? We had a night together? What do you mean?"

"At his house. You had sex. You told me all about it afterwards."

"My God."

"Yeah, I know. It was a bit of a shock. Anyway, when you went missing, I was questioned by the Inspector leading the case. I was so worried about you, I had to tell him about it. I am sorry, I really didn't want to."

Louise shook her head, "We had sex? I can't remember anything like that happening . . . although there is something."

"Don't try and force it. I shouldn't have said anything, especially if you can't remember."

"I can't quite believe it." Her forehead wrinkled, "Me and him, we had sex?"

Kym nodded, "But he's nowhere to be seen. Rumour has it he's left Harlow Wood."

Louise stared for an overlong moment. "It wouldn't have been him though, I'm sure of it."

"No, I didn't think so either. It's just the police were pressing me for any men in your life you might have had a recent relationship with, and I was frantic for you."

"Don't worry, you had to say . . . I would have done the same."

Kym watched as her friend's eyelids started to close, so didn't expand on her fears that because of her, Nick Feeney was sure to lose his job.

Louise drifted off to sleep. Kym quietly reached for her bag and made her way to the door. Even with her limited medical experience she could tell her friend's recovery was going to take some time.

48.

Louise

Had Kym left? She had been so pleased to see her friend but after about ten minutes of chatting she found it hard to concentrate. Her eyes had become heavy and closed of their own free will despite trying hard to keep them open. Some of the things Kym had said didn't make sense. Her and Nick Feeney? She found that hard to believe. Why couldn't she remember something as significant as that? The monitor bleeps slowed down as her breathing became shallow – she was beginning to recognise the tones, particularly as she drifted off to sleep.

Within an instant, she was back at Harlow Wood, staring at herself in the full-length wardrobe mirror. She was wearing her uniform and quickly tied her hair into a bun and gripped the hat over the top. The clock was ticking on the wall. It was huge with a large second hand. And the tick was loud. Where had the big round clock come from? It wasn't there before. The chimes rang out, indicating twelve midnight. They were loud. They'd wake up everyone in the nurses' home chiming as they were. She counted up to six and then fled her room. She had to get to the car park to check . . . the boot? What boot? Why was the boot important? Bottles, something about bottles.

As she stepped outside of North House, it was freezing cold. She should have brought her cape. Silly to forget it. And why was she wearing her slippers? There was a siren screeching. It was getting closer. Was it an ambulance? . . . no, it couldn't be. They didn't have emergency ambulances at Harlow Wood. Trauma cases were taken to Mansfield General as they had an A&E department. Maybe it was the police? Yes, that was it. It'd be the police. Her pace increased, she had to get there. But where was there? Where was she going?

She was running now, as best she could in her slippers. Danger was lurking, she just wasn't sure where. But she knew it was close. She checked her pocket for the car keys. They were there. Good, she could see inside the boot. See if there were any bottles.

The sirens were getting closer. Why was she running, then? The police would help her surely? She dodged the puddles. They seemed to get deeper the nearer she got to the car park. She was almost there. What was on that ledge at the side of the car park? It looked like Vanya. She was fast asleep. Her plaited hair was laid at the side of her. It was much longer than she remembered. She looked like Rapunzel from the fairy tale. It was almost the same length as Vanya herself. Should she call out to her to warn her of the danger? No, best to leave her, she had to get to the car. She could see it now. It was further away than she thought. Her legs were getting heavier, weighed down by the sodden slippers.

A noise made her turn around. Someone was following her, she was sure of it. Better to speed up. But the slippers were like lead weights around her feet. She looked down at her uniform she'd been wearing, but it was gone. She was now in a flimsy nightie. Was it the nightdress and pyjama party? Yes, that was it. They were trying to raise funds for the little girl to buy her a wheelchair and maybe send the family on holiday. As she passed a row of parked cars, Lloyd was waiting, rattling a collection tin. She didn't have any money though, and she needed to get to the car. It was important.

Lloyd called out to her but she ignored him. She'd see him later and explain. The car had seemed so much closer, yet now it was further away. Something was tapping her back. She reached to feel what it was. Her hair had grown longer and was in a plait, just like Vanya's. Who'd plaited it like that?

Sutty appeared next, stood next to a brown Mini talking to Mr Duffield. He smiled and waved at her, Mr Duffield didn't. Before she had chance to wave back, footsteps were catching up with her. They were close now. She wanted to look round to see how close, but she couldn't. She didn't want to see his face. But he was there. It was almost as if she was a feral animal – she could smell him. Smell the danger.

She reached the car. Nobody was going to stop her. She fished for the keys in her pocket. But they had been in her uniform pocket and that was gone now. The nightie had no pockets. She had to open the boot. She leant forward to click it. Miraculously it opened.

She screamed out loud. A man was hiding in the boot. He grabbed hold of her plait. Did he hit her? Or had she blacked out?

It was dark. The floor underneath her was hard. Hard and cold. She was naked. Fingers tweaked her nipples, hands rubbed the insides of her thighs. With a great effort, she managed to force her heavy eyes open. Someone was straddling her. She recognised the eyes. Tiny, hooded eyes, glazed and unmoving. Almost vacant, yet focussed on the task ahead. Pressure was tightening around her neck, rigid hands were forcing the breath out of her. She tried to move, tried to get air into her lungs before it ran out. Black specks appeared in front of her, growing in size to dots. Masses of black dots, coming together and joining up. And still the beady eyes glared.

"No . . . no. . ." she screamed, ". . . No . . ."

"It's alright, love," her mother's voice was telling her, "you're having a bad dream. Everything's alright."

Her mother's soft hands were stroking her hair. It felt nice. She slowly opened her eyes and took in her surroundings. She was still in the hospital bed. The monitor probe was attached to her finger and her arm was in a plaster-of-Paris cast supported by a sling.

"You're fine," her mum smiled lovingly at her, "don't worry, the doctors said you might experience nightmares or flashbacks. Here, have some water."

Louise sucked some cool water through the straw as her mum held the cup.

"Get the policewoman here, Mum, you have to get her to come, now."

"She will come, love. She comes every day. What is it?"

Louise swallowed, "I know who it is that tried to kill me."

"Alright, calm down. I wasn't going to say anything until they charged him, but they have actually got a man in custody."

"Please Mum, get Lisa, the policewoman here, quickly before I forget."

Vile images flashed through her mind, moving too quickly for her to process. But her racing heart gaining momentum was picked up by the rapid tone of the monitor.

Her lips trembled, "I know who it is."

49.

He lay down in the small custody cell. They'd quickly found his true identity, he wasn't entirely sure how. He'd been charged by his birth name with two counts of murder and one of abduction and attempted murder. For now, investigations were ongoing about other killings he'd done. From the moment of the first interview with Porteous when he'd answered every question with no comment, there was never any doubt he was going to be charged. Especially as they'd found the incriminating evidence of the knickers. The following day, he was going to be moved to a prison facility where he'd appear in court to face the charges, and placed on remand to remain in custody until his trial. That's what they'd said, anyway. As yet they had no idea he was dying. He was saving that little nugget. But once they did try and move him, he was going to say. By his own reckoning, it was highly likely he'd be taken to a hospital – the judiciary wouldn't want him dying on them. He surmised he'd be initially admitted for an assessment, but he was going to exaggerate his symptoms to ensure he stayed in hospital. Not that he'd have to do much of that – his body was worn-out, ravaged by the cancer.

His humiliation was now complete. In front of two police officers, he'd had to undress. His clothes were confiscated, his neck brace had gone, and the scarf to hide his protruding Adam's apple. The female persona of

Mrs McGee, matron of Harlow Wood, was no longer. He'd been exposed for who he really was. Eddie Major, a man living as a woman. Not by choice, but by a cruel twist of fate.

The officers had stifled their sniggers as he undressed. But their smirks and muffled laughs stopped as he stood naked in front of them and they saw for themselves he didn't have a penis. Breasts yes, but no penis. In its place, a huge unsightly scar. The humour turned to disbelief. They stared at him with incredulity, not quite knowing what to say or do. The younger officer handed over a green boiler suit for him to wear while the older one disappeared, no doubt bursting to tell someone about the freak of nature they'd charged.

The cell he was laid in was freezing. He pulled the blanket over himself. Not as far as he wanted to, that would expose his feet which were already numb with the cold. He couldn't sleep. The pain was severe in his bones and chest. His breathing was laboured. The question on his mind was how long had he got left. He wished he could close his eyes and not wake up. But he knew he wasn't quite there yet.

All the allegations Porteous had thrown at him were true. He had killed his father and several other women hence the need to move around England to escape capture. And coming towards the end of his life, he questioned himself as to whether he felt any remorse, but came to the conclusion he didn't. Killing was a compulsion, one he hadn't been able to fight. Once he came to terms with the terrible misfortune he'd had, the only pleasure he derived from his life was planning and killing young females. And he had no regrets – except for Angela. She'd been the only person he'd ever loved, apart from his brother, but was that really love he felt for him? He wasn't sure it was love, maybe closer to deep affection.

He recalled the officers' faces as he'd stood naked in front of them. He saw them trying to stifle bemused smiles. How could you be a man without a penis? It was unheard of. And it was to him too when he'd had to undergo a penectomy – surgical removal of his penis because of cancer. Maybe things could have worked out differently had he not ignored the small spot, rather like a mole that appeared on his penis initially. He'd not taken much notice, it hadn't hurt or anything so it was largely forgotten. But over a period of time, it spread and became larger. He wasn't sexually active, so he'd kept it private until the sore started weeping and soiling his underpants. When he eventually ventured to the doctors, the old boy hadn't seemed unduly worried which may have been because the condition was so rare, or he hadn't actually seen it before. He'd referred him to the local hospital and the consultant there had taken swift action. Following tests, he'd broken the life-changing news to him that it was cancer that had spread so far that all of the penis would have to be surgically removed.

It was devastating. Although he'd never been sexually active, he couldn't comprehend life without a penis. And the surgery had been massive psychologically. During the operation, they'd made a small opening between the scrotum and anus and redirected the urethra that carries urine. He was still in control of passing urine, but he had to do it sitting down. Apparently, so the consultant told him, this wasn't always successful. Some patients may have to have their tube redirected to their abdomen and wear a bag to collect the urine. He should have been grateful by all accounts, but he wasn't. He'd been angry. Furious. Ashamed. For months he hadn't been able to look at himself as his brother dutifully changed his dressings.

It took almost a year for him to become resigned to the surgery. He was still a man, but had always been an odd looking man and never indulged in sex. At school they called him endless names, often suggesting he looked girlish. During that year, it became evident that with help, he could easily pass as a woman. That was the first time he felt a sense of purpose. He began to believe that he may have been trapped in the wrong body and he should have been born a female. Maybe that's why he'd loved Angela's femininity. After months of deliberation, he came to the conclusion the best course of action would be to live his life as a female. The consultant, who'd carried out the surgery, supported his idea and helped him by prescribing hormone therapy. The medication helped with the development of breasts and his deep voice became much less masculine. He grew his hair and pretty quickly he started to appear feminine. He became quite adept at choosing clothes, styling his own hair, and applying makeup. He should have been, he'd watched and helped Angela for years. Maybe he'd always had a feminine side? He made the transition quite effortlessly once he'd come to terms with the hideous surgery. It took a while for him to gain the confidence to live openly as a woman though. Once he had, he started to apply for jobs. Initially office work, then he progressed to a matron of a girls' boarding school. He liked that. All of the posts were obtained by using false references supplied by him. He became quite adept at copying letterheads. His brother would pose as a previous boss if a potential employer wanted a verbal reference over the telephone. His brother was a shy soul; eager to please and basically would do anything he told him to. Not once did he ever question. Even when he suggested to him they live as man and wife for appearances. Some of the jobs came with live-in accommodation which suited them both. But his brother was never involved with the killings. He was complicit by turning the other way maybe, but that was all. Initially his brother had been taken from Harlow Wood to the station and questioned by Porteous prior to his own arrest, but quickly released, so his solicitor told him. It would have been a pointless exercise; he'd kept the killings from him so he knew nothing. He will have suspected, but he was confident he'd never have grassed on him to the police.

Footsteps approached and stopped at his cell door. He heard the keys rattle and slowly the door opened. Porteous stood in the doorway, accompanied by a uniformed police officer.

What did he want? He'd seen enough of him in the interview room. Nevertheless, he straightened up and moved into a sitting position.

Porteous cleared his throat. "You'll not be moved tomorrow as planned. You'll remain here in custody until we can arrange for a doctor to come and examine you in light of . . . any medical needs you might have."

Medical needs? Their terminology for a man without a penis.

"Once the doctor's assessment is complete, you'll be moved to a prison and placed on remand until your trial."

Where would they send him? A male or a female prison? They'd need the doctor's input but he was fairly sure it would be a male one even though, like a female, he had to sit down to pee.

He was weary and didn't want to go anywhere. Not to be a laughing stock when it hit the papers, he wanted no part of that. "You need to get me a doctor now." He stared directly into the Inspector's eyes, "I'm not well."

"Really? I'm afraid we've heard that before, many times. They all try it."

"I'm not trying anything," he said firmly, "I'm dying. I have terminal cancer and haven't got long left to live."

Porteous looked disbelieving initially, however his expression changed as he continued to stare. He could feel the sticky sweat beginning to forming on his forehead. It was as if for the first time the Inspector saw in front of him, a sick man. He kept his gaze steady but showed no emotion, "We'll have a doctor here in the morning."

Good. No way was he going to prison.

Porteous turned and walked out. The keys jangled in the lock. He was alone. No doubt until the following morning. But he was confident the doctor would come. The task ahead would be to convince him how ill he was. That wouldn't be difficult. Because he was clever, like the great Houdini, he always managed to escape and now was no exception. He'd been thwarted in his mission to take his own life, but the hospital was the next best thing. The nurses would be professional and care for him, unlike in a prison. There he'd be an absolute joke.

He lay down again. He felt warmer. Must be adrenaline running through him. His lips twitched into a half smile. He'd outmanoeuvred Porteous just as he'd outwitted the police for years.

He was never the thick piece of shit his father always told him he was.

50.

Kym

It was the day for Vanya's memorial service at Harlow Wood. It had taken weeks to organise. The recreational hall which had hosted the nightdress and pyjama party was set up in a completely different way, with a lectern, a huge vase of lilies next to it, and rows of seats occupied by second year students, ward nurses, admin staff, domestic staff and the canteen staff.

Kym held Guy's hand as they took their seats on the front row which had been reserved for Vanya's family. Mrs Beaumont was responsible for organising the event and had said those that had started their training with Vanya were to sit at the front alongside her parents. All ten of them were sitting together, dressed in their uniforms as they'd been instructed. After nodding to Vanya's mum and dad, Kym's biggest smile was reserved for her friend Louise, already seated next to them with her mum. Louise had told her that Vanya's parents had specifically asked for her to sit alongside them, which was a generously spirited gesture. They'd lost their daughter, but wanted to celebrate the fact Louise had survived.

Louise looked so much better. Although wearing her own clothes, she was still one of them. She'd been discharged from hospital and was recuperating at home.

They'd been talking regularly on the phone, and Kym had been sending letters. Louise had said she loved hearing updates about them all. It was great to see her back at Harlow Wood. Kym was hoping it might spur her on to return but she had a niggling doubt she wouldn't. It was probably preferable for her to start her general training in a completely different hospital.

Zoe had taken her place next to Simon. She'd appeared fine when she'd realised her and Guy were together. Guy tried to dismiss it all, saying he didn't think she was ever interested in him, but Kym knew differently. Fortunately, Zoe was fickle and had now moved onto a more permanent footing with Francis, the trainee doctor. Simon had, the last few weeks, appeared particularly friendly with Marie from their set. But it was hard to tell with him. He seemed to thrive on variety.

Sutty's voice caused Kym to turn her head towards the door. Lloyd was walking at the side of him, and following them was Nick Feeney. Kym nudged Guy who was reading the order of service sheet and he turned to look. Nick was accompanied by an attractive female, probably his wife. She wouldn't have known Vanya or Louise as she worked at Mansfield General, but maybe he felt the need for some moral support to attend. Louise had told her she still hadn't remembered their night together. Not in any great detail. She was aware of something, of maybe being in his house. But not the sex. Probably that was a good thing if he was back permanently with his wife. He'd already left Harlow Wood. Mrs Beaumont had told the class he was going to work as a charge nurse in Cambridge. He hadn't done

390

anything illegal with Louise, she'd been over the age of consent, it just hadn't been appropriate behaviour for a charge nurse and tutor. To her, it seemed strange he'd even returned.

The last to arrive was Mr Duffield, looking as odd as ever. For some reason known only to him, he was wearing a black bow tie. It had crossed Kym's mind, fuelled by Simon that he might have been responsible for the girls' abductions. He was certainly odd, but thankfully not a danger to anyone. Alongside him was Mrs Valance, the other nursing officer who'd been sick when they first started their training. She had taken over signing off ward assessments and had done so with Kym's first one she'd taken on the ward which she passed. It had been about holistic care of a patient. She'd been assessed by Charge Nurse Griffiths on the ward, dealing with the male patient's personal hygiene and his wound dressing. She'd loved the ward and was sad to be leaving. There was only one more week left on the placement, then they'd be back in school for a week, before moving to her next female ward.

The vicar took his place at the lectern. They all fell silent as he began the service with a moving tribute to Vanya. It seemed fitting. Although she hadn't been at the hospital long, she was part of the Harlow Wood family and it was right they were celebrating her life that had been cut short so viciously.

$* * *$

It was early evening when Guy and Kym had been for a walk and headed back to the gardens outside the School of Nursing. They'd been there that afternoon following the service as those attending had been invited to view the bench that had been erected in Vanya's memory. Since then, a couple of small bunches of flowers had been left on the seat.

Kym read the silver plaque again which Vanya's parents had suggested.

Vanya Mann 1977. Loved by all.

She stifled a tear. She'd done enough crying at the service even though it had been beautiful. Afterwards, as they had refreshments in the canteen, the vicar had been circulating and had the nerve to suggest forgiveness for Mrs McGee, whoever he she truly was. Seemingly, he was unconscious in a hospital and close to death. Kym couldn't help but feel angry that he'd escaped a long prison sentence and certainly couldn't think of forgiveness. In his guise as the matron, he'd sat in the interviews with the police as a so-called support to them. All along, while they were frantic about their friend, he'd known Vanya was dead as he'd killed her. And he'd had the audacity to urge Kym to tell the police about Louise when she went missing, and if she had a new boyfriend in her life. Yet all along, he'd been the culprit, blatantly sitting alongside the police, gaining information on the case. The police must surely have questions to answer. But he'd fooled them all. Harlow Wood had launched an internal investigation as to how he'd come to be employed by them in the first place. And his brother too as the handyman, who must have been a complete weirdo living as he did as a so-called husband.

Guy moved the flowers to the side of the bench so they had a space to sit down.

"So," she said, sitting close to him, "are you okay?"

"Yeah, course I am," he picked up an elastic band from the arm of the bench and started fiddling with it. "What makes you think I'm not?"

"Because we've talked about how well the service went and how nice Vanya's parents seemed to be, and we've said that Louise looks fine and how lovely it's been that she came back for the service, but apart from that you've seemed quiet today, as if you're thinking about something else. What is it? Tell me."

He swallowed. "You know I went home yesterday."

"Yeah, course."

He took a deep breath in. "I'm going to be leaving Harlow Wood."

She knew he would. He was far too bright to train as a nurse. Nevertheless, it felt like someone had thumped her hard in her tummy. What would it mean for the two of them? Were they going to break up? She raised her eyebrows, "You've had a better offer?"

"Sort of." He screwed his face up. "I think it's more that the old man was right. I was a fool to leave medical school."

"So, what are you saying, you're going back?"

"Yep, pretty much."

She sighed, "I always knew you would."

"You did?"

"Yes. Anyone can see you have potential. And that's what your parents can see. I'm pleased for you, honestly I am, but selfishly, I'm really going to miss you. First Louise and now you, I'll be like Billy-no-mates."

"No, you won't," he playfully nudged her shoulder with his, "you're too popular for that."

Her insides quivered. The thought of them parting hurt like mad. But it was right he should do what he wanted to do.

"You'll be a great doctor," she pasted on a smile, "anyone can see that."

"Thanks. I hope so."

"You will. And you'll be more mature this time. Although I'm not sure about you and studying," she grinned, "are you going to apply yourself, as you've not done much since we've been here."

His warm eyes lit up, he'd know she was right, he hadn't. "I'll have to. It's been easy peasy being here, so I haven't had to study, but I will over the next few years, that's for sure. Med school is full of theory before you even start on the patients."

"Where have you decided to go?"

"Leeds."

"I hardly dare ask," she swallowed the lump in her throat. "When?"

"February. But don't look so worried, I'm staying here until then so you're stuck with me a bit longer, yet."

"What do you mean staying here? How can you do that? If this isn't going to be what you're eventually going to do, you'll have to let them know."

"Yeah, I know, but not just yet. I've checked the contract we signed, I have to give four weeks' notice so I'll do that at Christmas."

"But why? Don't you want some time off before you start?"

"Nope. I want to stay here with you."

"You can't."

"Who says I can't. I'm not going anywhere, not for a while yet. Why would I?"

"Because it isn't what you want to do. You can't stay around for me. That isn't right."

"Okay then, I'll stay as I need the money."

"That isn't true, and you know it isn't. Honestly, Guy, you can't stay and work here just to keep me company. There's no need now all the hideous stuff is over."

"I know that," he tilted his head playfully, "but I might lose you to someone else, and I'm not risking it. I'm staying so you're not getting rid of me that easily."

"I don't want to be rid of you. I'm gutted you're going. It won't be the same without you here."

"Good. I don't want it to be."

"What happens . . . you know . . . when you do leave. Is it over for us?"

"What! Are you kidding me? Any more talk like that and I'll not be going anywhere."

Her heart lifted. She couldn't face a life without him in it now. Guy was the real thing.

"Don't tell me you thought it was going to be over between us?" he frowned.

"I didn't know what to think. I've only just heard about this. You've had time to work it all out."

"I'd never split up with you," he said softly, "you must know what you mean to me. My future's planned, and you're in it."

"Phew," she grinned, anxiety turning to elation. "That's a relief then because that's where I want to be."

He reached for her hand and placed the yellow elastic band he'd been fiddling with around the third finger of her left hand.

"What are you doing?"

"With this ring, I Guy Logan betroth myself to you, Kym Sullivan," she started to laugh as he wrapped the band around her finger once, twisted it and wrapped it again.

"You're an idiot," she grinned.

"Hey," he shook his head, "is that any way to speak to your fiancé?"

She smiled lovingly at him, her heart full of joy.

He leant forward and kissed her. It was right he moved on to reach his full potential, and she'd miss him terribly. But she was determined she was going to finish her training at Harlow Wood, in memory of Vanya and Louise who weren't fortunate enough to finish theirs.

"Come on . . ." Guy stood up and reached for her hand . . . "let's go and let the others know we're engaged and how much the ring has cost me."

"Don't you dare," she slapped his arm playfully, "they'll think we're crackers."

THE END

Acknowledgements

Although Harlow Wood Orthopaedic Hospital did once exist, all the characters in this story are fictional. Any similarities to anybody that worked at the hospital is purely coincidental – the storyline is entirely fiction and has only taken place in my head! My intention when writing this book was to recreate the hospital as I remembered it, but I have had to use *creative licence* for some of it to develop the plot.

When it comes to thanking those that have helped to get this book in good shape, there is a list of people. Firstly, and always top of my list is my excellent copy editor, John Hudspith. Writing a book is one thing, sharing it requires his skill. Brilliant insightful editors are a gift to any writer and I thank my lucky stars each day that I have Johnny guiding me. He constantly suggests ways to improve the story, but at the same time makes sure I keep my voice as the storyteller. He just has that innate ability to see how the story can be improved, which is what I'm striving for always.

I am fortunate to have the fabulously talented Jane Dixon-Smith design the gorgeous cover – and she never disappoints (JD Smith Design). To attract a reader to a book you need a special cover, and Jane delivers every single time.

To my beta readers, Nico Maeckelberghe and Lyn Wilkinson who have both been absolutely brilliant spotting the grammatical errors and finding those tiny mistakes that aren't evident to me. I read the manuscript how I think I've written it . . . not how it actually is. To have it fine-tuned is more than helpful, and an extra bonus has been their enthusiasm for the story – that has meant so much to me.

As always, my heartfelt and most important thanks and love go to my wonderful husband John, who never complains when I'm typing away like crazy and 'standards are dropping' everywhere!

I am extremely fortunate to be blessed with truly wonderful friends in my life, far too many to mention but they know who they are. They are always there for me jollying me along. What a dull life it would be without them in it.

2023 has been a year of numerous opportunities for me to give my talk, 'From Bedpan to Pen' to WI's, book clubs and luncheons. I wish I had words other than thank you to convey how grateful I am to every single person that has purchased my books at these events or downloaded Kindle copies. It is such a joy meeting so many enthusiastic readers who genuinely want me to do well.

Special thanks must go to all the bloggers who willingly share my books when they are released. These wonderful folks are out there industriously helping and directing readers towards my books and for that I want to say a huge thank you. With your help, more people read my stories and that's all I want.

Finally, to all my readers – I couldn't do it without you. Every email, review or message I receive saying you've enjoyed reading one of my books makes all the blood, sweat and edits worth it. Thank you most sincerely.

If you have enjoyed the story and are able to write a review on Amazon or Goodreads, I would be grateful. Each review gives the book greater exposure which I hope will attract new readers. Any author will tell you, that is primarily why we write. We just want readers to enjoy our stories and I'm no exception. So thank you in advance if you are able to write a few words about the book. And please do get in touch directly if you so wish. My email is *joymarywood@yahoo.co.uk* – I love hearing from readers.

Other books written by Joy Wood

Secrets and Lies
Getting Away with Murder
Who's Smiling Now?
April Fool
Chanjori House
Knight & Dey
For the Love of Emily

Milton Keynes UK
Ingram Content Group UK Ltd.
UKHW010013281223
435071UK00001B/11